THE HIGH MAPLES FARM COOKBOOK

T H E

HIGH MAPLES FARM
COOKBOOK

Favorite Recipes
and Reminiscences
of Farm Life

EDNA SMITH BERQUIST

Illustrated by Bonny W. Smith

The Macmillan Company, New York, New York
Collier-Macmillan Limited, London

Copyright © 1971 by Edna Smith Berquist

All rights reserved. No part of this book may be re-
produced or transmitted in any form or by any means,
electronic or mechanical, including photocopying, re-
cording or by any information storage and retrieval system, without permission in writing from the Publisher.

The Macmillan Company
866 Third Avenue, New York, N.Y. 10022
Collier-Macmillan Canada Ltd., Toronto, Ontario

Library of Congress Catalog Card Number: 79-135642

First Printing

Printed in the United States of America

To My Family

The High Maples Farm Family
Three Generations

GRANDFATHER AND GRANDMOTHER SMITH
William S. Smith   1842–1911
Lydia Sanborn Smith   1845–1912

GRAMPA AND GRAMMIE PAGE
Royal L. Page   1851–1927
Annie Osgood Page   1853–1939

FATHER AND MOTHER
Samuel W. Smith   1876–1957
Winnifred Page Smith   1877–1944

ESTHER AND JOHN
Esther Smith Weeks   1903–
John F. Weeks, Sr.   1903–

ROYAL AND VERNA
Royal W. Smith   1904–
Verna Friend Smith   1905–

EDNA AND HUGH
Edna Smith Berquist   1906–
Hugh G. Berquist   1896–

FORREST AND DOROTHY
Forrest A. Smith   1908–
Dorothy Weeks Smith   1911–1957

FRANCES AND SYDNEY
Frances Smith Wooldridge   1910–1969
Sydney Wooldridge   1910–1960

ELLEN AND DELBERT
Ellen Smith Page   1912–
Delbert L. Page   1910–

JESSIE AND HOWARD
Jessie Smith Naylor   1913–
Howard B. Naylor   1905–

ANNE AND DON
Annie Smith Dowling   1915–
Donald D. Dowling, Sr.   1913–

ROBERT AND MARY
Robert S. Smith   1920–
Mary Morgan Smith   1922–

GARDNER AND ALLYN
Gardner P. Smith   1922–
Allyn Robinson Smith   1924–

Contents

Recipes

THE HIGH MAPLES FARM COOKBOOK

Reminiscences One

❧❧❧

LIFE ON THE FARM

1

An Introduction to the Smith Family

OUR ANCESTORS on both sides of the family came to America before 1700. Among the one hundred and ninety known family names listed in our genealogy are several Scotch and two that are certainly Irish; the rest are English, evidently of the yeoman class. A few of our migrant ancestors were clergymen who left their homes in England partly because they were dissenters from the established state church. Others were craftsmen and one was a sea captain (he was Irish). Whatever their way of making a living, all at heart were tillers of the ground, impelled to migrate because there was little hope of acquiring land under the English system of entailment. Our ancestors were with those immigrants who came to the unsettled seacoast north of the Massachusetts Bay Colony and there helped establish plantations (as the new small colonies were called) in the area that is now southeastern New Hampshire. As the population grew, successive generations of our lines petitioned for land in the northern wilderness some one hundred miles from the coast, a region then considered western frontier. More than a century before our parents were married their great-great-grandparents brought their families to settle and farm the lands granted by His Majesty King George II and the heirs of John Tufton Mason, original grantee of the entire area.

The way of life on those New Hampshire frontier farms and the

changes that came about during the lives of the five generations following were part of our heritage. We often visited at our Grandfather Page's
where the farm operation was carried on much as it had been in Civil
War times. The barn loft and the wagon shed, the spacious house from
attic to cellar, all the rooms, all the nooks and the corners were
crammed with priceless memorabilia. That was something we didn't
realize when we were children, but having the curiosity of children we
naturally absorbed a great deal of history from our mother's parents.
Yet in some respects we have always felt that our lives were more
deeply influenced by our Smith ancestors.

Grandfather Smith died when I was a small child. Grandmother's
death followed within a few months. I remember them both but only
in a shadowy fashion. Some memory pictures: the molasses cookies
Grandmother used to bring out from her pantry when we stopped in
after school, and the hubbub when Grandfather fell out of the old
cherry tree at our farm. Forgetting the brittleness of his bones and
misjudging his considerable weight, Grandfather had climbed the tree
to reach the reddest, ripest fruit. I remember his beard and his white
hair and how he yelled when the branch split off and he landed on his
back with both legs sticking up in the air. He wasn't supposed to stuff
himself with cherries and that was why he had climbed up when he
thought no one was looking. I remember, too, how he was bound to eat
everything he liked, as much as he wanted, good for him or not, in spite
of Grandmother's worrying about his diabetes. My older brother and
sister remember our Smith grandparents only slightly more than I do.
The younger members of the family never knew them.

Sometimes when Father talked about his mother he used to say that
I was very much like her, yet Grandmother Smith was never more to me
than a shadowy, self-effacing figure, an appendage to Grandfather. With
him we were all well acquainted—his characteristics and quirks of
personality had left their stamp on us.

There was a general impression in the family that Grandfather had
been the typical male Smith, the embodiment of qualities predominant
in the line since his English ancestors. That Father resembled him in
many ways we knew. That we ourselves were pretty much Smith we
could not deny. All ten of us had inherited Grandfather's chin, which
was plainly shown in spite of his beard in the tintype done when he
was young. Father's was the same, firmly rounded with a deep half-
moon mark under the full lower lip. Apparently the chin was a true
dominant Smith feature (it is now being "worn" by quite a number of
Grandfather's great-great-grandchildren). Someone has said the set of
the Smith chin smacks of a managing nature—or the word might be
"domineering" if the critic meant the remark to be cutting.

We were almost as well acquainted with the old Smith ancestors as with Grandfather Smith himself. Father was one who always took a great deal of interest in his family genealogy. He liked to study history and he knew much about the early days in the townships of Sanbornton and Meredith where his ancestors had settled. In the fall of 1776 exactly one hundred years to the month before Father was born, his great-great-grandfather, Elisha Smith, had brought his wife and twelve children from the old home in southern New Hampshire to the log cabin he had built not far from the Great Bay of Lake Winnisquam. We used to pass by the site every spring when we went with Father driving cattle to summer pasture at Grandfather's old farm. Father would stop the horse to point out the hollow in the ground where the original log cabin stood. Nearby was the stump of a great willow tree which sprang from the wand Elisha once used as a walking stick along the miles of forest trail he followed on the way to work at his clearing. The big willow stood for more than a century, until a strong wind toppled it when Father was a small boy. A little distance back from the road was a large, square two-and-a-half story house with immense chimneys. It was the family's second home, a dwelling planned to shelter generations far beyond Elisha's time.

If we passed the place at the right time of day, we would cross the field behind the Bay Meeting House to eat our picnic lunch in the burying ground. No one had been there since last we came. Dead leaves had blown against the cut granite wall and drifted across the iron gate. Tall maples growing outside stretched their branches above the wall, partly shading the small graveyard. Father set the lunch basket and the stone jug of spring water on the wall beside the gate. While he ate his lunch and rested in the shade, we wandered about in the sunshine eating chicken sandwiches and doughnuts and feeling pleasantly sad about the long-dead children buried in the small graves marked by plain field stones, one at the head and a smaller one at the feet. Before we left, Father propped up the leaning headstones and cut the bushes that had sprung up around the graves of his ancestors, while we scraped away the lichens and traced the dates with our finger tips. He told us all over again about the generations of Smiths who had lived in the house by the willow tree. Last in the row of grave markers were the marble headstones of Samuel and Harriett, his wife. That Samuel was our great-grandfather who died in middle age leaving a large family of children for Grandmother Harriett to rear by herself. That was why the farm had to be sold out of the family, and that was how it happened that our grandfather brought up his family on a poor hill farm a few miles away in the town of Meredith. Grandfather might have done better if he had gone off to the city to make his living, the way his brothers did.

He was as good a craftsman as any of the Smiths. He could have done well as a clock maker or worker in a cabinet shop, but he never could have been happy confined indoors.

Father owned things that Grandfather had made. There was a big yoke for oxen and a small yoke to use when young steers were trained. There was a large hand sled (we used it to haul home the Christmas tree) and a very tiny sled that went with a pair of toy oxen Grandfather had carved from a piece of hardwood with only a jackknife for a tool. We never played with the little oxen. They were Father's treasures, not to be taken from the cupboard shelf. Father himself was good with his hands, though not as clever as some of his brothers. The Smith dexterity was inherited to some degree by every one of my four brothers and five sisters and, in some of Grandfather's descendents, it has been intensified to the point of artistry. For a share of that legacy I would gladly have given up all of the less-valued Smith characteristics, including Grandfather's chin.

Most of Father's memories were happy. He told often of the fun and the good food, not so much about the times that were hard. Grandfather was very good at making things grow in spite of the thin, rocky soil and the steep sidehill fields. Father liked to name over the kinds of apples they used to have, more than twenty varieties of bearing trees. Grandfather had a good maple orchard and always made enough syrup and sugar so they didn't have to stint at home; also he had "stirred" sugar to swap for white sugar and syrup to pay for other luxury items at the stores. They didn't have an abundance of fresh meat except at butchering time in the fall of the year, but neither did other farm families in those days.

Grandmother was one who knew how to do well with what was at hand. Father and the rest of his family used to boast about Grandmother's cooking. Her children admired her and were fully as proud of her family, the Sanborns, as of their Smith ancestors. Grandmother's married life was spent in the shadow of her strong-willed, arbitrary husband. The meals she served, the order of her days at home, her social behavior (on the rare occasions when she went out) were suited to Grandfather's ideas of what was proper and good. Yet as far as we know Grandmother was a happy woman. Hers was the life of the ordinary farm wife in the era when a man was master in his house. In that respect we have always been sure no Smith in the line exceeded Grandfather.

We all liked listening to Father's stories of olden times and the way of life when he was young. My sisters and I congratulated ourselves on not being born until a whole lot later.

2

"... an helpmeet for him ..."

WHEN SAMUEL STEPPED out into the early morning chill, thin fingers of light were beginning to streak the dim sky over the Belknap Mountains. There was hardly a stir in the air and it was too dark to see more than the outline of the barn's roof, yet habit made him look up toward the weathervane atop the cupola. He could feel the cold rising from the heavy white frost blanketing field and roadside. He knew there would be patches of ice crystals scattered over the surface of the road and a light skim of ice on the watering trough. The sun would come up bright into a sky without clouds; not long then before the crystals would dissolve drenching the withered grass, dripping from the dead goldenrod stalks along the side of the road. The crusty, porous spots in the dirt would be gone and the horses' hooves would again kick up little clouds of warm dust. The picture was there—whole, at once—in his mind's eye. He had no need to stop and ponder the weather's turn, yet he stood there on the back stoop for a while without picking up the milk pails, not lost in thought exactly but studying over in his mind what had gone before, how matters then stood with him.

Two years ago they had left the Meredith farm. What a job it had been—getting his father to let go and give up that old mountain place. Still his father never stopped complaining; it had been that way as long ago as Samuel could remember. ". . . scratching a poor living from this thin, sour soil. Ledges cropping out everywhere. Fields so rocky you could cross a whole acre without touching foot to the ground if you had a mind to. Blasted fool that settled here in the first place . . . should've known better than to perch the house and barn right up on the brow of the hill where the winds blow tough and tight all winter long. They cut through you like a knife, and get into the house in spite of the stoves going full blast, chuck full of dry maple chunks."

Nevertheless Samuel partly understood how hard it was for the older man to leave the land he had worked for thirty years. The family had mostly grown up there; it hadn't really been such a bad life, either. His father was afraid it wouldn't turn out any easier to make a go of this farm in Gilford, and he missed being able to look off in a wide sweep over the surrounding country. One thing for sure about the old farm on Meredith Hill—there wasn't a sightlier place in the whole county.

Now the hardest time was past. The move was made and they were well started on a much better farm. This big house could easily accommodate two families—he had looked out for that when he and his father were dickering for the place. The stand of pine on the west ridge was prime, ready for cutting. A portable steam sawmill was already set up over on the brook; teamsters and a gang of wood choppers had been hired. The sale of sawed lumber would bring in cash enough to make a sizable payment on the farm mortgage. That thought was a great satisfaction.

The weather would be clear he decided as he picked up the milk pails and started for the barn. A fine October day, just the right kind of day to be married.

Winnifred's dress was of fine-woven wool broadcloth, soft and smooth to touch. It was a misty, in-between color—not as green as new leaves nor as blue as lake water. The seamstress had copied a fashion plate from *The Ladies' Home Journal*, planning some moderation in the style, of course. The skirt was gored to fit smoothly across the front, gathered full enough at the back to swing gracefully as she walked; yet the dress was not really stylish, for the skirt was less than five yards around at the buckram-stiffened hem, cut short with not even a bit of train to drag on the ground. A more fashionable longer length would have been prettier, but she needed a skirt that could be lifted with ease to clear a muddy wagon wheel. The dress was completely lined with heavy sateen, sewn in with very tiny, very even stitches. The same sateen material had been used to cover the stays in the waist, and they were firmly anchored with the same beautiful stitching. The waist itself was cut modestly high at the throat. The sleeves were long and fitted close at the wrists, just a bit puffed and lifted at the shoulders—a slight nod in the direction of the fashionable leg-o-mutton style. For a touch of elegance, she had chosen trimming of deep blue silk velvet folded narrowly at the neckband, wider tucks for a band to circle the waist. Piping of the same blue velvet marked the top of the deep hemline; medallions of real French lace were sewn down the front of the waist to give a finishing touch.

Winnifred had paid the seamstress her fee without hesitation. Perhaps four dollars might be considered a high price for the sewing of a dress so plain, yet it was painstakingly made and fitted so smoothly. She remembered the elaborate gown she had worn the time she won the Prize Speaking Contest. How different a dress had suited her fancy then. It had been fashioned from a bolt of heavy white silk, flounced and ruffled. The dressmaker had filled in the neckline with a soft cloud of tulle ruching (the pattern had turned out too low-cut to be modest). She had worn long white gloves then and white kid slippers trimmed with rosettes sewn of tiny pearl beads. The same gown had been her graduation dress (she was a member of the Class of ’99, The New Hampton Literary Institute). Now the dress, done up in a cheesecloth bag, had long been hung away in a closet.

In the years since, she had taught the winter terms in a number of district schools, had made new friends wherever she went and always been asked back. Her summers had been adventurous interludes at York Beach up in Maine where she worked as a pastry cook. But that was all behind her now, and she was ready to begin a new life.

They would be married without any fuss—she had chosen a practical dress, one that would serve as a best winter dress for many years to come.

She was pleased with the house and the location of the farm where Samuel and his father's family had settled. The extra tenement was fixed up and ready for them to move right in. Except for the kitchen range, the furnishings weren't new or fancy (there were some familiar pieces from her parents' home), but everything was convenient and the house was snug. The well pump was handy to the kitchen. The shed held a plentiful store of wood sawed into lengths to fit the firebox of the kitchen range and there were piled-up chunks of maple, beech, and birch wood. One or two such chunks would keep a fire going all night in the front room stove, giving off a steady, even heat during the worst winter weather. Samuel made a practice of having the next winter's wood supply cut, hauled in, sawed and split and under cover early every spring before it was time to work the land. He took pride in having good dry wood stacked in the shed, always enough on hand to last two families all summer and through the hardest winter (with some left over to sell, usually).

When she first visited the farm almost a year before, Samuel took her down to the well-stocked cellar. He carried a lantern to show her the dark root cellar where the potatoes and vegetables were stored. He spoke of his plans for future crops, named over the varieties of apples that grew on the farm, talked of the different kinds of fruit they might grow in years to come. He pointed out the pork barrel still almost half full, packed so carefully the salted pork had kept in perfect condition, and mentioned the fat pigs out in the pen, about ready for slaughtering.

Winnifred knew that Samuel's main income was from his dairy cows —fresh milk taken into town every day. She would never need to worry about having plenty of milk and fresh eggs. She would have her own pen of pullets, of course, and from the sale of the eggs her pin money would come. She could see that Samuel was just as up-and-coming a farmer as her father—more modern in some ways. It was plain she was getting a good provider and in return she felt perfectly willing to pull her share in the yoke. So the idea of starting right off feeding a sawmill crew didn't worry her a bit. She agreed with Samuel—they couldn't turn down the chance to board the wood choppers—the money would be a real windfall. Of course her fine linen tablecloths wouldn't be used for awhile. Grandmother Osgood's fragile Chelsea china and the pink lustre dishes, Grandmother Page's silver spoons and the soft woolen blankets woven so long ago—all were packed away without regret. She spent the last of her teaching money for German silverware, crockery mugs and heavy dishes to set up table for the hands.

Winnifred awoke before light, but she lay without stirring until the sun's first rays touched the pane. She opened her window wide and looked to the mountains. On the other side, twelve miles away, Samuel would be doing his barn chores. She knew he would not come until nearly noontime, yet before the morning mist had all burned off her small valise was packed (the rest of her belongings had already been taken to the new home). She had packed the basket lunch, lingering awhile in dreamy anticipation. She had brushed her chestnut hair until it shone (it was so long she could sit on it) and pinned it in a coil on top of her head. She was waiting, dressed in her blue-green wedding gown, when she heard the rattle of the team coming down over the hill. She marveled that Samuel had come so quickly—he must have started his chores an hour early. She saw that he was driving his father's speediest horse, the Colt, hitched to the light buggy. "What a beautiful October day!" she thought. "What a wonderful day to be married!"

They came up through the woods of Grant Mountain and drove out into the open countryside, brilliant in the autumn noon. At a spot where a great clump of white birches cast a patch of flickering shade beside the road, Samuel reined in the Colt, slipped off his bridle and tied on the feed bag. While they ate chicken sandwiches and apple turnovers, the Colt munched away on his oats. A wind came up to rustle the sweeping branches of the birch trees and shake loose a shower of bright leaves that twisted aimlessly in the currents of air, then floated downward one by one to light, soundless as a flight of yellow butterflies. A little time for talking and dreaming, then they drove on.

Elder Munsey's home was on their way, just over a mile this side of the farm. The minister's wife had readied her parlor for the marriage, raised the shades, taken the dust covers from her horsehair parlor suite and polished the mahogany trim (it was carved in the stylish grape design). Winnifred and Samuel were married there, standing before the marble fireplace. As they finished saying their vows the chiming of the mantel clock sweetly marked the hour. Then came congratulations and a gift for the new home from the minister and his wife. After slipping a folded bill into the minister's hand, Samuel handed Winnifred into the buggy and they drove on home.

The sun was not far down in the western sky—time enough before chores for Samuel to help her get settled. Winnifred hung her wedding dress away in the upstairs bedroom closet and changed into a new print housedress. She chose the pink sprigged one with the double ruffle around the skirt; she wanted to look especially nice—they would be by themselves for this one night only. Samuel went out to do the milking. She set about getting supper.

The next day and for many days there came from the hill the ring of axes, the sound of trees crashing down, the shouts of teamsters logging to the mill beside the brook, the circular blade's long-drawn whine as the logs were sawed into boards. Winnifred heard with half an ear as she got on with her baking. She must be ready to feed twelve hungry men crowding into her kitchen at six o'clock to sit down at the long trestle table. And how they would eat! Small mountains of potatoes pan-fried with crisp salt pork, fried meat heaped high on big platters, dozens of fluffy baking powder biscuits. And on top of all that, generous wedges of pie—apple, squash, or pumpkin. She was accustomed to cooking for a crowd and she liked to see the sawmill hands enjoying her food. These woodsmen devoured with gusto all that she set before them. No wonder! They were used to the greasy, coarse fare dished up by a slap-hazard man cook, meals stirred together on a makeshift camp stove.

At Winnifred's table they sat down every morning to a breakfast just as hearty as last night's supper. They heaped their plates with Red Flannel Hash and hot suet Johnnycake, sweet and moist, baked in thick sheets and cut into big squares. Good corned beef and plenty of vegetables went into the hash. Lucky that Samuel had planted extra-long rows of carrots, beets and onions last summer and the late potatoes had yielded better than usual. Each evening after supper Samuel would get out the old wooden chopping bowl (scooped out of basswood so long ago no one remembered who had made it), and he'd help her chop up the meat and vegetables for the breakfast hash. Even so, Winnifred had to be up long before light to get the oven hot for baking and the coffee to boiling. Every other morning she mixed up a double batch of dough and fried several dozen doughnuts. Nothing would keep up a man's strength and spirits like fresh hot doughnuts, she knew. A couple of those doughnuts and a big slice of cheese made a welcome addition to the meat sandwiches in the men's lunch pails. The bread must be started early every day so it would rise and be ready to go into the oven in the early afternoon. She baked six loaves at a time, reckoning half a loaf to each woodsman's lunch pail.

Every bit of the board money they put into the savings bank; that made all of the hard work worthwhile. In the years to come the farm would be making a living for two families, so Samuel must add to his herd of milking cows. He needed a new mowing machine, a more up-to-date horserake, seed for next season's crops—there was no end to his list. She never found time during the daylight hours to do fancywork or take a rest—not even so much as a little cat nap—but she always had plenty of energy and she enjoyed working. She had a hired girl to come in during the day and bring in water from the well, keep the woodbox filled, wash up the dishes after meals. It was a help to be spared so much of the drudgery, and as for fancywork, that was something she never had taken any interest in. She'd rather be out in the garden or off picking berries in the fields and woods. Next spring she would surely be able to get outdoors again to help Samuel in the garden and start some flower beds around her side of the house (the other side was her mother-in-law's). Thank goodness the men were pleasant to have around. Although they were ignorant backwoodsmen only recently come down from Quebec with the idea of improving their fortunes where pay was higher and the climate better, they were men of native gentleness and courtesy, always laughing and gay. They made the evenings merry with story telling and singing, along with the music of the harmonica and jew's-harp.

One November day the job was finished. The shrill whining of the saw was stilled. She no longer heard the men shouting as the trees came crashing down. The wood choppers came to say goodbye, told as best they could in broken English with a Canuck accent of how they had enjoyed her good food; then they shouldered their axes and followed the mill to a distant, untouched stand of timber. The long trestle table was taken down and stored up attic. Then she could admit to herself that she was a little tired, but she pushed out of mind the thought of the pain that sometimes caught her as she stooped to make a bed or reached up to put away the dishes. She refused to believe that it was always there waiting to pounce, often became an insistent nagging by late afternoon.

On these late November mornings Samuel felt no temptation to linger before taking the clean milk pails from their place on the window shelf by the back door. Often when he started for the barn low-hanging clouds entirely shut off the mountains from his view. Always he felt the sharp bite in the air, positive prophecy of early snowfall and hard winter weather ahead. It was his custom still to gaze off across the field beyond the barn toward the ridge where the noble stand of pine had been, but he did not regret the cutting of the tall trees. He looked not at the raw gash in the hillside but into the future.

His fancy roamed over the farm as it would be in years to come, all the while he was doing the barn chores with the ease of long habit: The smooth, worn handle grasped and the milking stool set beside the first cow in the tie-up line. The first warm streams of milk, rhythmic music in the bright pail held between his knees. The foaming, full pail emptied into a larger one and set up on the shelf. Then to the next cow, placidly chewing her cud, and so down the waiting line to the last.

Bright and clear were the pictures in his mind's eye. The brush piles left by the lumbermen all cleared away and burned, the high pile of sawdust gone—put to good use as bedding for the cattle in winter. Summers, a flock of sheep pastured on the hillside. (Sheep would crop down the low-growing bushes, would do well in that rough new pasture where cattle would pretty near starve to death. The flock would be close to the barn, in no great danger from roving dogs.) And there would be early springtimes, the best time of year, when the maple sap started and the boiling down was going on. His foresight had saved the small rock maple trees growing among the pines. He had asked his mother to strip up an old red flannel petticoat so he could mark each sapling with a flag of warning, and in that way keep every precious maple safe from the bite of the axe. It would not be many years before they would have a maple orchard larger than the one on the old farm in Meredith. His father took on so now about the lack of maple sweetening; he did hope the old man would live to see the time when they could again freely use maple syrup and maple sugar. Next spring he and Winnifred would start small, plan to do the boiling down in a pan on the kitchen stove; but in a few years, by the time their boys were big enough to help, they would be putting out six or seven hundred buckets at least. They would build a good sap house with a roof vented for the steam to escape, buy an evaporator and make fancy syrup that would bring the top price. The whole family would work together; most of the children would be boys although they might have a girl child or two (he supposed Winnifred would be glad of a daughter for company in the house). He guessed he could make a living for half a dozen at least (some of his ancestors had as many as twelve or fourteen children).

But this was foolish wool-gathering—somewhere off in the future. He had plenty to be thankful for right now. He had Winnifred, surely the right wife to help and comfort a man. Pretty lucky for him she hadn't chosen that city slicker who had been so sure of getting her. Now that they were settled he was looking forward to winter. Working out in the snow and cold kept a man feeling alive, made him value the warmth inside—companionship and comfort through the long winter evenings. Next week would be Thanksgiving and they were invited to eat with his folks. Just this once more, his mother had offered, she would do all the cooking so Winnifred could get a good rest. They would have all the old favorites: roast chickens, cranberry sauce, potatoes and gravy, pumpkin pie, mincemeat pie, too, and of course, her custard pudding (the family called it "plum puddin'" because of all the raisins she put in). Oh, it would be a real Smith family feast. Just thinking of all that good food was enough to make a man smack his lips!

For him that day of thanksgiving and feasting did not come. Instead, it became a sad time never recalled in after years, a happening to be rooted up and cast from memory. On that day his young wife lay near to death in the hospital.

Early in the morning two days before Thanksgiving, Samuel was roused from heavy sleep by her stifled moaning. He did not know how she had tossed, unable to sleep, didn't realize that she had not been well for many days. Sometimes burning hot and then too cold, she had tried all through the night to ease herself of the pain that would not let her go for a moment, held hard possession no matter how often she turned and twisted her body. When at last she had tried to slip out of bed quietly, not wanting to disturb her husband so early, the pain had struck with a ferocity that felled her. It was so that he found her, kneeling, holding herself against the bedstead unable to rise.

His helpless, frantic shouts brought Mother Smith rushing in from her side of the house. She got Winnifred back into bed, bathed her face and smoothed the tumbled bedclothes. Samuel's mother had learned to nurse the sick and minister to the dying long before she was a woman grown. When she was young, families living miles away from any doctor's help had to learn how to meet emergencies by themselves. She had the knowledge passed down through generations of pioneer women and the skill of long experience. As soon as she touched the fevered body, noted how the limbs were contorted by agonizing pain, she realized that here was an illness beyond the help of any soothing potion such as she could administer. The doctor must be called at once, urged to come without a moment's delay. In no time, it seemed, she had rung up Central and raised Dr. Abbott, the family doctor who had helped bring all five of her children into the world. Mother Smith had great confidence in the old doctor because she well knew that he would never refuse to go out on a call, no matter how far he must travel in bad weather or how late at night the knocking might come at his door. He would work just as hard to save the life of some ne'er-do-well, poor as a church mouse, as to cure the most prosperous merchant in town. Of course, some people disliked him because he gave short shrift to women who suffered from nervous vapors and the like. Such vague ailments he was likely to treat with a sarcasm so caustic that memory was bound to sting after the physical ailment was long forgotten. This time he came, not stopping for any breakfast, not sparing his horse on the hills. Yet when he entered the sickroom he was unhurried, his manner calm and confident. His examination was thorough. Even after he appeared to be finished he sat long by the bed, deliberating, asking Mother Smith a question now and then, Winnifred herself could not have answered for she was tossing restlessly and murmuring, seeming to wander in her mind.

When at last they came out of the sickroom into the kitchen where Samuel waited, the old doctor's look was bleak and forbidding yet his tone was kindly, and he gave his diagnosis in every day language so that Samuel could not fail to understand his meaning. He had found an obstruction, an abdominal swelling most unnatural. He had no doubt it was a fast-growing tumor which was interfering with the bodily functions and so was building up poisons spreading rapidly throughout the sick woman's body. All he could do was to leave some pills which would quiet her and ease the pain somewhat. He felt that he must tell them straight out, though it was a hard thing to say, that never had he been able to save a patient so afflicted. Yet he felt there was a chance to save her life—but only if the tumor could be removed at once. It would mean she must have an operation to be performed by a surgeon at the hospital. Samuel would have to sign a paper giving his permission. That was the law. The doctor realized that Samuel might hesitate to allow any surgery to be performed on his wife. He knew that some people were dead set against it because they had such a horror of the surgeon's knife; others held religious scruples—thought such a thing was like flying in the face of Providence. He knew, too, that none of the other older doctors in Laconia would recommend surgery. It could be they were afraid of being blamed if the patient did not recover. As for him, it was a chance he'd have to take. Even though he himself couldn't do the operation he didn't believe in sticking entirely with the past. His own son, now studying at a university, would become a surgeon he hoped. Of course when he was young, all the doctors had learned their business the same way—beginning by driving about with a doctor making his round of calls, observing, and reading the doctor's books on medicine. He knew that Samuel and his mother had confidence in him and in the old remedies, but he wanted them to know, too, that a good many people now alive and going about their everyday affairs would have been laid in their graves a long time ago except for the help of some surgeon's scalpel. He had spoken bluntly because there was no time to lose. The decision must be made quickly. It was up to the patient's nearest of kin.

Samuel could not answer. The blow had come upon him so suddenly that he could not really take in the doctor's meaning. He felt stunned, unable to think clearly. Certainly he was not up to making a decision which could mean the life of the woman he had married such a short time ago. The doctor went away and left him sitting there at the kitchen table, his head bowed, face buried in his hands.

As soon as the telephone call came through that morning, Winnifred's father set out. He drove his team at a punishing speed all the way up from Gilmanton. He met the doctor returning to town and stopped him to learn the particulars of Winnifred's illness. The doctor's report left him shaken and distressed. He urged his weary horses onward, for he felt the time was short. His daughter would need all the help and comfort he could give and he must try to bolster up

Samuel's courage, plead with him to get Winnifred to the hospital quickly. He did not even unharness, just left his team standing, lathered and trembling with exhaustion. As he hurried into the house he saw that the decision had already been made. A horse had been harnessed and hitched to a light wagon, ready now at the hitching post beside the doorstep. It had not taken Samuel long to get hold of himself. He could not stand by, doing nothing, and let his wife die— he must allow the surgery, must take the chance no matter how desperate a gamble it might be.

Winnifred roused up a little when her father came into the room. She knew when they lifted her, wrapped in blankets, and carried her to the wagon. Father Page drove while Samuel supported his wife, cradling her in his arms, trying to save her from the jolting of the wagon. The doctor's medicine had taken its effect. She drifted in vagueness, not always aware of where she was, hardly feeling the rough places in the road. By the time they reached the hospital she was barely conscious, so she did not know when they carried her in and placed her life in the hands of the surgeon.

They could only wait.

Winnifred's father appeared to be far away in thought as he sat there on a bench in the small anteroom. Maybe he was lost in a reverie of years gone by. Surely he was praying for the life of the daughter he loved so dearly. Samuel took the waiting hard, for patience was not in his nature. He walked back and forth continuously, up and down the hallway. Whenever he came back to sit briefly, the older man spoke, offering words of comfort, but Samuel's restless pacing was not abated. He took out his watch over and over again, then at once forgot what the hands had told him. He felt that time had never dragged on so slowly. Afterward, he could never remember how many hours passed nor tell how long it had been since he had eaten. He knew that it must have been late at night for the lights had been lit a long time before the doctor came to tell them that Winnifred was still alive. The operation had been very complicated, the most difficult he had performed. It had been necessary to keep the patient under anesthesia beyond the period of maximum safety. However, she was young and her heart was strong. They must hope for the best. No use for them to remain here any longer, better to go home and get some rest because she would be unable to recognize them for some hours to come. While the effects of the ether were wearing off, she would suffer from nausea so that she would need constant care and attention. It was best to let the nurses watch over her.

When they came back to the hospital late the next afternoon they were called in for a consultation with the doctor who had operated. He wanted to prepare the relatives before they went in to visit the patient. He told them that he was sorry he could not give them better news. Everything possible was being done. Other doctors had been called in to give their opinions. The patient had lost a great deal of blood, had been slow to recover from the effects of the anesthetic. He had hoped and expected that she would respond more quickly, but the fact was that she had not really regained consciousness, seemed to be sinking deeper into a coma. He gave them to understand that he believed her condition would worsen. They would be allowed to keep constant watch by her bedside if that was their wish.

When Samuel saw his wife lying there motionless and already so far away from him, he was ready to give up hope. The pillow on which her head rested was no whiter than her face. Nothing was left of the sparkle and glow of health; all the youthful energy had drained away. He leaned close over her and spoke her name. He thought that he saw a slight movement of her lips but he heard no sound. Then he took both her hands in his but felt no answering pressure. He was most deeply hurt by the sight of her strong hands lying there so limp, the square, capable fingers already weak and helpless.

Samuel had never learned to find comfort and help in prayer, and he could not ask that Winnifred's life be spared. It was not that he was an unbeliever, for he felt always a Divine Presence in the whole out-doors, but he knew that the rain fell and the sun shone with impartiality on the fallow fields of the slothful and on the crops of the diligent. He was a firm believer in the old saying that God helps those who help themselves.

It was Father Page who sustained and comforted him now. The older man had known the full measure of sorrow and loss, yet through-out his life he had held to a faith serene and unchanging. He had never doubted God's goodness nor the final wisdom of His ways. He felt sure that God would not take Winnifred away until her work here on earth was finished. She had been given the strength to come through the operation. Samuel must pin his hope to that, for it was a good sign. They must stay with her—wait and pray for her life. They took turns at her bedside through that night and through Thanksgiving Day. Two nights more and another day her life wavered, seemed ready to flicker out, until the hour came when she knew them, spoke their names. When they could believe with certainty that she would live, Samuel went home to take up his work again and Winnifred's father went back home to Gilmanton, feeling old and worn-out, in need of a good rest.

The doctor allowed Winnifred to leave the hospital a few days before Christmas. The weather was unusually cold for the time of year and there had been several light snowstorms. Enough had fallen to make good sleighing on all the roads. When Samuel set off to bring Winnifred home, he was driving the Colt hitched to a cutter. He saw to it that his wife was warmly dressed—in her heaviest coat, his fur cap with the earlaps pulled down and warm mittens to protect her hands. He tucked the buffalo robe carefully around her feet. Winnifred said she felt fine. It was wonderful to be out where the cold stung her nose and made her cheeks tingle. She enjoyed the sunshine on the fresh snow. The glare didn't bother her one bit. She was so thankful to be going home.

Her strength came back so slowly that she was often impatient. She sometimes said she was as weak as the baby kitten Samuel had brought in from the barn. He told her it was one the mother cat wouldn't own, but it was really to help keep Winnifred amused. She hardly stepped out in the snow all through January, didn't go upstairs for weeks. She seldom thought of the broadcloth dress for she never was able to go anywhere. She supposed it was still in the upstairs closet where she had hung it on her wedding day. Finally she began to take an interest in her house plants (Mother Smith had slipped some new varieties for her), and when the mailman brought around the seed catalogues she helped Samuel plan next summer's garden. They picked out seeds that were claimed to be hardy and best yielding, then sent the order off right away because Winnifred thought she'd like to start some plants in the house—cabbage, lettuce and tomatoes, maybe some asters, too.

Spring came early that year. When the weather broke, right after the first of March, Samuel tapped the maple trees near the house. Winnifred wanted to go out to help, but Samuel thought she'd best be satisfied to stay inside and help with the boiling down. He had the tinsmith make a pan to fit right on top of the kitchen range. He saw to it the woodbox was kept filled. He brought the sap into the house, while Winnifred kept the fire going and tended the boiling sap (she dropped in a bit of butter now and then to keep the pan from boiling over and making a mess all over her stove). Samuel was usually around when it was time to syrup-off, so she wouldn't have to lift the heavy pan and pour off the boiling hot maple syrup. They made enough syrup that first year for the use of both families. Winnifred cooked down the darker last-run syrup and stirred it into damp sugar to use in cooking.

While he was taking up the sap buckets, getting them washed and stored away for another year, Samuel was planning ahead to the spring work. He had made a good start toward clearing the brush from the sheep pasture, but it would need a new fence all around. The cow pasture fence would need mending—patching fence was a job that had to be done every spring before the cattle could be let out to pasture. He would need to decide which fields to plow, what ground should be seeded down, where it would be best to plant corn and potatoes.

Winnifred was not quite ready to tell Samuel that she too had begun looking forward to a natural event. She felt pretty sure they were going to have a baby, but she couldn't be more than three months along, and she wanted to see a doctor before letting Samuel get his hopes up. Not that she was frightened or worried, because she was familiar with childbirth and the care of babies. She was the oldest in her family, the only girl, twenty years older than her youngest brother. She had, in fact, assisted the doctor when her mother's last baby was born. The boys had learned early to depend on Winnifred for comfort, because their mother was a headstrong, impatient woman bound to spend her days working in the garden or tending the stock. She put the younger ones' care onto Winnifred's willing shoulders. Winnifred's gentle, patient father saw how things were, but he never could stand up to his wife. She had her say about everything, indoors and out. Winnifred hadn't minded, for she was a natural-born mother and she loved children, had always planned on having a family of her own. She wouldn't have considered going to a doctor this early if she hadn't been so sick last fall. It would be best to consult the doctor who had operated.

One morning she remarked to Samuel that she might drive in to Laconia that afternoon. There were a few small things she needed in the dry goods store—some sewing notions. At the same time she could do the week's grocery shopping and save him the trip. Besides it would do her good to get out of the house. She hadn't been in to the stores all winter long.

She went first to the doctor's office. He was doubtful when she told him she thought she was pregnant, but his examination proved that she was right. The doctor was a plain-spoken man who made no effort to spare Winnifred's feelings. He just told her bluntly that she couldn't have this baby, perhaps might never be able to bear children. He would certify that the pregnancy must be terminated, otherwise her life would be in grave danger. And if she had any idea of risking her own life by trying to carry a child to full term, she'd better consider the possibility that the baby might be malformed. She should go home and discuss the matter with her husband, make plans to come back to the hospital—the sooner the better. Winnifred paid his fee and walked out of the office. She was so upset that she unhitched the horse, climbed right into the wagon and headed for home, forgetting completely about the grocery list in her pocketbook.

She was halfway home before she made up her mind. She kept remembering something she had dreamed a few nights before. In the dream she was outdoors in a sunny, grassy place. She was running and beside her, holding on to her hand, was a baby, a rolypoly, perfect baby who laughed and crowed and ran along with her, light as thistle-down, bare feet hardly touching the ground. She woke thinking, "What a funny dream! A baby so young couldn't possibly run." It was her baby she had dreamed of—this baby she was carrying. She knew she could not allow the doctor to destroy its life. God would not have let her get well, allow a baby to start, unless He had meant for her to bear children. She pulled on the reins to turn the horse around, and she drove right back to see another doctor.

This time Winnifred went to a younger doctor, one who had assisted the surgeon at the time of the operation. Dr. True listened to her story, asked her a good many questions, then made a careful examination before giving his opinion. He respected the older doctor's skill and his judgment. However, he himself had been present at the operation and he did not believe it would be impossible for her to bear a child. He could see that she had made a remarkable recovery and he could find nothing abnormal about this pregnancy; everything seemed to be progressing well. He advised her not to worry about the danger of having a malformed infant. That was something that very rarely happened, couldn't be predicted. If it should happen in this case, he felt sure the child would be stillborn, would never breathe. He wanted to see her again in a month or so.

Winnifred hurried through her shopping, eager now to tell Samuel the news. She'd just say they were going to have a baby; the doctor thought it would be in the early fall. She decided to put all worry out of her mind. She would have her baby and it would be healthy. She knew she could depend on God's help and the assistance of Dr. True.

Winnifred continued to feel well all summer. She spent some time outside every day taking care of her flock of chickens and working in the flower beds. She picked berries, even helped Samuel with the vegetable garden. She began to feel uncomfortable and heavy toward the end of summer—that was to be expected—but she wouldn't sit around idle and see the crops go to waste. The baby clothes had been finished weeks ago, folded away in a dresser drawer. She kept busy doing some preserving, making pickles and quantities of piccalilli to sell. The hotel in Laconia was glad to pay her two dollars a gallon for all she could make. The tomato plants were bearing so heavily they couldn't possibly use all the crop themselves. When the garden was threatened with heavy frost in mid-September Samuel picked all the green tomatoes left on the vines. He brought in four bushels heaping full; Winnifred said she felt like getting right at the job, so she went to work making more piccalilli and wouldn't stop until she had tomatoes and onions all cut and the piccalilli cooked up and put down cellar in stone crocks.

Mother Smith recalled an old saying: "When a woman takes a streak of dusting around with so much energy, you can be sure it is a good sign the baby is about due." She wasn't a bit surprised when Samuel called her that same night. She could tell things were going along normally, so she let Dr. True get his sleep out. As it was, he got there in plenty of time to deliver the baby. The minute Winnifred heard her baby's first loud, indignant cry, she knew everything was all right. She felt so worn-out that she just shut her eyes and went to sleep without knowing whether she'd had the son Samuel wanted.

Samuel was only a little disappointed when Dr. True told him the baby was a girl. Winnifred and the baby were both fine and, after all, there would be more children—plenty of time for boys. Mother Smith said her first grandchild was the most wonderful newborn infant she had ever seen. The baby was so large (she must weigh more than ten pounds) and so well developed that most people would take her for a month-old baby. Her skin was not red at all, just a pretty pink, and she had lots of hair. Samuel didn't have any special girl's name in mind so he let Winnifred decide. She already knew what she'd name the baby if it was all right with him. She had always liked the story of Esther in the Old Testament. "Esther" meant "a star," she had read. She thought it was pretty, and a good name for a first-born child.

Esther was a perfectly healthy baby, her Grandmother Smith's pride and pet from the first. She didn't even have one colicky spell and wasn't so very fussy when she was cutting teeth. She was a lively baby, a handful during the next summer when she was creeping all over the house. She was always climbing up onto chairs and tumbling off, constantly getting into the lower cupboards to pull out all the cooking dishes and scatter them around the floor. Samuel often carried her up to the barn or down to the garden when he went to pick vegetables. She liked the outdoors so much that he had to put up a little gate at the door to keep her inside and out of danger. Before she was a year old she was running about, then there was no keeping her inside the house.

Winnifred had a hard time trying to bathe and dry the little girl for she would wriggle out of her mother's lap and run laughing out into the sunshine without a stitch of clothing on. If there were any rain puddles left beside the road she would splash mischievously in the mud. Running after the child was a job for Winnifred, because she was heavy and awkward, far along with her second child.

Three days before Christmas a big, healthy boy was born to Winnifred and Samuel. This time Samuel had a name already picked out. The baby should be named for his two grandfathers. Of course his first name should be William after his Grandfather Smith, because he was the first Smith grandson. Winnifred agreed, although she really felt that William Smith was too common a name. The boy would be sure to have a nickname like Willie tagged on when he got older. She herself liked to speak of her baby as Royal, after her own father. The baby's eyes were so dark that for a little while she thought they might turn out to be brown like her father's. She had always longed for a baby with laughing brown eyes to take the place of the lost little brother she still mourned, though he had died when she was only eight years old. Samuel soon forgot that he had insisted on his father's name for the baby and took to calling him Royal, too. Not until then did Winnifred write in her Bible. On the first line of the page entitled "Family" she had written "Esther Marion, September 18, 1903." Now on the second line she wrote her son's name, "Royal William, December 22, 1904."

That was the way the family began—the story as she told it to us years afterward. She sometimes let us take the blue-green wedding dress from the trunk in the attic, where it had been packed away years before along with her white silk graduation dress. We laughed at the old-fashioned style. The dress was so heavy and stiff, so very wide around the skirt. We marveled at the tiny, even stitches and rubbed our faces against the soft blue velvet trimming. She told us she had never worn the dress again—the belt wouldn't go around her waist after her second baby was born. We'd better put the dress carefully back in the trunk up attic. Someday our own daughters might value it just for a keepsake.

❧ 3 ❧

The Bow in the Cloud

Winters are long in New Hampshire and spring there is a most capricious season. Just as a matter of custom, we always used to check the weather on Groundhog Day, but we didn't take any stock in the notion that the woodchucks came out then to look around. Some years the snow was so deep it would have taken a week to tunnel through. Even if the ground happened to be bare, we felt no woodchuck was foolish enough to leave his warm, underground burrow and look for his own, or any other shadow, early as the second of February. And, supposing the Old Farmer's Almanac forecast an early spring, we still believed it was good sense to be resigned—plenty more snowstorms and a lot more than six weeks of cold weather lay ahead.

I remember how eagerly I always watched for the first signs of warmer weather. Sometimes I used to despair, sure that winter would linger on forever. The icicles hanging from the eaves melted a bit, only to grow longer and heavier again; the frost on the windowpanes stayed thick; the snow was too deep and too solidly drifted ever to melt away. My mother used to say that I minded the cold worse than the others. Whenever we played outside in the snow I nearly always gave up and came in ahead of the rest. My brothers and sisters might have rosy cheeks and sparkling eyes but not me—only my nose got red! It ran. So did my eyes, and my face was inclined to take on a sickly bluish cast. Often when I came in shivering, my mother would pamper me a little, get me some hot catnip tea or some cocoa. No doubt I liked the extra attention, enjoyed having her fuss over me. I liked being all by myself, too, huddled up close to the comfort of the tall Round Oak heating stove. I'd put my feet up by the opening into the low ashpan. Sit there dopey. Feel my numb toes coming slowly back to life. Blink at the glowing coals dropping down through the grate into the grey ashes below.

How wonderful the sun felt when finally the icicles began to drip and run away in little streams! Some years we'd have a few of those thawing days before the end of February. Even so, March always seemed to "come in like a lion." As I remember, we often had the worst storm of the season about that time. Yet even while the northeast wind howled around the corners of the house and drifted our roadway full of snow, we took comfort, knowing that winter's back was broken. One day soon the weather would be right. A morning would come when Father would say, "Time to tap the maple trees."

Maple syrup time—how we did enjoy that season. . . . Fragrant steam rising from the evaporator in the sugar house. On the kitchen stove Mother's big pan of hot syrup boiling up into heavy, bursting, golden bubbles—almost ready to pour off and stir into sugar. And how we ate! Hot maple sugar dipped onto clean snow, forming little puddles that hardened in a moment. Too sticky to chew, just right to melt away on our tongues. Cold yet biting-sweet, brittle and smooth, a sort of lollipop that we called "Leather Aprons" and ate by the panful. And the sugar cakes that Mother made—little scalloped and heart-shaped ones to gobble at once or to hoard and nibble away, whichever we pleased. A glass pitcher brimming full of new maple syrup on the table at every meal.

So much hard work for the grownups—tapping the trees, gathering and boiling down barrels and barrels of sap to make syrup, and then more boiling and stirring to make the sugar—all that meant nothing to us children. We had only the fun. In those days when our maple orchard was young even the trees nearby the house were tapped. Our "Big Maple," the noble tree that sheltered the house and yard, used to have four buckets hung around its great trunk. On a fine sap day we could stand on our front piazza and hear the sap beginning to run. "Dri-ip, dr-r-op. Drip, drip, drip." On those mornings we got up early and dressed quickly, hurried through breakfast so we could run out into the sunshine. By the time Father came in from the barn chores to eat his breakfast, we'd be back, ready to tell him what kind of sap day we thought it would be. The early morning snowcrust would hold so we could slide on our Flexible Flyers down the hill and across the field, then climb the slope to find out if the sap had started in the main sugar orchard. We'd go around to some of the biggest trees, lift up the covers and peek into the buckets. Sometimes when the gathering team had not been around since early the day before, a few of the buckets would already be running over. Then we'd hurry back to tell Father how the sap was going to waste on the ground, but first, if we happened to be thirsty (and we always *were* thirsty), we'd drink from the bucket's rim—big, satisfying gulps of crystal clear sap, freezing cold and just faintly sweet.

A good sap run could never be expected to last more than a few days. Winter was sure to come sneaking back, changing everything with a touch of cold magic. The sap in the buckets was frozen into cakes of sweet ice, and the droplets falling from the spiles were turned into small glass pendants. Other times a storm blew up in the night, and we'd wake to find the dingy, snow-covered fields were frosted over with fresh white. Jaunty caps of snow were perched atop every bucket cover and on all the fence posts. Cottony puffs decorated the drooping branches of the evergreen trees. A "sugar snow," forerunner of more good sapping weather, Father told us. We didn't mind late snow; it never stayed long—even helped to melt away old, hard-packed drifts. Some years the first robins arrived before we could see much bare ground. Of course, we were always very glad to see the birds come back, but we wondered how they expected to find any worms when ground was still frozen hard. We begged Mother for bread crumbs to throw out. We worried and wondered where they stayed at night.

Almost before we'd had time to catch a breath, it seemed, we were through March and into April. A pair of bluebirds showed up and began looking over the hole in the apple tree down beside the woodshed. About that time we always had a day or so of warm rain to take off most of the snow and ice. Then we could hear the brooks again. One night at suppertime Father would say, "Sapping's about done. Go outside and listen—the frogs are peeping."

From the wet hollow at the bottom of the lower field, first one, then another, then another timid "peep." Then more and more, quickly joining in. A week later the full chorus would be starting up every night just before dusk. The deep vrooming notes coming in now and then were made by the old bullfrogs, we thought, and the young ones were the chorus of peepers. We used to argue about the frogs' song. Somebody told us it was a sorrowful chant.

"Paddy gaw' drunk! Druunk! Druunk!," the big old ones harped mournfully.

"Weeep. Weeep. Weeep," the little sopranos lamented endlessly.

I never heard it that way at all. The frogs croaked every evening; the roosters crowed at daylight; and the birds sang all day because they were happy that spring had come to stay. I knew it because I was so glad myself. Springtime was the freshest, greenest, prettiest— the very best time of year—and it was all mine.

"April showers bring May flowers"—only a tarnished old rhyme, but to me it was the music of poetry. I suppose I must have learned it even before I could say the words. I loved the warm sun and the warm rain. I watched for the opening of each new blossom. While there was still a piece of old snowbank left along the garden wall, little green shoots began pushing up through layers of soggy, dead leaves. One day I forgot to look, and when I went back I saw a whole bed of Snowdrops nodding their pearly heads at me. A clump of tall pussy willows grew beside the stone wall. I stroked their silvery catkins gently with one finger and discovered something wonderful: The furry velvet was as soft as a real kitten's ear! I stayed very still to watch a bluebird bringing wisps of hay to the old apple tree and I saw that his feathers were made of the deepest, purest blue in the whole world. I walked under a maple tree—just for my pleasure a little breeze came by and let fall on me a shower of tiny scarlet blossom pieces. Whenever I came near their hiding places, the pink and white mayflowers peeked out from under dusty-green leaves, offering their dainty perfume to me. Wherever I looked, whatever I saw was all for me.

Whenever I think of my lovely New Hampshire springtime, memory reaches back to the long, long ago when I was only four and a half years old. I must have been a dreamy, imaginative little girl. I'm sure that's why I secretly pretended that I alone could feel the beauty and the wonder, while all the time another part of me knew it *was* only pretend. I'm certain I never truly supposed that I was a special anybody. There was always "we," never just "me." My sisters and brothers and me.

All of us were so glad when the time came to shed our wrinkly, long-legged underwear. We watched so eagerly for the first flush of green to show in the bare brown fields, and we begged to go barefoot when the new grass was scarcely high enough for a field mouse to nibble. We knew it was much too cold. We knew our mother's rule: "Look at the mountains. When there's not one bit of snow to be seen on the mountains, then you may go barefoot."

From our back piazza we looked for the morning sun and watched the snow line receding up the Belknaps. So close we could make out the fire tower on the middle one, three rounded mountain humps marched in a row like the bears. Gunstock and Belknap, two bigger mountains, followed by Whiteface, a ledgy, "baby" mountain. In the spring afternoons clouds would gather and a quick shower would shut us off from the mountains. Oftentimes the sun would come out before the rain was all done. Then we'd see a rainbow, maybe just a pale gleam of color lasting only a moment or two, or it might be a perfect brilliant arc with one end touching down in the pine grove just up the lane. If we ran quickly, we said, we could surely pass right through the shimmering colors and find the pot of gold hidden there where the rainbow ended. We were matter-of-fact children so of course we couldn't take fairy stories seriously. We knew that the pretty colors were made by the sun shining through the raindrops, but I liked better to think of the story my mother told us. "The rainbow is God's sign," she said. "His promise to us that the snow will always melt away. Every year spring will come again, bringing the warm rain and the sunshine to make the crops grow. It's God's token, His 'bow in the cloud.' The Bible tells us so." After awhile, it would be May; by then, all the late wild flowers would be blossoming, the trees would be leafed out and not a bit of snow could we see on the mountains. Then we would gleefully unlace our shoes and take off our heavy black stockings (never to put them on again till fall, except for Sunday School), and we would run barefoot and free on the soft green grass.

There were five of us then. I was the middle child. Sometimes when we were gathered around the supper table our mother would smile fondly at us, shake her head and tell us a rhyme. She used to hear it when she was young, she'd say:

> " 'When you have one, you take it and run
> When you have two, then you make do
> When you have three—you stay where you be.'

"I used to think four would be a nice family—two boys and two girls. Here I am with five of you!" Then, so we would know for sure she wanted us all, she'd laugh (she had a way of throwing back her head and laughing most heartily). None of us ever questioned her love or felt that she had any favorites, and we never begrudged the special pleasure she took in the little ones.

My mother used to say that my younger brother, Forrest, was the happiest, least bothersome baby and the busiest little boy she had ever seen. He went about inside the house and outdoors talking along to himself or singing scraps of tunes without words. Wherever he went,

close behind him followed our baby sister, Frances, his little shadow.
The fall before, while she was still creeping, Frances had done her best
to keep up by scrabbling along on all fours. Now that she could run
around she was never left behind. It was comical to see the little boy,
not even half past two himself, putting on such an air of condescension
toward his dumpling baby sister. He graciously accepted her to be his
slavey and nicknamed her "Little Tine." She still just pointed at the
rest of us when she wanted to make her wishes known, but she had
tried to say "Forrest" right after she had learned to say "Mamma."
While she followed her brother everywhere, smiling so sweetly and
watching with such adoring eyes, she kept remarking smugly to no one
in particular, "For'st bad boy! Bad boy, For'st is!"

Esther and Royal were old enough to help with the barn chores.
They had already learned how to milk, taking turns on Old Pansy
because she wouldn't kick and didn't care how long they sat there on
the milking stool—tugging away, working to fill up a one-quart tin
dipper. They could halter the stubborn calves and lead the balky little
creatures along on a rope willy-nilly. They were learning to harness
and drive the horses, how to climb up on a box high enough so they
could force the bit between the horse's teeth, reluctant though the
animal might be. How to back him carefully between the wagon shafts
until the traces could be hitched up. Yet there were hours of playtime
every day when they could go wherever they pleased all over the
farm: Clear up to the cupola on the roof of the barn to look out over
the tops of the tallest trees as far as the horizon stretched toward the
four points of the compass. Through the fields to climb over the stone
wall, squeeze carefully under the strands of barbed wire on top, and
go down to play where the pasture brook ran swift with icy cold
snow water, overflowing its banks in freshet. And wherever they went
I followed, a constant tagalong trying hard to keep up.

I was too young then to have regular chores either inside the house
or outdoors. It was several years before my father discovered that I was
no earthly use around the barn. I might sit forever on a milking stool
beside the most resigned old cow, struggle as hard as I could and never
fill one small cup with the warm, sweet milk. Even the gentlest horse
could sense immediately my abject cowardice and would begin to act
up, tossing his head so the bridle wouldn't go on (even if I happened
to have it right side to) snorting his contempt and blowing flecks of
sticky foam into my face. I might hammer and pound away at a
hundred nails without getting a single one to go in straight. Then,
when the day came that my father finally gave up he would tell me,
not unkindly, that I'd best go into the house to help my mother with

the babies and I'd go—happy because the barn would still be a fine place to play and I was forevermore free from the hated barn chores.

We spent almost as much of our growing-up time in the big red barn as we did in the house. The upper floors smelled of hay and grain, even when the cattle were all out to pasture and the fodder was nearly all used up. The only place I didn't care to go was the far end of the cellar underneath the cow tie-up. I didn't like to be anywhere near the stinking manure piled up there. I knew the land soaked up that good fertilizer to make the heavy windrows of clover hay drying in the July sun and the fields of oats bending thick gold heads in the August breeze, but I never wanted to think anything that smelled so nasty could help to grow the juicy ears of green corn and the sweet little garden carrots we liked to pull and crunch right up to their ferny green tops, not minding at all the bits of clinging black earth.

I disliked the odor of the animals, too, and was a little afraid of them. I suppose that's why I never really tried very hard to milk a cow or learned how to manage the horses. When I was small, the cows looked so big to me and there were so many, jostling each other as they were let loose from their stanchions. They crowded and stumbled and slipped down the narrow chute-way to the long stone watering trough in the barn cellar. They sank their noses deep into the water and drank noisily, then pushed roughly out through the barnyard gate. Their hoofs were enormous. What if one came smashing down on my bare feet? I took care to keep me and my toes well out of the way! The horses were supposed to be gentle, but they stamped loudly and impatiently in their stalls and sometimes lashed out at each other with an iron-clad hoof. At times they bared their teeth and let out shrill whinnies at me. Probably they were only hungry for their hay and grain, but I wouldn't go alone into their stalls nor walk behind them for dreading that I might be stung across the face by a long switching tail. I got over the fear as I grew older, but I never lost that feeling of uneasiness around animals. My feelings were shared by some of my sisters—I know that now, although we never used to speak of it. Farm girls who are fearful and inept around animals had better be ashamed to admit it.

Yet I wasn't really a timorous child. As far back as I can remember, in the summer before I was five years old when I spent all my days following the older ones about, I wasn't afraid of bugs or mice or any of the creatures of the fields and woods. I wasn't scared of the dark nor timid about high places. Though I wasn't aware that they felt any concern for me, I suppose Esther and Royal must have watched out for my safety. I felt privileged just to follow and watch, and I thought I was taking care of myself. I couldn't have been much trouble for them because I was never reckless or daring. Once I did know real fear—a swift, paralyzing terror—but it was not for myself that I was afraid.

We had been playing in the barn one morning. It must have been early summer because the scaffolds were bare and the bays on the barn-floor level were so empty of hay we could play hide-and-seek in the dark corners. On the wide floor just a scattering of fine old chaff was left where in wintertime Father pitched down big piles of hay from the scaffolds. Esther and Royal had gone up to the cupola and back. I followed along, the way I always did. Why they had gone I never afterward remembered; perhaps they planned to scan the distant hills for smoke signals, thinking to warn the settlers if the tribes were making ready to go on the warpath. Maybe there was no game and, instead, they were searching among the castoff farm tools on the high floor for a piece of scrap leather or a pair of small wheels. (They were forever building wagons out of boxes and putting together straps and old buckles for a harness or rigging up a hitch for a pet lamb or a gentle heifer.) I went up there just for the fun of it. Climbing up so high was both risky adventure and play ritual to me.

Run quickly up the first safe staircase to the lowest scaffold. Turn a sharp corner and keep going fast up the next short flight taking care to hug the closed-in side. Step out onto the wide boards of the second floor, an open platform high above the first level. Turn right a few steps to look down through the tall window-opening at the roadway below and across to the attic windows of our house, partly hidden behind three maples standing in a row. Then about-face and stop a moment to consider whether to go on. Just ahead stretches a wide opening with narrow walkways on either side. Nothing to hang to going across. In haying time that opening is needed so the big fork can be pulled down to the load below. That fork is hanging out of use now, like a great dusty spider in its rope web high up under the ridgepole. Crossing by the big hole is scary, but the next stairway going up is on the other side, so don't hesitate too long and never, never look down to the hard barn floor so far below. Walk steady. Keep right along the center plank. Place each foot carefully straight ahead. And so across without getting even a little bit dizzy! Take a deep breath before going on up to the cobwebby third floor and across the squeaky, dusty boards; then climb straight up the tiniest stairs and out into a square, safe little room right under the sky.

That day we had gone back down to the barn floor and were just ready to go out the big front doors when we heard something that made Esther and Royal pause. When the noise came again they turned back and so did I. We looked up and saw Forrest out on the narrow walkway beside the big hole. He was smiling and chuckling, pleased with himself—that was the little noise we had heard. He crawled farther out, leaned over and kept laughing at our scared faces. Then he lifted one fat little hand and waved at us, said "Hi" and something that sounded like "Foo'dya!" I don't know what Esther and Royal said, but somehow they got him to hold still right there until they could reach him and lead him safely down the stairs. I couldn't do anything at all to help— just stood there stock-stiff, not able to close my mouth and make even a dry whisper come out. But the inside "me" was churning every which way. I pictured my little brother falling, falling down to the hard floor. I saw him lying there, a crumbled heap with his chubby arms all twisted. I hurt all over because I knew he would never again open his eyes and I knew for sure that I would be blamed, and I could not deny that it was all my fault. I remembered how I had heard something in the hole under the stairs as I came down. A rustling that could have been made by a cat, or a hen scratching up the chaff. If only I had bothered to look I would have found the little rascal hiding there. For a long while afterward we didn't tell our parents about that narrow escape. I never told anyone, not even Esther and Royal, that I had half-known Forrest was hiding there. I felt too guilty.

I soon forgot to blame myself and the memory faded until it was no more real than an old nightmare. I was barely old enough to be responsible for myself, let alone worry about the younger ones. That bad experience should have taught me to value my little brother, but it didn't. I played happily with him and the baby when the older ones weren't around; the rest of the time he was just *there*, the next younger one. I felt superior because he slept in a crib and always wanted my mother to do him up in a blanket and carry him in to bed to take his nap. He wouldn't give up drinking his milk from a baby's bottle, either, but he chewed up the black rubber nipples and lost them, too, so we were always having to hunt one up when he went to bed. Probably I was jealous underneath, because he was bound to crowd into my mother's lap whenever she was rocking my baby sister, so there was never any room for me. I couldn't remember back to a time when I had been the baby of the family and had been rocked to sleep. If it bothered me I didn't realize, because I liked to think of myself as a big girl. I had what I needed—my mother, so nice and soft to lean against, always ready to soothe rumpled feelings or bandage a cut finger. Once that summer I did get a notion to play the baby. That one time was enough—it turned out such a fizzle I never tried it again.

None of our near neighbors had any young children so we had always played at home. Then a new family with a girl about my age moved into the next place down the road. One day the mother called up to invite someone down to visit, because her little girl was lonesome. My mother told me I might go if I liked, only get cleaned up first. I washed my hands and face, but I was too impatient to wait until she could brush my hair and braid it over again. I never even thought about my dusty feet until I saw the little neighbor girl was wearing shoes and stockings, just like Sunday. She had a big hair bow and tight curls that bounced on her neck when she flounced herself about. Her name was June. A pretty name, but how funny to be named for a month! Her mother mostly called her pet names like "Honeybunch" and "Junie-baby."

At first I didn't have a good time. My feet were so dirty and they felt so big! I didn't know where to put my hands or what to say, so I just kept still and listened to the mother going on in her high-up, tinkly voice. Junie talked a lot, too, but she couldn't say her words any better than my little sister. That's what I thought at first until I caught on—she was just talking babyish on purpose. After we had a cambric tea party and ate some cookies that I didn't like, the mother said we could go outdoors to play. I felt better outside, especially when I found out Junie couldn't do any of the things I did all the time. She couldn't skip rope or pump herself in the swing. She couldn't go into the pasture for fear of muddying her shoes. She let out a little scream when she saw a fuzzy brown caterpillar, and she dasn't hold a grasshopper I caught to squeeze for molasses. And the way she took on—wrinkling up her nose when she almost stepped on some horse droppings in the road! But how pretty and dainty she was! Her hair was so shiny and curly (mine was stringy and mouse-brown). She was wearing clean white stockings and black patent leathers on her little feet. Her ruffled pink dress was too short to cover her knees. My dress was a hand-me-down plaid gingham that Mother had tucked up. I had liked it fine, but now I saw it was way too long (Mother always left plenty of room for growing), and it hung off me like an old grain sack. It didn't take me long to decide that Junie was the cutest, prettiest little girl I had ever seen, and I longed to be exactly like her. I knew I couldn't have light-colored, flounced dresses or get my mother to put my hair up in rags every night, but I could try to walk like Junie and I could learn to talk the way she did.

I practiced all the way home. Once I forgot and began to skip but I slowed right down and went on taking dainty, short steps. I tried wrinkling up my nose and holding my little finger out the way Junie did when she drank the cambric tea. I made up conversations so I could answer myself with a baby lisp like Junie's. I couldn't wait to show off to the older ones. I was sure it would be such fun.

I didn't have long to wait. As I came up over the hill I saw that

Esther and Royal were working on one of their contraptions up by the barnyard, so I headed toward them. There on the ground, right by the barnyard gate, I saw a big soupy cowflap. Of course I didn't usually make any fuss about a natural thing like cow manure dropped in the road, just took care not to step in any with my bare feet. But not this time! I let out a soft little cry of horror—anyway that's what I meant it to be. Esther and Royal looked up in surprise and watched with open mouths. I wrinkled up my nose (just like Junie), lifted my gingham skirt and minced past, exclaiming "haw'wid, nassy stuff," achieving just the right effect, I felt. I had made an impression all right, but not what I had hoped. Both of them stood and glared at me. Then while Esther looked on in scornful silence, Royal began his own performance. He put on a stupid, grinning face, held his arms close and stiff and let his hands flap loose, went back and forth posing, and teetering and squeaking silly things at me, "Poor itsy-bitsy dirl! So her was f'wightened, was her? Whatta nassy, nassy ole cow!" And then in his regular voice, only meaner, "Huh! You little dummy! Think ya cute, dontcha?" Esther was just as mean. She kept on laughing loud. Then they turned their backs and walked off, leaving me hanging my head and pouting out my underlip. Serve them right if I should go in and tell Mother how they had plagued me. I would have, too, if I had thought it would do any good, but she would never pay much attention to our complaints about each other, especially not near mealtimes. She'd only tell me, "Never mind them. It will all be forgotten tomorrow. Run along now. You know your father always wants his supper on the table when he comes in from the barn, and I'm hurrying to have it ready." I stood there awhile, hating Esther and Royal, thinking up ways to get even with them. Then I gave up. Might as well get used to it. I wasn't little, or cute, or pretty. I was nothing but just plain me! All that thinking had made me hungry, so I went into the house to see if supper was ready and found it was.

We always had a good hot meal at suppertime the same as we did at noon and in the morning. In those days most families ate three square meals a day, even city people, I guess. My father wanted to have plenty of good food set on the table. He never believed in stinting, except when it came to drinking milk. That was because the money from the milk check was his only steady year-round income. Anyway, he thought only babies needed milk to drink. He didn't care about it himself. Said he'd rather have good spring water to drink with his meals. So that's what we all drank, because Father had the say about the food that went on the table (and most everything else, too). Mother got around him some, though, by letting all the children have their bottles as long as they wanted. Forrest didn't give up his until he was so big he was ashamed and used to hide behind the door while he was sucking up his milk.

All the milk from our farm, except what we used at home, was sold to a milk peddler who lived about a mile away. Every night after supper when all his barn chores were done, Father hitched one of the horses to the express wagon, loaded on the full crates and drove down to leave the milk and bring back empty milk bottles. One night he let me go with him. I remember especially because it was the only time I ever felt close to my father when I was little.

We had all gone to bed and the others had fallen asleep but somehow I couldn't, so I got up and came downstairs just as my father was getting ready to take the milk. The evening was cool, so Mother dressed me and put on me my little red coat with the wide double collar (I called it my coat with angel wings). By the time the milk was delivered and we started home it was very dark and I thought it must be very late, the middle of the night probably. I felt very queer being up when all of the others were at home in bed. I snuggled up close to my big father, stared hard into the dark and listened while he talked about the stars. He showed me the Milky Way and pointed out the Big Dipper and the North Star. If you could tell where the North Star was you'd never be lost, he said. I kept looking and looking, watching the twinkling stars until my neck was tired. Then I listened to the tree toads and the crickets. My father said you could almost tell it was August by the way those crickets were singing. It seemed to me there must be millions and millions of crickets down in the grass all scraping away, loud and mournful. Afterwards, I always disliked crickets and hated to hear them begin to tune up, because I knew that summer was almost over. Warm weather never lasted half as long as it should. I didn't want to think summer would ever end.

When it came September that year, I stood at the top of the hill and watched Esther and Royal going off to school, swinging their lunch boxes. They were happy and excited. I was left with nobody to play with, only the little ones.

❧ 4 ❧

A Growing Time

T HE SUMMER after Annie was born Mother decided we ought to have a family picture taken. She knew Father wouldn't give up the best part of a good hay day. As far as that went, he wouldn't agree to get dressed up in his suit and stiff collar on any kind of day, unless for something a good deal more important than a picture-taking session. Mother really didn't care, because she didn't want to be in the picture either; she said she was past the age when it was any fun to be photographed. What she wanted was a good picture of us children so she could remember us as we were right then. Although it wasn't mentioned, we had an idea the family photograph was to be used as a show piece.

Whenever Mother's or Father's old acquaintances or down-country city relatives came to the farm, we were called in—except for anybody lucky enough to be helping Father (usually Esther and the boys)—to be counted over and appraised. The little girls were certain to have dirty faces and hair hanging frowzily. Our feet were either dusty or muddy, depending on where we had been playing, and there were always some bandaged toes and skinned knees in the lot. Mother was proud of us and didn't seem to mind. The dirt was fresh; we all looked bright and certainly healthy. But every time such visitors came I hated it. My little sisters' grimy appearance was my blame; bad enough, but not nearly as shameful as going around without shoes and stockings myself—big girl as I was. I tried to keep me and my big bare feet as inconspicuous as possible, glared at my little sisters when they squirmed or scratched, and suffered through each exhibition. Mercifully it never lasted long. The visitors were polite, amazed at the size of our family and soon bored. The talk shifted, and we escaped outdoors.

Afterward I was mean to the little girls for awhile, made them wash their faces several times a day; then we slipped back into the comfortable old ways and I kept on going barefoot until school began. The family photograph would show us all dressed up, might possibly make me look pretty, at least prove we did have shoes and stockings to wear. I didn't expect to be consulted about the picture-taking and I wasn't, but if anyone had asked I would have said I was in favor. I guessed the others were, too.

One August day we drove down to Laconia. After hitching the teams in an alley, each of the older children took a younger one by the hand and followed Mother (she was carrying Annie) around front to a building on Main Street. We climbed up a steep flight of stairs to the picture studio, a peculiar-smelling room without any windows, except one you couldn't see through up in the ceiling. It was a job to get changed (Mother had brought our Sunday dresses and the boys' jackets in a cardboard suitcase) because the place, already cluttered, became pretty crowded with the eight of us and Mother and the photographer, a fussy little man with fluttery hands. Esther and I got behind a cloth screen to help Frances, Nellie and Jessie; then sent them out one at a time to sit on little stools so they wouldn't get their dresses mussed. While Royal and Forrest got on their suit coats and neckties (Royal knotted Forrest's twice but still it was crooked in the picture), Mother was sitting over in the corner with her back turned so she could change Annie's diaper and put on her pink lawn dress. As soon as Esther and I got our white dresses buttoned up, I took Annie while she helped Mother smooth the little girls' curls and tie their ribbons. I tried to brush Annie's hair into a wispy curl on top of her head, but I had to keep stopping to dab with my handkerchief at her fat little chins (she was cutting a tooth and she drooled). Then the photographer posed us in front of the screen: The boys were like two steps standing at one side, heads held stiff, looking straight ahead; Royal, the taller one, with his right hand placed on Forrest's shoulder; Esther next to them, sitting on a small hard settee with me right beside her; Frances standing up on a stool close behind us, roguishly puffing down the backs of our necks, knowing very well we couldn't turn around to make her stop; at our knees Nellie and Jessie plumped onto low stools, hair bows standing out perky and crisp, everything else about them babyish curves—fat cheeks, jouncy curls and dimpled elbows; Annie was put on Esther's lap so I didn't have anything to do with my hands.

After the photographer had poked and pushed at us enough to suit him, he got under the black cloth that was thrown over the big camera sitting on three high skinny legs. We thought he was going to take the picture so we pulled up the corners of our mouths and tried to look happy—all but Annie whose mouth was already opened in a little round O. He wasn't anywhere near ready! He kept popping his head out to flap his hands at us, running over to poke at our heads a little, all the while whistling and tweeting and smirking at us. We supposed he was trying to be amusing, thinking to make us look pleasant, but he was so dumb-acting we felt kind of ashamed. Out of the corner of my eye I could see that Royal's eyebrows were up, a sure sign he was pretty disgusted. Finally the nutty little man got back under his cloth, said, "Look right at the camera. Tweet - Twe-e-ety - Tweet! Everybody smile! Hold it, now," and squeezed the rubber ball. He grabbed something out of the camera and went quick into a little dark closet. We thought he was finished so we stopped breathing in and let our shoulders slump. But he came right out again and we went through the whole business another time or two. When we got downstairs after the picture-taking we were so tired we climbed into the wagons without quarreling about who was to go with which team. What was more remarkable, no one said anything about going to Keller's candy store, and there it was right down the street.

Mother must have been pleased with the pictures; she got the photographer to finish up two different poses. I supposed the rest were satisfied with the way they looked. I didn't ask and they didn't say. As for me, after I took one look, I tried to forget the whole business, was careful to be somewhere else when the photographs were brought out to show. My picture was just ordinary, didn't show me a bit prettier than every day. I hadn't smiled or even succeeded in looking pleasant— you would have thought I was more worried than anything else—my eyelids kind of droopy and the corners of my mouth turned way down. It would have been different if I could have had Annie sitting on my lap. I would have been a lot more important in the picture. I wouldn't have cared so much if I didn't look pretty. Of course Esther was two years older, but at home I was the baby tender while she spent most of her time helping Father. Whenever we went to Sunday School or anywhere that we took two teams, she and Royal took turns driving one of the horses, but I always went with Mother and held Annie.

Annie was born in October, my birthday month, but that wasn't why I had come to feel she was my special charge. The fact was, I hadn't valued her at all when she was a tiny baby, could never recall much about her birth. At the time I was taken up with school, and anyway a new baby—another baby sister at that—was no novelty in our family.

I found out where babies came from a long time before we had Annie. Kittens and lambs and calves were being born on our farm right along—nothing mysterious about it any more. But having another baby come was pretty hard on the younger ones. Nellie and Jessie got under the table and stayed for almost a whole day. They didn't want anything whatever to do with the strange woman who tried to make them come out from there and eat some dinner. They didn't want a new baby, either. They wanted Mother to come downstairs and feed them.

The way I remembered it, I had felt just about the same at the time Nellie was born. Of course I was much younger then and not very smart (I hadn't begun to go to school). I was sure Dr. True had brought the baby I could hear crying up in the south chamber. We had had a bad surprise when we came downstairs that morning. Out in the kitchen slamming around getting breakfast was somebody we scarcely knew—a Mrs. Smith, a relation of Father's family, we had been told. Right off she said to us, kind of mad-like, "Dr. True was here early this morning. Now you've got a new baby sister. Your mother is tired and she's resting. You children are to leave her alone. If I catch one of you sneaking up there, I'm liable to skin you alive!"

When Father came in from the barn I watched him pretty close to see how he was taking it. He didn't seem a bit surprised, just sat right down and ate his breakfast the same as always. He told Esther and Royal to hurry up and get ready for school so they could go with him when he took the milk. After they left, Forrest and Frances went out to play. I could have gone with them but I didn't feel like it. They wouldn't be doing anything that was fun, just playing in the sawdust down by the icehouse or monkeying around with Father's tools out in the corn shed. Forrest would, anyway. Frances would be following along after him watching what he did and acting like she knew what he was saying. They were satisfied as long as they were together. Nobody was lonesome but me. I kept getting more so and more so all the morning.

Father didn't take us when he went up to see Mother at noon. All the time he was eating dinner he didn't mention our new baby sister once, but he joked and laughed with Mrs. Smith (she seemed to think a lot better of him than she did of us). He told her he would like to sit around awhile and visit about old times, but he had to get back to the corn piece. It should have been finished before now if there was anything to the old saying about getting the corn planted when the white oak leaves are the size of a squirrel's ear. She tossed her head and rolled her eyes at him and said the way she had heard it was: Plant the corn when the apple blossoms fall on the hill. He didn't think it made much difference either way—high time he got the seed into the ground. Then he went out without taking any more notice of us.

After awhile when Frances got cross and began to fuss about seeing Mother, Mrs. Smith gave her, and Forrest too, bottles of milk, told them to go into the back bedroom to rest and take naps if they wanted. She still acted mad, looked hard at Forrest out of her black eyes, said, "Great big boy. Ought to be 'shamed, sucking on a nipple. If it was my doing, you wouldn't still be drinking milk from a bottle. Neither would your sister." Forrest wouldn't be shamed by a woman he didn't even like, and as long as he didn't care, Frances didn't either. After they were gone I began to feel lonesome again.

I couldn't think of a thing to do, so I stood in the middle of the front room, listening for the baby's crying—but she wasn't. Inside the house there were no sounds at all. Outside a big green fly was buzzing and bumping against the window screen, trying to get in, I guessed. From somewhere in the maple trees a robin was scolding and off in the fields lots of bobolinks were singing. I could hear Father making the horse pull the corn planter along the rows. His voice sounded funny and faint, though I knew he was yelling loud, "Giddap. Get along. Gid-dap now." Mrs. Smith came in carrying a pitcher of water and some towels over her arm. She went right by me, on through the front hall and up the stairs, didn't seem to notice me waiting there lonesome. I couldn't stand any more of that. I went around, sneaked up the back stairs, and tiptoed soft and easy along the back hall taking care not to make the boards squeak. I stood outside the door to the south chamber listening and waiting, quiet as a mouse. After a very long time, probably more than an hour I thought, Mrs. Smith got through with whatever she was doing and stopped talking to Mother. When I heard her go out the other door and start down the front stairs, I lifted the latch ever so careful, pushed hard on the door and went in.

When Mother opened her eyes and saw me standing by the bed she was even gladder than I thought she would be. She wanted me to tell her what the others had been doing, so I did, as much as I could remember, but mostly I told her about how I didn't have anybody to play with and there was nothing for me to do and how we wanted her to come downstairs and get us something to eat because Mrs. Smith was mean to us and we didn't like what she cooked. While we were talking she put her arm out and let me lean against her. On her other side was a small bundle I knew was the baby wrapped up in something blue, but I didn't say a thing about it, just made believe I didn't notice anything was there. After awhile Mother told me if I wanted to I could come around and climb up on the bed and she would show me the new baby sister. I didn't care a bit about looking at her, but I could tell Mother would feel bad if I said so. While she was undoing the soft blanket, I scrounched on the edge of the bed with my feet under me so she wouldn't notice they were too dirty to be there on the white sheets. She told me we would call the baby "Nellie" but her name was really Ellen Genevieve—for some relations of hers and Father's we children had never heard of. I was discouraged right then. That name was such a pretty one, so long and important-sounding. If they had been going to think up a name like that, why couldn't they have done it sooner so they could have given it to me?

The baby was hardly worth seeing, she was so little. Her arms and legs were not round and cute at all, more like bent-up sticks. She was badly wrinkled all over and red colored, almost as dark as chimney bricks. Of course I knew better than to think new babies could walk or talk, but this one just lay there with her face all puckered up, wouldn't open her eyes and her mouth was shut tight, too. I didn't understand how a crying loud enough for me to hear downstairs could have come from that tiny little thing. Mother kept on talking about what a nice baby sister she was, so strong and pretty and healthy. I could see it wouldn't be a bit of use for me to say anything so I kept still until she turned the baby over to show me the back of her. That was when I saw the two big purple spots right below where her head was hitched on to her shoulders (she didn't seem to have a neck). That was the worst of all! Nobody could make me think a purple-spotted baby was worth having. I was going to say so, but Mother saw how I was feeling and said, quite fast, "Those little birthmarks don't amount to anything. A short while and they'll be all faded out. Nellie will be soft and round and sweet-smelling. You're big enough now so you can hold her, rock her to sleep if you want to. Don't you think you've been up here long enough? I'll tell you what—let's not say anything to the others about your seeing Nellie first. Let's keep it a secret for you and me."

I would have done it, too, only when it was time for Esther and Royal to be coming home from school I happened to be out in the dooryard playing so I ran to meet them at the top of the hill. Before they could say anything, I told them, "I went up to see Mother and the new baby ahead of you. We're going to call her Nellie but her name is really Ellen Genevieve, and she's going to be the prettiest one in the whole family!"

The next time it was Frances who told Esther and Royal and me how Dr. True had come and left us a new baby sister. When we got home from school on September eighteenth, the day Esther was ten years old, Frances met us at the top of the hill—so excited and proud anybody would have thought having a baby sister come on our oldest sister's birthday was something she had planned all by herself. When we went up to see Mother we found out she was just as surprised as the rest of us—about the birthdays, not the baby. She was surprised, too, because she had thought we would surely get a new brother instead of another sister this time. I didn't know how the rest felt, but I didn't care at all. Done up in her soft blue blanket that new baby looked just right to me. She was wrinkled and pretty red, but of course I knew she was supposed to look that way at first. Her cute little face was round and so was her chin, the same as Nellie's and everybody else's in our family. All over her head was pale yellow hair, so downy soft I had to feel it to be sure it was there. When she opened her dark blue eyes and looked right at me, I liked her very much and I couldn't believe it when Mother said she didn't really "see" anybody yet.

Of course it wasn't so much fun having the birthday supper without Mother there, but we thought it was lucky she had baked Esther's cake and frosted it before she knew our baby (her name was Jessie) was going to be born on September eighteenth, too. After we had finished eating, the woman who was taking care of us said Mother wanted us all to go to the south chamber so she could read us some more of a story book, the same as she did every night. We were glad, but when we got up there Esther and I were bothered (Royal was some, too), because Frances and Nellie were bound to climb on the bed. We knew very well they would be leaning heavy against Mother, bumping up and down, maybe poking with their fingers at our little Jessie. We tried to grab them and haul them down, but Mother wouldn't have it. She said, "Oh, let them stay. They only want to be close. They'll be good, I know." They weren't very, but we couldn't do anything about it except glare at them while we tried to keep our minds on the story.

Mother came downstairs much sooner than she had when Nellie was born, and right away everything was just the same as before we had Jessie. It seemed so to me anyway, but once when a friend of Mother's was visiting I overheard some talk I didn't like. The friend was speaking to Mother in a scolding voice, "—never heard the like! Four young ones on the bottle at once, two of them in diapers. I don't see how you manage. With a family so big you ought to try to make it easier on yourself. Of course you haven't asked my opinion, but I'd say you should take Forrest's bottle away from him—such a big boy, no sense to it. Frances could just as well drink her milk from a cup, too. I hope you don't mind my saying this, Winnie, but seven in ten years is entirely too many. That's something you'd better think on." Mother answered so polite and quiet I couldn't hear all she was saying— something about not minding the bottle washing or the diapers, either. She told how when Forrest was so sick, that time before he was two years old, Dr. True had been afraid they couldn't save him, and if they did he might not be able to walk; how she had made up her mind then she wouldn't ask for another thing if he could only learn to use his legs again. And she said it was such a pleasure to see how sturdy he was. She wanted him to keep drinking milk. She didn't care how long he hung on to his bottle, or how long the little girls did, either.

As soon as I had a chance to get Mother alone after the friend had gone I asked her why that woman who was visiting had talked as though the little ones oughtn't to suck their bottles, and if she was try-ing to make out there was something bad about having so many in the family. Mother just laughed and said, "Oh, she didn't mean anything by that talk. She thinks because she's such an old friend she ought to tell me how to run this house. I didn't pay any attention to her, and don't you."

So after that I didn't. But I really couldn't understand why the younger children made all that fuss about drinking milk from bottles. When I was born, Mother had gone to the hospital in Laconia and I never had a bottle. What the connection was I didn't know because Esther and Royal were born at home and they didn't have bottles. The important part was that nobody but me had been born in the hospital in Laconia. Sometimes Mother said she was sorry she hadn't put me on a bottle, too, because I didn't like milk and didn't eat a good break-fast. Sometimes when Father noticed that I wouldn't eat oatmeal, he called me a "scrawny young one" and offered me money—as much as a dime—if only I would eat a small dish of hot cereal before setting off for school in the morning. I never would. Yet I was pleased because he had singled me out that way, and I couldn't help reckoning how many pink-striped candy sticks, rolls of Necco wafers, or long licorice ropes I could have bought, if only I had eaten the oatmeal and had the dime to spend at the store down on Casino Square when school was out at noontime.

Esther and Royal and I began school in Laconia because there were so few children in our part of Gilford it was cheaper to pay our tuition, instead of opening the one-room rural school up the road from our farm. When Forrest was old enough to attend, there were enough more pupils in the district so the schoolhouse was fixed up and a teacher was hired; but those who had started in the graded schools of Laconia were allowed to keep going there if their parents wanted them to. Mother was pleased that we could, even though it was hard to get us to school in stormy weather. She was sorry the younger children would have to go to a country school where there would be only one teacher for all eight grades, but it was better in another way, she thought, because they could have a hot meal at noon. Esther and Royal kept on in Laconia and so did I, except for a spell when Mother thought I ought to be nearer home and not have to eat cold sandwiches for lunch.

But that was a later time. The fall Annie was born I was in the fourth grade at Gilford Avenue School, a mile and a half from home. We had all begun school there but Esther and Royal had been changed to an upper-grade school farther away. They drove to school, left the team in a nearby, unused barn, and went over there at noon to feed Jim or Belle (whichever Father hadn't wanted to use that day) some oats and a bag of hay brought from home. Instead of riding with them, I decided I wanted to walk home by myself and Mother said I could, as long as the weather was good.

Always before I had gone along with somebody older, so at first I was afraid when I started home; but pretty soon, when rough boys standing on the sidewalk would holler nasty words after me, I would make out I didn't hear and keep walking right along until I really was out of earshot. Then I could go on, climbing up the hilly dirt road, seeing all sorts of things I had never noticed before: The heavy golden-rod stalks bending low and beginning to turn brown; frost asters bloom-ing everywhere along the roadside—fringed, dark purple flowers on tall, thickly-clustered stems; others, on spiky stems, colored soft blue; low-growing white frost asters—little star-like flowers sprinkled under-neath the blue and purple. And the leaves got prettier every day. Some maple trees turned red all over; some stayed dark green (except for a few spots of orange and yellow) until their leaves blew off. Oak leaves were mottled with black and rusty red; on the pasture hillside, barberries flamed orange-red; sumacs and wild blackberry vines turned a velvety purple-red, prettiest but quickest to become dry brown and drop off. I didn't mind that it was uphill walking all the way home—except for Bennett's hill, the last rise before our own steep hill. It wasn't because I was tired of walking when I got there, but I was short of breath because I couldn't get over being afraid of Bennett's grizzly dog. He never failed to come rushing out to the edge of the road, bristled up and barking fiercely, showing his sharp teeth, hanging out his great red tongue at me. My heart pounded and I felt kind of shaky but I never ran (Mother said if I did he would know for sure how afraid I was). I kept to the far side of the road, pretending I was looking at something over beyond the stone wall. He followed along on his side of the road barking, threatening me until I was over the top of the hill and could breathe easy again.

In just a few minutes I was climbing up our hill, hungry as I could be. If Mother had been baking, I could smell the fresh bread as soon as I came into the house. She would cut two thick slices for me and spread on lots of butter and grape or apple jelly or peach jam, whichever kind she had been making. When she wanted to make hot applesauce for supper, she would send me down to the Porter tree in the lower field. While I was picking up a panful of apples, I would eat one or two of the biggest, ripest right through from the speckled yellow skins down to the delicious "water" cores. On the way back to the house I would go around by the late pear tree to see if any ripe fruit had dropped on the ground. If none had, I would reach up and shake a low bough until one fell. Even if the pear wasn't very ripe, I would eat it, skin and core—all but the seeds. When it was time for supper I would be as hungry as the rest (they had eaten lunches, too).

Sometimes on those early fall mornings when we came out of the house to start for school, it was as though we were on a high, sunny island with all around us a sea of chilly mist that we must go down into. The trip to school didn't take long (when I rode with Esther and Royal), but even when the fog had lifted before we came to Gilford Avenue I felt shivery. Sometimes when I took my lunchbox into the schoolhouse my teacher would let me stay and help her instead of going outside to wait until the first bell rang. My teacher was not as old as most. She smiled a lot and wore frilly shirtwaists with a little gold watch pinned on front. When I made mistakes, she showed me how to do better, and I began to get more arithmetic and spelling papers with stars than I used to in third grade; but what I liked best of all was reading in storybooks. My teacher thought I was a good reader, maybe the best in the whole grade, because when the superintendent came and sat in the back of the room and she was having us take turns reading out loud, I was usually the one she let read the longest. On Saturdays, when I didn't feel like playing, I could read to myself from Mother's poem book, or Esther's Ruth Fielding books, or a story from *The Youth's Companion*. I was relieved to be rid of babyish books, pleased because I could think many more long words. I didn't bother Mother when she was working, didn't complain that I had nothing to do. I was so busy enjoying school and liking the outdoors that I hardly took time to feel sad, the way I usually did, because all that was so lovely would soon be gone and winter would come.

Back in the summer I had known Mother was going to have another baby but not when, and I wasn't curious enough to find out. After I got home from school one afternoon in September, I heard Mother making a remark about the baby when she was talking about the corn cutters coming. As soon as the ears on the tall stalks of corn were fully developed Father (and other farmers who raised ensilage corn) hired a gang of men to cut down the corn with sickles. Hod Berry would come with his gasoline engine and set up his corn-cutting rig next to the tall, round silo that was attached to the barn. The heavy, cut stalks were loaded onto horse-drawn racks or carts and driven up to the silo where old Hod Berry (we children said his name "Hodberry") and his helpers had the dangerous job of feeding the stalks (ears still on) into the sharp cutter-knives where they were chopped to bits, then blown through a big pipe to fall through a hole high up in the silo. After school and on Saturdays the boys helped inside the silo tramping round and round, working to pack the green fodder solid so it would keep good until fed to the cows during the winter. The boys liked that job, but Father made them take short turns because it was hard work. They came out tired, covered with bits of green, smelling as though they had been soaked in corn juice.

Corn cutting was a noisy, fascinating, exciting time. We girls would have liked to stay up at the barn watching, but Father wouldn't allow his girls around such a rough lot of men. The swear words they yelled at each other—and at the teams—were often loud enough so we could hear them over the noisy putt-putting of the engines, anyway. Hod Berry was a skinny, oldish man with snags of teeth and a gnawed, grey moustache stained dirty yellow (he chewed tobacco and spat). But when Hod Berry and the other men came in to eat dinner, after washing up in an agate basin outside the kitchen door, they were as quiet and polite as you please. They hunched over their plates, shoveled in Mother's good food, saying not much of anything to each other except once in a while some remark like: "How 'bout sending them beans down this way?" or "Soon's you feel like lettin' holt of the brown bread, we could use some over here." Mother made sure the serving dishes were kept full—more hot baked beans from the two large earthen pots, heaped plates of sliced brown and white bread, vegetable hash, cold boiled beef, sliced ham, pickles and chili sauce. For dessert the men had big wedges of hot apple pie, then almost everyone took a second piece. Mother put on such a big spread because she knew the same gang went around to a number of farms. The men would boast about her food, but some of the things they told about what they got to eat at other places wasn't a bit complimentary.

One afternoon in September Mother was talking on the telephone to the neighbor woman who sometimes came in to help out. "I'll need you to wait on table and help wash up the dishes," Mother was saying. "We'll have at least twelve, probably for three noon meals—and you know how those men eat. I'll be able to manage the cooking, if only this one will wait until after the silo is filled. You remember how it was two years ago when Jessie, my youngest, came at this same time in the fall. I just made it then through the busiest part of September, but I don't know about this year—everything is later. For awhile, when it was so wet in June, Sam was afraid the crops weren't going to amount to much, but now the corn is so tall and heavy he is wondering if the silo will hold it all."

Annie was obliging. She waited all the rest of September and through the first week of October before getting born.

As I said before, I didn't pay particular attention to her at first, because I was too busy with my own concerns and, anyway, I had seen plenty of new babies. Nellie and Jessie got over being jealous as soon as Mother could give them some attention again. As for the rest, nobody minded about having Annie except Father. He went around glum, not saying much pleasant for several days. We all knew what the trouble was. He wasn't mad because the family kept getting bigger; he was downright disgusted because Annie was another girl, instead of the boy he had confidently expected. The way he acted, anybody would have thought it was somebody's fault because there were six girls and only two boys in the family. Mother was aggrieved by his attitude and showed it. She wasn't one to hide her feelings when it came to anything concerning us children. For years afterward the matter was a bone of contention between them—not a serious quarrel, but a thing dug up now and then to spat over.

Father was prompt about coming to his meals, particularly at midday. When the clock struck twelve noon he expected the food to be dished up and on the table, cooling off somewhat (he never could abide putting into his mouth any food more than lukewarm). If a household emergency had caused the least delay he was annoyed and would be sure to make a sarcastic allusion to the abundance of girl help, "All these girls standing around idle—should at least be able to get some food onto the table." It was always the same, even when we were obviously all busy or were not anywhere in sight. Then, invariably, Mother would be irritated and to get even she wouldn't sit down at the table. She would stay out in the kitchen, rattling pots and pans in the sink, muttering ladylike imprecations just loud enough for Father to get the drift.

Sometimes when he had hired extra hands to work in the hayfields and was planning to take a short nooning to make sure the cured hay would be got into the barn ahead of threatening thundershowers, Father would send Esther into the house at a quarter to twelve. "What are *you* doing in *here*?" Mother would ask her in mock surprise.

Although she knew very well it was a leading question, Esther would answer in seeming innocence, "Father sent me in to help you get dinner." Of course the table was already set and the food on the stove almost done but Mother, letting herself get flustered, would have everybody within calling distance scurrying around while she shoved kindling wood into the kitchen stove and stuck a fork into the potatoes already boiling furiously in the iron kettle; and at the same time she would be going on about the unreasonableness of men in general, Grandfather Smith and his various ancestors in particular.

As Mother saw it, Grandfather Smith was entirely to blame for each and every one of Father's shortcomings. According to the story she told us over and over (she got it from Aunt Mary, Father's only sister), Grandfather had been greatly influenced by a moneyed Smith aunt, a childless old harridan who had harped away constantly on the one string: "Girls ain't worth raisin'." This unfemale old person, who often came to visit when Grandfather's family was young, never let up lecturing Grandfather on the proper way to bring up his boys—Aunt Mary's existence she ignored. Father and his brothers, so Mother told us, were taught to regard women as their menials, fit only for scrubbing the kitchen floor after their barn boots had tracked in cow manure, standing over a hot stove frying the enormous quantities of meat and fish required by their almost insatiable appetites and raising the boy babies they fathered. Mother usually ended her denunciation of the Smiths by remarking it was a pity anyone had bothered to raise the old aunt who, she supposed, must have been born a girl baby herself.

Neither Father's tempery explosions about "so many lazy girls lying around doing nothing," nor Mother's spirited manner of retaliating much affected my sisters and me. We were irritated or sympathetic by turns, but didn't take any of it to heart. Perhaps we had heard the theme so many times over we couldn't believe it went very deep. At any rate, not one of us developed an inferiority complex, but of course that may have been because we were at least half Smith ourselves.

When it came to housework, Mother used to say, Father was probably the most unhandy man that ever was. He couldn't sweep a floor or wash a dish. He could build up a fire in the kitchen stove and get a teakettle of water to boiling, but if he had to get meals for himself he would starve to death inside of a week, she believed. (She didn't count the buckets and buckets of popcorn he fixed for himself and us children on cold Sunday afternoons.) He never in his life warmed a baby's bottle, and wouldn't have the slightest idea how to go about changing a diaper, so it was just as well he wasn't at all disturbed by the babies' crying at night, could sleep right through when three or four of the children were sick, all fussing for attention at the same time.

We recognized the exaggerations as well as the truth in Mother's not wholly serious grievances but we didn't then understand that the real reason she allowed her babies—and all of us whenever we were sick—to be so demanding and possessive of her was because she wanted it that way. Until long after they were well able to run around on their own two feet all day, she lullabied her children toward sleep in her armless old rocker and carried them upstairs to bed, cuddled in soft blankets. Although it was often near midnight before she put the breakfast cereal on to cook and finished up the supper dishes, she never failed to read us an evening story—a chapter from one of C. A. Stephens' books about life on an old farm up in Maine, or some favorites from *Poems Every Child Should Know*, or the latest installment of a continued story in *The Youth's Companion*. Mother certainly never neglected any of us and if it could be said she had any favorites, it was always the baby or the one who, right then, didn't seem quite as strong as the others and so needed her most. It was true that she did favor us children over Father in some ways, but she was never heedless of his well-being. She appreciated his promptness in coming to the table, so she tried always to have his meals on time, and she strove to make the food she set before him suit his tastes exactly. She didn't expect or really want us to believe Father was quite the hard, unreasonable man pictured by her sometime complaints.

Father needed and insisted on having help from the boys and all of us girls (even me) with the numerous outdoor chores the year around. He made us learn to tell weeds from the carrots, beets, parsnips and spinach in his long garden rows. Nobody ever, even once, pulled plants instead of weeds. He taught us as well to know and enjoy the flowers and edible plants that grew in field and wood. He valued the songbirds so much that when he saw the parent birds frantically darting and fluttering, as the sharp mowing machine blades came nearer their nests in the grass, he would carefully mow wide around the spot, leaving the grass tufted high, marking a nest of bob-o-link or meadow lark, warning off whoever came later to turn and rake the hay. Among the tall pines in the lane he built us a 'camp' of old boards—play quarters first for us older children, then for the younger ones, summer after summer. On crisp Saturdays he let us play day-long games of 'fox and hounds'—racing through the empty fields, over stonewalls, across rocky gullies, up the pasture slopes. When the leaves were falling, we had time to go off hunting chestnuts, beechnuts, and butternuts. Sometimes he went with us to more distant woods, and then we brought home a treasure of hickory nuts to store in the corn shed where they could dry out and be ready for cracking, safe from plundering red squirrels and chipmunks.

When the cattle were all driven back to the barn from the summer pastures and the snow had come, the outdoor choring and playing was different, not so good in some ways. There was the cold to struggle against and I, for one, felt its bite much more keenly when there were paths to be shoveled and wood to be carried in than when I was helping the boys build a snow fort, my mittens wringing wet, my hands icy and numb. I dreaded the few steps across the road to carry the hens some grain and a pail of water or to gather the eggs, yet I thought it was pure fun to help pull the boys' heavy traverse sled all the way back up the road to the top of our hill after the swift, flying coast down the half-mile stretch. While I was still quite small, Father had permanently excused me from chores in the barn because it was plain to him I would never be anything but a bother trying to help with the horses and cattle; but I always played there with the others, most often in winter. We raced along the barn floor in front of the milking cows in their stanchions, scrambled up the built-in ladders to the highest scaffold right under the frost-rimmed ridgepole, swung on ropes, jumped from scaffold to mow to bay, crawled on hands and knees through the tunnels the boys had cut in the best hay. Father was always threatening to put a stop to our wild romping in his barn, but he never got to the point of forbidding it.

What I set out to explain in this chapter was how I became the sister who did the most baby tending and taught the younger ones their manners. I didn't mean to bring in so much about the work and the games we played, because a good deal of that was later on. I wasn't going to tell about Father—the things he did and didn't do—but after I did I could see I had left out one of the best parts about him. I should have mentioned how, when the little ones were cross and tired as could be, raising all kinds of a row and bothering Mother about getting supper, Father could get them to calm right down and be good just by taking them on his knee and reciting one of his story rhymes.

Father wouldn't always tell a story, only sometimes when he was in the right mood. That was one of the reasons his story telling was such a treat. The badly crushed self-esteem of a little girl who had thrown herself on the floor, crying and stiff with resentment, rejecting with angry kicks every attempt by an older sister to appease, could be restored as if by magic when Father coaxed the little one to come sit on his knee and listen to the tale of Mister Fox. Father could be so dramatic—lifting his eyebrows, rolling his eyes, pursing up his mouth to make his voice come out mellow and round on the big O's. He made the characters so vivid, so improbably quaint. The bold fox, polite as could be when he raided the poultry yard, saying, "Madam Goose, and by your leave I'll take you away without reprieve and carry you home to my den O!"

Next to be seized, the black duck fearfully and futilely crying out, "Quack! Quack! Quack!" as Mister Fox swung her over his back with her legs hanging dangling down O! (Father quacked loud and startled, exactly like a scared duck.)

Old Mrs. Slipper Slopper jumping out of bed, and out of the window, popping her head. Imagination showed her plain as anything— long nightgown ballooning in the breeze, grey hair stringing out of her night cap. At that point Father mimicked precisely her quavery old voice, "John, John, John! The grey goose is gone and the fox is off to his den O!"

Mister Fox, scorning the blast of John's horn, both loud and shrill, remarking airily to himself and the moon, "Very pretty music. Still I'd rather be in my den O."

The conclusion was foregone and very familiar. Father smacked his lips as he told with a flourish how the fox sat down with his wife and did very well without fork or knife. And the little ones picked the bones O!

Then Father set his own little one gently on the floor and came to the table to enjoy his supper in peace.

❧ 5 ❧

"...to Grandmother's house we go..."

ONE SUMMER NIGHT some years ago the farm buildings at Mother's ancestral home were burned to the ground. What had caused the fire was a mystery. It couldn't have been one of the sudden electric storms that so often came sweeping across the Belknaps and down into that part of Gilmanton, because the entire night was starry, we were told, without even the distant flashes of heat lightning commonly seen at that time of year. It happened before the period when there was a known firebug loose in the county, so there wasn't any real reason to believe that particular fire had been purposely set. But it was talked around that the absentee owner of the place (which he had bought for a summer retreat after it had changed hands a number of times following the years when it was our grandparents' home) had insured the buildings heavily and wasn't unhappy about the fire. That section of town had become run-down; descendants of the old families had moved away to New York City or California. The pastures and fields had grown up to bushes, were fast returning to forest lands. Except for the loss of taxes on the buildings the ignominious demise of what had once been a gracious, well-kept farmstead made no difference to the people of Gilmanton. Nor to anyone else, for that matter, except to all of us and our Page cousins who remembered the pleasure of visiting there.

Esther especially regretted the fire and mourned the destruction of the big two-and-a-half-story house with ell built by our great-great-grandfather, Deacon Moses Page, nearly two centuries ago. Because she was the first-born grandchild, Esther has the longest memories of our grandparents and their farm home. She is also sentimental about all fine old-fashioned things, yet she is not given to sentimentality in general, but is a completely practical person with a no-nonsense kind of philosophy that does not permit brooding over what cannot be changed. Very soon she was consoling herself and us.

"Perhaps I ought not to care," she began her reflection. "Maybe now I can go back to remembering the way it was when we used to have so much fun there. You and the others who were away so much in later years probably didn't realize how the place was changed after Grampa died and Grammie came up to Gilford to live with our family. The Massachusetts people who bought the property never did any real farming, although for awhile they tried raising horses—trotters, I believe. They had their horse trailers painted with gaudy signs—a king's crest with the name Royal Page Farm in fancy gold lettering—trying to make out that our Pages had once been servants of royalty, instead of the good, plain old Yankee stock they were. The inside of the house was torn out—wainscoting and old bricks—all the antiquity discarded, everything modernized. The first owners couldn't have cared much for the place; they didn't stay long in Gilmanton nor did any of the others who lived there afterward. You remember how Mother would never go back, how she always asked Father to take another route when they went to Gilmanton to decorate the graves or to attend the August Old Home Day celebrations over on Meeting House Hill. Now I can understand why, and I think she did the right thing. It was her way of keeping her memories unspoiled."

It seemed to me that what Esther had said was right for us too, because what we valued and wanted to keep unspoiled were our childhood memories. They did not change because the buildings were gone. And I thought that if only memory pictures were made of tangible stuff I could collect bits and pieces from Esther; and Royal and Forrest—the older boys; from Frances, Ellen, Jessie and Anne, the sisters in a row who used to be called "the little girls"; from our youngest brothers, Robert and Gardner, Mother's last babies—once "the little boys" of our family. I would have some of Cousin Archie Page's memories and a great many of my own.

I would featherstitch the many bits together carefully to make a bright-colored quilt, or perhaps a wall hanging. There would be pictured Grammie Page, her pet piglets and her garden with the double-ruffled, variegated petunia blossoms, well-weeded vegetable rows and silvery grey-green sage bed. Grampa Page with his pair of driving horses hitched to the buckboard would be there, and again Grampa in the cutter with the stallion, Black Beauty, between the shafts, harness bells jingling as he pawed the snow. There would be the fan-lighted doorway, shaded by the sweeping branches of two majestic elms, the back door under its little grape arbor—all the fascinating places within the many-roomed house, the long weather-beaten barn and the carriage house and woodshed.

My fancy woolgathering was foolish and entirely unnecessary. I had always been able to remember very clearly exactly how everything was down at Grammie Page's when I was twelve or thirteen, to my mind the best time of life to visit one's grandparents at their old-fashioned farm. Let the others keep what was theirs.

Whenever Grampa Page drove up to Laconia, he planned his business and trading at the stores so he could take midday dinner with us. Our farm was only a few miles out of his way, an easy drive for the sake of seeing us children and visiting with Mother. He enjoyed Mother's cooking and took great pleasure in drinking cup after cup of the good, strong tea Mother fixed for him. It wasn't that Grammie couldn't cook —she always made wonderfully good things for us to eat when we were visiting there—but when she and Grampa were alone she wouldn't bother. As for tea, she somehow had the notion that both coffee and tea should be classified with strong drink, just as injurious to the system—also a needless extravagance. Once her mind was set on an idea, she never let go. Tea and coffee were evil substances, therefore banished from her home. Mother was grieved to know her father was deprived of the small comfort of a hot drink with his meals, and when he came to our house she did her best to make it up to him.

Grampa Page's appearance was not imposing, yet he had a certain gentle, natural dignity. He was a rather small man with just enough silvery hair to make a soft fringe around his head. He was a trifle bow-legged—not really a disadvantage—only it caused him to walk with a slightly rolling gait, but this also made his knees very comfortable perches for two small grandchildren when he sat down in a rocking chair. He was a master storyteller and mimic and he treated us children as his equals. We were accustomed to seeing him dressed in working clothes—faded blue shirt and checked overalls or loosely fitting dark cloth trousers held up by worn suspenders. He seemed completely indifferent to the clothing he wore, although he was never disheveled or unshaven, and of course he did have a "good" black suit which he wore when he took the steam cars to attend a session of the State Legislature in Concord. He was as much at ease with the smooth-talking politicians there as when he was dealing with the rough cattle buyers and unscrupulous horse traders who had long before passed the word among their kind, "Watch out when you're trying to make a trade with Royal Page. When you think you're way ahead of him, you're liable as not to find yourself coming out with the short end of the stick."

Grampa usually arrived for dinner about the time we were finishing the meal. While he put his team in the barn, Mother reheated the food and made a fresh pot of tea. After some brief conversation, Father went back to his work, but we stayed to listen. While Grampa ate, the littlest one sat on his knee, watching with fascination the old-fashioned manipulation of knife and fork. The rest of us grouped around the table in position to see and hear. Grampa's white moustache quivered and his merry brown eyes laughed with us while he ate and talked and cuddled the baby and gestured and drank hot tea. Grampa didn't like to be interrupted while telling a story, so whenever he wanted more food he would keep right on with his yarn, just throwing in an absent-minded, "Let's have. Let's have!" at the same time stretching out his arm in a beckoning sweep over the table. Confusion followed because our long table was laden with many dishes. We didn't want the story to be interrupted either, so each would make a silent guess and quickly pass a dish to Grampa. Then he would have the sugar and the salt, more hot tea, another thick slice of warm bread and the butter, the dish of crispy-brown fried potatoes, the platter of pink ham slices— everything offered at once. He would make his selection tranquilly as the story proceeded. The same thing would happen once or twice more before he ended the story and finished his dinner with a wedge of apple pie, served hot and swimming in maple syrup.

In summer two of us—one older to look after the younger—were generally asked to go home with Grampa for a visit until his next trip to Laconia. While he went out to see to the team, we hurriedly got ready. Riding with Grampa was special because he drove a pair instead of going about with a one-horse team as we usually did. Sometimes when the mare, Silvermane, and her harness-mate had baby colts born at about the same time, Grampa would let the young ones go along too—each running free, gamboling beside its mother. We thought that very exciting because all the people in the streets of Laconia turned to watch as we drove through the city.

The stories Grampa told as we traveled along made the twelve-mile trip go so quickly we didn't mind the bumps in the road, never noticed when the afternoon shadows began to grow long. Soon after leaving

Laconia we reached the foot of Marsh Hill where Grampa always stopped to water the horses and let them rest before starting up the steep winding incline. From a pipe set into the hillside, spring water gushed endlessly—crystal clear, overflowing the round wooden watering trough at the side of the road. While the horses sank their noses deep into the water, drinking and blowing, we climbed down from the buckboard to find the tin dipper that hung beneath a sign nailed to a nearby pine tree. We took turns drinking cupful after cupful of the clear, icy water until we were really too full for comfort, and we read aloud the verse on the signboard:

"O, weary Traveler stay thy feet.
Take from this fountain pure and sweet
A cup of water in His name,
Free to rich and poor the same.
Then go thy way remembering still
The Wayside Spring beneath the hill."

Who had written the verse? Who had lettered the sign and hung the dipper? Nobody knew. The Good Samaritan had gone without waiting for thanks or leaving his name.

As the horses settled into the traces for the pull up Marsh Hill, Grampa began to spin out an entrancing story, never the same as last journey's tale. It might be he would take us to a long-ago time in a far-away part of the world where gallant knights jousted in the lists and fair ladies shuddered and sighed for the mailed riders unhorsed, applauded and rewarded the heroes who triumphed.

More often Grampa took us back to live for a little time in the early days when our ancestors came to settle in this region. While the horses traveled toward Grant Mountain, we were imagining ourselves far up the mountain side amongst the thick-growing trees, together with a party of men following the tracks of a fearsome wild creature. We knew it must be a panther, surely the last of those huge cats that would ever roam this part of New Hampshire. For weeks the ruthless marauder had laid bloody waste for miles around, a wanton destruction of the sheep and young cattle in the pastures. The panther must be killed or there would be hungry families come winter. The leader of our party, that clever woodsman Jesse Towle (a great-great uncle of ours) knew the panther would be extremely dangerous when brought to bay. Out of breath from hurrying, we reached an open spot where we sighted the dogs leaping and baying frantically at the foot of a tremendous oak. Up there, stretched along a thick limb, was that a long grey shadow? Or what? An eerie, long-drawn scream stilled the dogs and turned them momentarily to bristled-up statues. It was the panther, treed and desperate. We saw him crouching, powerful tail lashing. We felt the fire of his wicked yellow eyes. Our scalps prickled and our blood slowed. Why didn't the men fire? They surely must know the panther was about to leap. Was the powder wet? Half a dozen flintlocks flashed at once. Through the smoke we saw the little body slacken, begin to let go, tumble to the ground. Fiercely burning life changed in a moment to a heap of dirty, yellow-grey fur. Uncle Jesse's job was done. We turned away down the mountain, leaving the growling pack worrying at the dead cat.

Then we were happy to relax for a bit and be just us, on the way to Grammie Page's, living in a modern, civilized world where fierce creatures no longer roamed the woods.

A mile or so more and we were down over the "saddle," traveling through leafy hardwoods—white birch, oak and beech. Grampa began another story. He said his grandfather had grown up on the original Page farm in Gilmanton—the buildings had been hereabouts. As our horses quickened their pace, sensing the homestretch was near, we stopped to watch a boy clothed in linsey-woolsey ride bareback up the forest trail. We saw him dismount, tie his horse to a tree, shoulder his axe and head toward a stand of trees the size to make good fireplace wood. We were with him when he spied the two rolypoly cubs at their scuffling play, tumbling about in a little hollow where last year's leaves lay thick. The mother bear was nowhere in sight. It was easy to imagine what was going on in the boy's mind: "How simple 'twould be to capture those wee bears and carry them home. What a surprise for Pa and the rest!"

And it was clear his mind was made up. Closer and closer he crept. My, but he was a clever one! Not a twig snapped beneath his cautious feet. Swoosh! The baby bears were caught up in his stout homespun jacket. Axe forgotten on the ground he was racing down the slope hanging tight to his wriggling bundle. How those cubs did squeal. What a crashing and a roaring when the old she bear woke and came lumbering from the thicket of fir trees where she had been sleeping. That foolish boy better drop the cubs and run for his life. He ought to know he didn't have the ghost of a chance to outrun an aroused mother bear. Then one little cub struggled free and dropped to the ground. Without turning to look, squeezing the other one under his arm, the stubborn boy kept on running. While the old bear stopped to nuzzle her whimpering baby our hero reached his horse and made off home with his prize. There Grampa's story ended.

"But, Grampa, whatever became of the cub he saved?" we asked.

"Oh, he kept it until it was half-grown. It made quite a pet but was always a great nuisance around the farm. The boy's folks were glad when the yearling bear didn't come back to the farm after holing up for the winter. . . . Now we're almost home. You've all talked enough so I want you to be quiet and not be bothering your grandmother with so many questions."

Grampa was joking, of course. None of us would pester our grandmother with idle questions; we wouldn't think of sassing her back when she delivered long lectures which we silently rejected because what she preached was contrary to Mother's teachings. The farm was her domain, the place where she was absolute ruler. At home Grampa was in all ways subservient, a henpecked husband if ever there was one. Grammie's reputation as a bossy woman had spread all over town many, many years before any of us were born, but only the near neighbors and a few old friends had as much as a telephone-visiting acquaintance with her because she rarely went away from home. "Royal Page let his wife get the upper hand when they were first married and she's been backing him down ever since," people said. "She has him right under her thumb. It's her house, her cattle and her farm."

There was a good deal of truth in the talk. Grampa wouldn't let any man run over him, but even we children could see how it was at home. Rather than cross Grammie, he would settle for peace at any price. She was bound to manage everything in the barn, so the easiest way was to let her. He was good about helping her in the house and there, too, everything went as Grammie said. No wonder we always spoke of our visits as "going down to Grammie Page's."

The arrangement was not entirely to Grampa's disadvantage. He could do what he liked—go out among people, carry the farm produce to market and buy the grocery staples, manage his lumbering operations without her interference. He was free to attend county fairs or political meetings without having to worry about getting home in time to do the milking as other farmers did. He got a good deal of fun out of a lifelong contest of wits with her, constantly circumventing her rules and prohibitions in cunning, harmless ways. Hidden away in a hayloft or atop a high beam, he kept a store of fancy, boughten cookies, bananas or out of season fruits forbidden by Grammie because she thought such luxury items sinfully extravagant for farm people. His booty he often divided with us, making us his merry conspirators with the mock warning, "Now don't you dare say a word about this in front of your grandmother!"

Grampa's irrepressible sense of humor, the constant joking and storytelling which so captivated us, often irked Grammie. She felt obliged to keep a watchful eye on Grampa when we were around lest he drop his work to engage in time-wasting play with us. One rainy afternoon in summer when several of us were rummaging in the loft over the harness room (a part of the long, closed-in shed which joined the house and the barn), we discovered a hanging rope connected to the great schoolhouse bell mounted on the roof above us. We were immediately inspired with the idea of playing train. Brother Royal appointed himself engineer-conductor and began pulling the rope to make the bell clang in loud, strident tones while he kept bawling out, "All aboard," in his best imitation of a trainman. The rest of us mounted the narrow open stairway and took places on upended boxes. Tickets were ceremoniusly collected and Royal was about to resume his energetic pulling on the bell rope when we heard a slurred, unfamiliar sounding voice calling from below stairs.

"Hey, youse! Jush hol' up thar. Doan start thum cyars. 'M comin! Acomin' ri'long." It was Grampa, playing a drunk man. Up the stairs he staggered, nearly bumping us off our seats as he went weaving along the aisle of our imaginary train. He turned his pockets out one by one, scratched his head, looked comically dismayed as he pretended to hunt for a lost ticket, all the while mumbling and rolling his eyes. To see our Grampa capering in this ridiculous fashion tickled us so much that we dissolved into wild hilarity. But the train game was broken up a little too late.

The clanging of the long-unused bell on the roof and the racket in the loft had set the hens to cackling hysterically and alerted Grammie. She burst upon us with a shower of angry epithets, "What's all this commotion? Sakes alive, Royal, as if you had nothin' better to do! Old fool, carryin' on like a school boy!" We didn't hear the rest. We had scattered as quickly and silently as a covey of frightened baby partridges.

Yet in her own way Grammie was really fond of us, though not as individuals. In her mind we were lumped together as Winnie's children, a fresh generation who might, if only she persevered, be led into the ways which she considered morally right. It was her pleasure as well as her duty when we were visiting to teach us the value of hard work and economical living, to feed us well though not necessarily at regular meal times. She heartily welcomed her grandchildren, one or half a dozen at a time; but she never let anything upset the rhythm of her working day so she often became absorbed in weeding her vegetable garden, milking the cows and skimming cream from the full pans left sitting from the previous milking, repairing the calf pen, or watching over a litter of newborn pigs. At such times our presence was likely to slip her mind, giving us blissful, unrestricted hours to play and explore the premises wherever fancy led us, indoors or out.

To look at Grammie Page, a stranger might have doubted her ability to halter and lead a stubborn heifer, gentle a spirited colt or stop a runaway horse. Her open brow and light blue eyes would have given her a benign expression except for the firmness of her chin and the narrow line of her mouth, and as soon as she spoke there was no mistaking the metal beneath the surface. She had a high-pitched voice that could reach Grampa's ear as far away as the other side of the big hayfield. A small woman, made shorter by her permanent stoop, she must once have been a slender, tiny-waisted girl, but of course we could never imagine her any different from the way she looked all the time we were growing up. Her voluminous flannel petticoats—wool for winter, cotton for warm weather—lent her a false bulkiness. Her fine straight hair, never showing the least touch of grey in the black, was pulled back and twisted into a tight knot. Her high-topped, soft-leather shoes, her grey, calico-print "wrapper" seemed always to be the same clothing worn year in and year out.

If she had put on trousers or overalls her work in the barn would have been made easier but in spite of having preempted a dominant role on the farm, the very idea of showing her limbs in men's pants outraged her sense of propriety. To keep her skirts clear of the dirt in the cow tie-up, she hoisted her petticoats above her ankles, wrapped a clean grain sack around her middle and secured this barn apron at her waist by pinning it with a large nail. She disdained women's hats as too fancy and not at all comfortable. In summer she went about bareheaded, carrying a black umbrella to use as a sun shield when she was berrying. On the rare occasions when she was induced to leave home in cold weather she squashed onto her head a shapeless old felt that had once been Grampa's. It was a very suitable hat, easy on her head, Grammie always made a point of remarking, and she never failed to add that she hadn't been a bit bothered when one of the neighbor women had scoffed at the hat saying it was a thing *she* wouldn't even wear to a dogfight. Grammie's one dressy outfit was a black wool broadcloth skirt that barely cleared the floor and a high-collared foulard shirtwaist adorned with the only piece of jewelry she ever wore—a round, antique gold pin, beautifully chased and centered with one piece of rosy coral. (Grammie's lovely old pin is now the cherished possession of her namesake, my sister Annie.)

Before we went off to pay a visit to her old home, Mother always reminded us that we must be careful not to cross Grammie in any way or do anything to ruffle her. Mother wasn't truly afraid that we might arouse our grandmother's ire and be horsewhipped as in years past her younger brothers often were, but she could never forget that her mother was an unreasonable, unpredictable woman and she could not forgive what she considered the mistreatment of her father. Perhaps Grammie had become more tolerant than she was when her own children were young. At any rate, she was always good to us and never administered a punishment worse than a light scolding. Of course we walked warily in her home, never rebelled against her crotchety ideas even when we thought them unreasonable, old-fashioned superstitions.

Every time a thundershower came up, Grammie acted half-scared to death. She watched apprehensively as the thunderheads rolled up on the distant horizon. When the first flicker of lightning tongued out from the gathering clouds, she cut short our berrypicking or games of I Spy on the wide lawn and around the buildings and hustled us inside. After planting us on the capacious feather bed in her bedroom and telling us to stay put, she pulled rubber boots over her shoes and went pacing nervously through the house, closing windows and doors. When all was secured inside, she hurried down the steps into the woodshed and along the passageway to the barn where she shut the big doors and fastened them tight. Then back again she came muttering, looking nervously over her shoulder, glancing out the window, starting back fearfully as the lightning flashed. We rather enjoyed those daytime interludes. While rain pelted the windows and thunder rolled overhead, we whispered and scuffled in the billowy feather bed or engaged in pillow fighting on the sly. Lightning storms that came up in the night were another story, no fun at all. At the first faraway rumbling, Grammie would be up getting dressed, making Grampa get up, too. She would come up to our rooms, go around banging down the windows, firmly shaking us awake, urging us out of bed. Kerosene lamp held high, she would shepherd us ahead of her down the ell-chamber stairs. Making it down that crooked stairwell in bare feet and trailing night gown wasn't easy for a sleep-drugged child, because the stair steps had been narrowed by years of accumulations—piles of newspapers, bags of dried sage and catnip, ancient cheese hoops, antiquated kitchen tools, boxes of rolled twine. Grammie didn't believe in throwing away a thing because, she said, "You can never tell when it might come in handy." When we were all safely gathered Grammie would have us sit on the backless kitchen chairs and there we would perch, droopy-eyed and dopey as roosting chickens, barely aware of her shrill monologue punctuated by the peals of diminishing thunder. Not until the storm had rolled far off across the Belknaps and the crickets were chirping outside would she allow us to grope our way back upstairs to bed.

Grammie Page certainly was a woman of numerous contradictions. When there was a harness to be repaired or a calf pen to be built, she could do as good a job as most men, but she also excelled in many branches of housewifery. No woman in town made better cheese or sweeter butter. When she was young she had dyed the wools and drawn the patterns to make the hooked rugs on her parlor floor—one had a garland of roses and mixed flowers with beautifully blended coloring; another pictured a lifelike prancing horse with flowing mane; others were done in intricate geometric patterns. Laid away in chests and high-boys were hand-hemmed pillow slips, fine linen chemises and pantalets edged in dainty crocheting or tatting. That her work-coarsened hands could ever have done anything so fine seemed incredible, for when we knew her she thought fancywork pure time wasting. She was proud of being able to paint and paper a room unassisted. She was given to driving up nails, the best way to keep things neat in the kitchen, she said. The buildings were filled with the possessions of three generations, but everything was kept in order, even up attic. At first glance, Grammie's kitchen appeared an extremely cluttered place with clothing and utensils hanging on large nails, piled-up back copies of the weekly newspaper and dishes always stacked on the table. It was an orderly kind of clutter. The vinegar bottle, salt and pepper shakers, ironstone sugar bowl and pressed-glass syrup pitcher were always set in the exact spot on the table. The kerosene lamps on the shelf above the wooden sink were lined up just so—the low bedroom lamps placed inconspicuously toward the back, next the bull's-eye glass, at the front the prettiest lamp with the ruby glass fount; the wicks were always trimmed, the chimneys shining clean. Nobody was allowed to displace a single stick of wood in the pile beside the kitchen stove. Grammie wanted everything right where she could put her hand on it.

She was fond of animals but wouldn't have a dog because she couldn't stand having her floors muddied up with dirty paws. More than anything else she enjoyed working with horses and cows, but her real pets were her pigs—in our opinion the most unlovable of all farm animals. She did have a cat, or rather there was always a cat—the same one as far as we knew—that lived somewhere about the place. This enormous, yellow tiger Manx named Wow maintained a friendly though distant relationship with Grammie. He kept the barn and out-buildings free of rats and mice; she gave him fresh warm milk for supper. When she came into the house after helping Grampa do the evening milking, she filled Wow's dish, always left sitting by the walk-way at the foot of the steps leading to the kitchen. Wow was never there waiting, mewing for his supper in the obsequious way of an ordinary cat. He had to be notified. Grammie sent out a prolonged, shrill call, "W-OW, W-OW, W-OW, W-OW!" Sometimes she had to repeat the summons a number of times before the stately, tailless tomcat materialized and leisurely began to lap up his milk. Grammie's unique way of calling the cat intrigued us and we sometimes tried to imitate her, but could never get Wow to come. And when we attempted to pet him, coaxing him to be friends, he wouldn't stay and purr around our legs. He gave us no thanks, just a disdainful glance from his amber eyes, then turned away and we were left to watch his haughty rear end disappearing around the woodpile. When we went to look, he had vanished.

Grammie Page was a wonder at making things grow; she liked picking berries and helping harvest the crops, but she didn't enjoy cooking the food. Yet when she had a mind to, she cooked expertly, without a bit of bother. For us she prepared the most delicious, most bountiful food ever set before hungry children. When the weather was cold, she gave us rich chowders, delicately spiced homemade sausage, bits of tender salt codfish in cream sauce, potatoes cooked in their jackets then peeled and doused with butter and cream, pancakes with maple syrup or small, fried "spoon" cakes for dunking in the warmed maple syrup. In summer we ate wild strawberries with clotted yellow cream, blueberries and milk for supper, raspberries and wild blackberries, blueberry pie running over with juice, apple pie flavored with lemon, baked in a crockery plate and eaten with crumbly homemade cheese. For lunching at any time of day or year there were big crinkle-edged sugar cookies, doughnuts rolled in sugar as Grammie lifted them, sizzling hot, from her iron doughnut kettle; and, when we helped with the churning, fresh buttermilk and to go with it, "common" crackers spread with sweet butter. Seeing us enjoying her good food was all the thanks she wanted.

We never forgot Grammie's food and her kindness to us, but not until many years later did we understand the reason we couldn't love her as we did Grampa: We never could feel easy with her. She talked *at* us, but he understood our feelings and knew what we were thinking. We remembered his twinkling brown eyes, his many stories and how his droll way of telling them had tickled us. We remembered adventures of the road . . . a runaway horse, the long cold ride in the pung when we drove down after school on a Friday afternoon in winter, getting dumped from Grampa's light sleigh right into the middle of a big snowbank when Black Beauty reared and the sleigh tipped over, how the snow always stayed late in the woods of Grant Mountain, how cool those woods were in summer and how scary it was to ride down over the "saddle" at dusk when the screech owls were calling. Each had his favorite memories; we could reminisce endlessly.

What I remembered most fondly was the big white house. It was my second home, a place where in a way I felt a sense of belonging more truly than in the farmhouse where our family lived. When I was visiting there without any of the others and Grammie was working outside, I liked the feeling of being alone in the great house—so many rooms with nobody in them but me, the tall grandfather clock in the dining room and the other one in the front hall keeping me company as they ticktocked the hours away. I didn't really understand why the house never seemed empty and lonesome. If I had been pressed for an explanation, I might have been able to say how I could feel the presence of many others—not ghosts or anyway not the frightening kind—but something left there, impressed on the house by all of the Page children who were born and grew up or died in childhood within its walls, something brought by each of the brides who came to spend a lifetime there, raise a family and be buried from the parlor.

When I was old enough to consider myself a young lady, I put away childish memories of happy times at our grandparents' old farm home. I didn't even recall which season of what year I had last visited there, but the house would never let me go. Time after time I dreamed of being there. I went in at the kitchen door, through the swinging doors of the pantry to the long, cool dining room, heard the chiming of the tall clock, sat down at the parlor organ and pressed the yellowed keys, looked through the downstairs bedrooms before I went into the front hall and mounted the wide stairway to the second floor. I searched through all the rooms there—were there five or six?—the high-ceilinged, airy front chambers, the small cubbyhole rooms, the windowless back bedroom and the chamber over the kitchen ell. I did not know what I wanted, only that it was something precious there in the house.

I never found the treasure I sought in my dreams. The end always came when I opened the door and started to climb the attic stairs.

❦ 6 ❦

Decoration Day–1916

WHEN I WAS a little girl in the time before the first World War, our town was mostly a farming community, the same as other New Hampshire country towns. Father's farm in Gilford was only two and a half miles from the main street of Laconia, the 'City' where he sold produce and bought groceries and grain. Farther away by a mile in the opposite direction, lying close under the Belknap Mountains, was Gilford Village, just a hamlet with a dirt road for a main street, a few homes, a schoolhouse and a store that sold sundries. The ancient town hall was there, a newer, nondescript building that was the Grange hall and two white-spired churches with bells calling the congregations to worship on Sunday mornings. The Village was the center for a good many community gatherings. Church suppers and Grange sociables in winter, picnics on the Fourth of July and a big celebration every August for Old Home Day—but that wasn't begun until later years. At the time we older Smiths were quite young and our family went about with horse and buggy, we looked forward most eagerly to the first summer holiday, the yearly free dinner and Decoration Day exercises over at the Village.

Automobiles were not then commonly used on our dusty, winding roads. The loud honking of a warning horn heard 'round the bend was enough to startle even the steadiest horse so he'd shy and rear in fright. Then, everybody moved at a slower pace and people had time to be neighborly. Even though it was planting season, most of the farmers in our town took a whole day off on the thirtieth of May. Each family took big baskets of wonderful home-cooked food for the dinner, always served at the Grange hall. We children decorated small wooden baskets to place on the Old Soldiers' graves. The order of the day never varied. First came the parade led by a brass band hired from Laconia or a nearby town. Then the dinner was served, and a little later in the afternoon people gathered on the Green over in front of the Town Hall to listen to the patriotic orations. Between times, the band played old, old tunes like *Battle Hymn of the Republic* and *The Girl I Left Behind Me*. Lots of new ones, too. The grownups who were working on the dinner committee stayed at the hall getting the tables set up and the food ready to serve while we marched in the parade up to the Pine Grove Cemetery. The noonday dinner was freely and generously served to all who came: the little cluster of Civil War veterans, the officials of the event, the dignitaries who were there to make the speeches, the bandsmen, the townspeople and all their visiting friends and relations. Plenty of food left so the children could eat their fill at the last table, along with the grownups who had taken a turn at serving. How well I remember what good times we had.

The year is 1916. There are already eight of us Smiths. My tenth birthday won't be until the next fall; Esther and Royal are older; Forrest is just younger. Then come the four little girls (Annie, the littlest one, is the baby just beginning to creep). School has been let out for the afternoon so we can gather wild flowers for the baskets we will carry in the parade next day. We are the luckiest ones because our schoolhouse (District No. 12) is just a stone's throw up the road, set right on Father's land beside our cow pasture lane. We know just where to find the flowers that will make our baskets the prettiest. To the pasture and over the hill for the wild lily of the valley, flower stalks of fuzzy white and green leaves shining in big patches on the sunny slopes below the pines. Then down into the woods beyond the lower fields to spy out where the earliest pink lady slippers' delicate blooms are hiding in the leafy moist spots. Deeper in among the taller trees to look for late-flowering painted trilliums. Beyond, on the meadow's edge, whole banks of pale anemones sway. (Pick their fragile blossoms gently and don't squeeze or they'll never last until tomorrow.) Pull lots of trailing evergreen on the way back. We'll twine it over the baskets—greenery nests for our flowers. But we have only pink and white blossoms. Shouldn't we have some yellow? We must cross the field behind the barn and go to our secret spot, the place where the dogtooth violet grows. Climb over the stone wall to Uncle Charlie's pasture (take care not to get caught on the barbed wire fence!). Where the sun's rays slant into an open place just before the thick, dark woods begin, we come upon a crowd of rare golden blossoms nodding gently on slender stems above their heart-shaped leaves. Now all we need is moss to line the baskets. We find some under a fir tree and go home satisfied. Frances and Nellie and even little Jessie help trim the baskets but the baby is just a nuisance. She keeps pulling off the flower heads! When the baskets are finished we carry them down cellar and set them on the cool dirt floor. There they will stay moist and fresh overnight.

We are all up early in the morning. Father has lit the kitchen fire before daylight and gone out to do the milking. Mother has breakfast to get and the oven must be kept hot to finish baking the beans she is preparing for the dinner at the Village. She will take the big earthen pots from the oven just before we start. Father will wrap them in many layers of newspaper, pack them into bushel baskets. The pots won't break and the beans will keep steaming hot, come out smelling delicious, all mingled with salt pork and sweetening of maple syrup. We children are dressed before the sun shows over Mount Belknap. We have not really worried about the weather; still it is a relief to find it will be beautiful—warm and blue and sunny with little white wisps of cloud in the sky. Perfect weather for the first holiday of summer.

Right after breakfast Esther and the boys go out with Father to hitch up the teams while I help the little girls put on their best clothes. Patent leather shoes are shining bright (rubbed with Vaseline last evening). Three small pairs for Frances, Nellie, and Jessie. Two bigger ones for Esther and me. Now just button up three little dresses of rosebud dimity and tie hair bows into three perky butterflies. Then pack Annie's extra baby things into a wooden soapbox, a good-sized one so Mother can keep her in it while we are marching in the parade. On the way to the Village I will hold her on my lap; she is 'my' baby and Mother depends on me to tend her.

We are ready and so are the teams. Mother will drive steady Old Belle hitched to the two-seated carriage we call the "Top Team Buggy." The little girls and I will go with her. That leaves the horse Jim and the Democrat wagon for Father. The Democrat wagon has two seats and an extra-long body so there is room for Esther and the boys and all the baskets. Of course, both Esther and Royal can manage horses very well, but today Father will do all the driving. Jim is not a mean horse, but if he should get the least bit frightened (he's such a skittish creature), he's likely as not to bolt, or let fly with his heels and kick in the dashboard.

Today the three-mile trip to Gilford Village will seem much shorter than in wintertime when our hands and feet and noses get so cold. There is so much to see along the way we don't mind Old Belle's slow pace a bit. We have time to spy out even the tiniest flowers growing beside the road, the dainty blue-eyed grasses and the low-growing blueberry bushes (just now their sweet small bells are opening). Up on the flat we see places where the wild strawberries grow thick in the grass. We 'mark' the patches of white bloom so we can find the big ripe berries in mid-June. We aren't allowed to tramp down the good grass in the hay fields just to pick wild strawberries, but Father doesn't mind when we hunt them here along the roadside where the grass is coarse and must be cut late by hand scythe anyway. We remember how sweet the wild strawberries were last year. A handful, ripe and red on the long stems, made a pretty bouquet but it smelled so good we had hard work to keep from eating the berries one by one before we got them home to show Mother.

A quarter mile more, up the rise then down, and we pass the Big Willow Tree. The boys came here earlier in the spring to cut wands for making whistles. Esther could make good willow whistles. Mine didn't work. I tried, but not very hard. Anyhow, I cut myself with the jackknife and gave up right away.

A little farther on, standing all by itself is a ramshackle old house with not even a flowering bush in the yard. We have heard people say in early times it had been an Inn, a coach stop where the passengers could rest and eat. There were barns so the drivers could change their tired horses for fresh teams. All the big set of buildings rotted away and blew down, leaving just this one forlorn part which now houses a family much larger than ours. Mother studies the place with a worried little frown, looking to see whether any of the children are in sight. She thinks perhaps they often go hungry. She wonders aloud if there will be enough food left from the dinner so she can leave a basketful on the way home. We barely glance at the house. Why should we worry about other children when there is so much wonderful springtime? More than we can see and hear and smell, more than we can possibly drink in. On the opposite side of the road is a long steep hill where maples and white birches and pines grow thick, almost to the top. Away up on the shady slope a peewee slides his plaintive notes on a silver thread—first down the scale, then up again. The little girls' quick eyes catch a sparkle of brilliant red on a green pine branch just over the stone wall. Mother answers their exclamation of delight. It is a scarlet tanager, a shy and rare songbird. One quick flash of jeweled beauty, then he flies away on sooty wings and leaves us feeling sad. How can we know that one glimpse is enough? He has left us a lovely memory, a precious gift to keep forever.

The next half mile of road runs through the fresh green pasture land and fields of prosperous farmers. Jim and the Democrat wagon ahead have gone out of sight, hidden by a curve in the road. Along here Father will be looking over his neighbors' plowed ground, pointing out to Esther and the boys where this season's crops are being planted. He knows these farmers are proud of their fine fields and heavy crop yields. He will admit that some may have better potato crops, but he has yet to see the year when any neighbor can raise corn to equal his. His stand of fodder corn is always taller and heavier; his field corn bears bigger ears, yields more bushels to the acre. Our sweet corn is almost always the earliest, and Father always has more plantings coming on so that we have fresh green corn to eat from August until the first killing frost. And Father has raised his own popcorn ever since be began farming (his first seed came from Grandfather's old place). How we do enjoy those big bowls of tender, buttery, hot popcorn on cold winter Sunday afternoons!

But we ourselves take no thought for the crops to come. It is May and summertime will be forever. In every dooryard we pass, the lilac bushes are in heavy bloom. The purple clusters hang full, just beginning to wilt and fade a bit. It seems they must be spilling all their last perfume at once into the passing breeze for us to breathe as we drive past. We say, half pretending, it smells so sweet and strong we're a little bit dizzy when we try to watch the greedy, gold bumblebees weaving from flower to flower along the roadside.

We are approaching the place we like best, a stretch of road where the view opens wide. Across the fields we can see Lake Winnipesaukee's broad blue waters and soft green islands. Far away to the north the misty blue of the White Mountain ranges. High over all—Mount Washington's peak, lofty and clear in the morning air. But we cannot see its very top—the snowy peak is hiding in the clouds. Then I remember a Psalm Mother sometimes reads to us from her Bible and I know the meaning of the beginning words, "I will lift up mine eyes unto the hills from whence cometh my help," only I will always think "mountains" instead of "hills."

A small wind ripples across the grass, puffs away at the gone-to-seed dandelion heads and shakes an apple tree as we pass by. Dandelion down fills the air; it brushes our faces with fairy fingers. Pale apple blossoms blow all around us, falling onto the little girls' dimity dresses. Pink petals lie on Old Belle's black mane; one lands on Annie's baby nose. Hating to lose our mountains, we keep turning to look back until the horse carries us around a bend into a woodsy spot where we feel the cool dampness coming up from the thick underbrush. Tall brakes grow in rows beside the stone wall. They march along in rows like soldiers with furled plumes on their helmets.

Around another curve, up a short rise and we can see our own familiar mountain range again, but it is not the same as at home. Gunstock has moved around and is hiding Belknap, so near it isn't blue anymore. We can almost see the trees. The evergreens are great streaks of darkest blue-green reaching high up the sides. The wide gold-green zigzags lower down are the hardwoods just beginning to leaf out.

Father and the others are not far ahead of us, starting to dip down over Schoolhouse Hill into the Village. We pass the Grange horse sheds and the watering trough and catch up when they draw to a stop in front of the Grange hall. Royal and Esther help Father unload the baskets. Forrest shepherds the little girls across the road to the Village store. They will have time to spend their nickels for strawberry ice cream cones before the parade forms. I carry Annie into the Grange hall kitchen to stay with Mother.

Father is helping set up long tables in the dining room. The committee ladies are hurrying back and forth, taking food from the baskets and reckoning up quantities. The kitchen stove is already hot; the warming oven and the big bottom oven are both crammed with bean pots of all sizes. Loaves of brown bread are heating in two big, steaming kettles on the stove top. I stop to watch the ladies. They look so fresh and nice in their print dresses with aprons all ruffly and starched. But I mustn't get in the way. I quickly set Annie down in her box. I tell her, "Be good," and I go over to look a minute at the row of pies sitting on a wide shelf. There are pies made from apples that have kept firm and flavorsome stored all winter down in good dry cellars. One or two old-fashioned dried apple pies, too . . . some that must be mincemeat and half a dozen made from canned pumpkin. I don't spend much time looking over those common kinds; I have eyes only for the "fancy" pies, the ones we hardly ever have at home. Of course we all like Mother's pies just fine. We have pie most every day, too. Sometimes Mother makes four or half a dozen at a time, especially apple and all kinds from fresh berries. Our family can eat two whole pies at a meal (there are usually twelve at table, counting the hired help), so she can't often take time to fuss over cream fillings or meringue toppings.

All the Gilford ladies are good pastry cooks, but their soft pies are the ones to boast about. Whenever there is an occasion like today, quite a few ladies bring their most special creations. Some share their receipts but others make a big secret about what ingredients they put in. How good all those fancy pies look! There are real lemon with inches-thick delicate golden meringue, velvety smooth custard pies, cream pies I just know will melt away if I take a bite. Pies with whipped cream toppings so thick there's no telling what filling is underneath. There won't be any of these pies left by the time we children get to eat at the last table. This one look is all I'll get. I feel just like reaching up and sticking a finger into the whipped cream to get a lick. I don't, though. I put my hands behind me and go on outside.

Pupils from other school districts are already gathering for the parade. They are all children we know, maybe not by name but by their schools anyway: the Village School, Liberty Hill, Lily Pond, the Mountain School (District No. 9) and a few East Gilford pupils, from down back of the mountain. It won't be a long procession, but for us it is exciting enough. When the man who carries the biggest brass horn coiled round his shoulders blows one loud blare through the wide mouth and the drums give a short roll of beats, we run quickly, pick up our baskets and get into line at the end. Next to the bandsmen are the Old Soldiers waiting for the open buggies to be driven up, so they can ride in the procession. Maybe that is to do them honor or perhaps they are too old and weak to walk even such a little way. Their faded blue uniforms flap loose on stick-thin arms. Crooked canes are held in twisted, shaky old hands. We whisper, saying they look a lot like the scarecrows on Father's new-planted corn fields. Yet we wouldn't think of snickering at them. They look very proud and fierce standing there, trying so hard to keep from stooping. But we give them only a fleeting thought. What can a holiday matter to such old, old men?

We begin to feel sticky and hot waiting in the dusty street. Our shoes, so shiny a little while ago, are gray now. Small damp ringlets hang over the little girls' foreheads. It bothers me to see their white stockings so grimy, wrinkling loose down around their ankles. No time now to pull up stockings and dust off younger ones' shoes. The parade will be starting. We'd better practice marching. Left-right. Left-right. I-Hada-Good-Job-And-I-Left! LEFT! LEFT! LEFT!

From up beyond the Town Hall comes a rider, wheeling in to head the procession. It is Captain Von Lilienthal sitting easy and straight on a shining chestnut horse, mane and tail braided with ribbons. We don't know much about Captain Von Lilienthal for he only lives here in summer. We think his thick white hair, small pointed beard and wide-brimmed soldier's hat make him look grand. Somebody from Lily Pond School tells us that horse is a real war charger. The Captain rode him at a famous battle in some far off place, "San Jew-on Hill," or something like that. Anyway we are very lucky to have a brave soldier and his spirited war-horse leading us.

Now we are a real parade and off we go. At the head is the big chestnut horse, lifting his hoofs high in a steady prance right in time with the music. How beautiful the flag is! High on its staff, silken colors float in the sunshine! The horses pulling the buggies plunge. The drivers rein them in sharply. We children on the tail end have crooked off a little to one side so we can see toward the front and not get dust in our eyes. Along the Village street, by the small white church and the dooryards with their picket fences, past the red brick house with the tall elm and on beyond Sawyers' farm. Up the steep bank (take the younger ones by the hand here) and through the wide iron gates into the cemetery.

There the procession halts. We scatter, hunting for the graves where small flags fly over iron G. A. R. markers. Others have been here before us. After we have placed our baskets, the cemetery is like a big flower garden, stretching clear over to the pine trees along the fence. We go back and listen quietly while the prayers are said. At last they are ended. The cornet's long, sad notes for the dead float far out over the air. Then we hear—like an echo quickly returning, all changed to gladness—the bursting song of a lark flying distant and high over Sawyers' meadow. The sharp sweet smell of warm pine needles is in my nose. My eyes are stinging and I feel a lump in my throat. I hunt in my dress pockets but cannot find the handkerchief Mother tucked there this morning. Some of the others are blinking, too, pretending they have to scuff their dusty shoes on the grass. Then (I imagine) I see something else. The wrinkled old men and the buggies are gone. In their places are tall young soldiers, really only boys in new blue uniforms crowding around the flag. They are laughing and joking as they fall into line behind one who blows on a cornet and one who is a drummer. They are going far away from home to fight—perhaps to die. I think of how they did fight so long ago and how many did die. It was for us so we might be here safe at home, close under these friendly mountains. Everyone in our whole country could be free, and nobody in our part of the world would have to worry about war ever again.

After the parade is over, we find the waiting tiresome until the grown-ups have finished eating. At last the tables are set up for the fourth time and we are called in to eat. We needn't have worried; there is still plenty of food. Platters of pink ham slices and cold boiled beef cut nice and thin, white pea beans baked with molasses, cranberry beans, kidney beans, yellow eye beans baked with onion mixed in. Some kinds we like well enough but none are as good as Mother's. We spread the hot steamed brown bread with gobs of yellow butter, help ourselves to favorite relishes. There's Mother's piccalilli (she brought a big jarful dipped from the two-gallon stone crock she keeps down cellar). There's chowchow, good but mustardy enough to make your mouth smart. Sweet pepper relish, red and green all mixed together. Cucumber pickles cured just right so they have kept crisp all winter long; some are plain, others flavored with dill or mustard and brown sugar. There is a dish of my most favorite pickles—dark, sweet slices made from ripe cucumbers peeled and cooked with sugar, vinegar and lots of spice. All the kinds look so good I make a pig of myself and finish up eating more pickles than beans. Nobody takes any of the homemade grape ketchup. We always think it smells delicious when Mother is making a batch, but we like the tomato ketchup from the store much better. Not even one piece of lemon meringue pie is left. I really was hoping there might be, but now I'm surprised to find I don't care. Somehow we aren't hungry for dessert.

Right after we leave the table, we begin to be very thirsty and go back into the hall to ask for more nickels so we can buy soft drinks over at the store. The pretty colored soda bottles are packed deep into a big tank of iced water. Moxie, Root Beer, Orangeade, Grapeade, Lemon Lime, Ginger Ale, Sarsaparilla. We count them over before we choose. It's hard when there are so many tempting flavors. We hesitate awhile, then decide and plunge an arm quickly into the coldness to fish one out. I choose Moxie. I don't know why; I've tried it before, so I ought to remember that I don't really like the strong taste. I have hard work to finish the bottle, the same as always. Over at the Grange hall we could get good spring water. We would like it better, too, but then we'd miss the fun of buying.

Mother and Father are still over there in the kitchen working with the rest of the committee, washing up the dishes and dividing the leftovers—part to take home, the rest for needy families. They are talking and visiting, having a good time while they work. They don't seem to mind missing the speaking and the band concert that's going on over where the crowd has gathered. We don't go over either. It is more fun to play games with some of the other children, out of sight of the grown-ups. When we get tired of the games we go down to the Village brook where the boys show off, skipping flat pebbles over the water. We plump down on our stomachs close to the waterfall, trail our fingers in the clear water and watch quietly, hoping a fat brown trout will rise to snap at the water bugs skimming over the pool. We hear the band music faint and far away. If we listen for the clapping we can tell when it's time to go.

The sun's rays are slanting from the west by the time Mother and Father are ready to start home. We are all dirty and tired. The little girls squabble over who will get to sit with Mother on the front seat. Annie is too sleepy to be cross. She snuggles against me and naps all the way home; maybe I take a little cat nap too. Old Belle keeps close behind the other team. She is impatient to get home to her hay and oats, so she blows and paws the dirt when we stop at the place where Mother wants to leave a basket of food. As we come down over the hill toward home we see the cows waiting in the lane. Forrest climbs down from the wagon to open the pasture bars. The cows follow the teams down the road to the barn. Esther and Royal change their clothes in a hurry, go out to help Father with the milking. I unbutton three dirty little dresses and untie three draggled hair ribbons (shoes and stockings were pulled off the minute we started for home). Mother gives Annie her bottle and puts her in the crib. Father says, "Don't bother to set the table for me tonight." He eats sitting on a stool in the pantry—a cup of hot tea, cold sliced meat, bread and the two doughnuts left in the pail on the pantry shelf. We have cocoa and toast. We don't even ask Mother to read us the usual bedtime story. We just wash up a little and go upstairs without being told.

After that May we began hearing more about the battles in Europe. Of course we knew all along about the war over there, but it seemed so far away it could never affect us. We read about refugees and the many ships that were being torpedoed by German U-boats. Mother felt very sorry for all those poor people who had lost their homes. We ought to make more effort to help them, she felt. Father said he was more worried about the chances of our getting dragged into the fighting. Whenever visitors came, they'd sit on the front piazza and argue about the war. Most all the men agreed with Father on one point: Our country should stay out of foreign nations' affairs; their wars were none of our business. Father was relieved when Woodrow Wilson was re-elected President because we had kept the man in the White House who had promised again and again in his campaign speeches that our country would not get involved. But it didn't turn out so, of course. It wasn't six months before President Wilson was forced to ask Congress for a Declaration of War against Germany.

At once we were all caught up in the fighting spirit. Patriotic speeches and sales of savings bonds took the place of food and fun the following May. The National Guard made ready to leave for Camp Devens in Massachusetts. We knew they would soon be going overseas. Mother's youngest brother, our Uncle Otto Page, was with them, also two of the neighbor boys who were old enough and our hired man (we children missed him the most because he was Irish and was always laughing and joking with us). A poster outside the post office in Laconia showed Uncle Sam big and stern, pointing his finger right at us and saying, "I WANT YOU!" Of course we knew he wanted men to enlist, not us children, but there were other posters urging us to save food and scrap iron and money to buy bonds and saving stamps. They said, "YOU must all buckle down and do your bit" and we did, along with everyone else in our town.

Nothing in Gilford was ever quite the same after the war. Some time in those years "Decoration Day" was forgotten and we began speaking of "Memorial Day." There was still a parade and the younger children carried baskets to decorate the graves, but the buggies and the little handful of old, old men—the last of the "Boys in Blue"—had gone with the years. Their places were taken by young veterans in khaki carrying the flag, marching smartly to the cemetery, standing at attention while "taps" was blown. Our parents and their friends tried to take up again the friendly old custom of serving a community dinner, but it was no use. News of the free meal had spread and strangers from as far away as thirty or forty miles drove to the Village in their automobiles. They didn't go near the cemetery, just got out at the Grange hall and crowded in ahead of everybody else. They ate their fill, then drove right off without even a "Thank you."

Later on we had many good times at the Village—church suppers, Grange parties, dances at the Town Hall and the Old Home Day celebrations in August. The dinners then were put on by the Mt. Belknap Grange as a money-making project. Mother and Father often served on those committees and solicited food, although it was not all given. By that time the food didn't interest me nearly as much as our Old Home Day dramatic productions—and the boys I might meet at rehearsals. We weren't sorry to give up riding to the Village behind a horse. It was so thrilling to be riding along in a car at twenty-five miles per hour that we never once thought of all we had lost. We could not hear the birds' songs coming from deep in the woods. We went by too fast to take any notice of the small busy life beside the road. The fact was, we young people forgot the good times we used to have when we drove with Old Belle and the "Top Team Buggy" to the Decoration Day exercises, but our parents never stopped regretting the loss of the happy community gatherings when the food for the dinner was generously given and freely shared with all who came to observe the day.

❦ 7 ❧

We Are Ten

WHEN MY LITTLE SISTER Annie was past her fourth birthday and Mother hadn't had any more babies, I made up my mind Annie was going to be the last. Father's disappointment because we were unevenly divided—six sisters and only two brothers—didn't matter to me. The way I looked at it, eight was a great plenty. When I learned we were going to be nine pretty soon, I was dismayed and disgusted. How Esther or Royal or any of the younger ones felt about the prospect I didn't know. They kept their thoughts to themselves and I did the same.

It wasn't that I thought having one more in the family would crowd us. The house was big, as comfortable as other farmhouses, more convenient than most. At that time no other home in our neighborhood had running water and a bathroom. I wasn't afraid that Mother would be unable to take care of us or that Father would fail to provide plenty of food however big the family might become.

My resentment wasn't rooted in jealousy. Of course we often had jealous, angry feelings toward one another, but even in the midst of a fight when we were name calling and hating each other fervently we knew it would all blow away and after awhile we would be playing cozily again. When a sister told a brother, "I'll never ever speak to you as long as I live!" she meant "for at least fifteen minutes." When a brother hurled a biscuit or some heavier object in the direction of a sister whose taunts had unnerved him, his response was a spontaneous reaction, not a deliberate attempt to score a hit. If I complained to Mother that Royal had spat in my ear on the way home from school and she soothed me in an absent-minded manner but said not a word to him, I was irritated but not surprised. I knew that she knew what I meant was: Royal had tormented me by pretending that he was about to spit in my ear. If I accused her of always taking the side of the younger ones, right or wrong, she wouldn't exactly deny it but would gently remind me that I was older and bigger and shouldn't make a fuss over something that didn't matter. I would be angry at her but not for long. The truth was (though we would have been the last to admit it), we were a close family—all willing to accept responsibility, each proud of brothers and sisters.

I had always been especially fond of my little sisters, liked reading to them, making them mind their table manners. I was chief baby tender for Annie. After she was perfectly able to run wherever she wanted to go, I let her impose on me, kept on lugging her around on one hip until Mother, fearing I would begin to grow lopsided, made me stop. When Annie was old enough so she ought to have been trained but seemed determined not to be, I used to set her on the pot chair a dozen times a Saturday, coax and entertain her so she wouldn't jump right up and skip off, leaving the pot empty.

Having another baby to help take care of wasn't what bothered me. I simply felt that it was very embarrassing to belong to such a peculiar family. There was Esther, almost seventeen and halfway through high school, and everybody else except Annie already in school. And there was my mother, really pretty old, about to have a new baby, likely as not another girl, at that. My little sisters could let it out to everybody if they wanted to. From my point of view the situation was nothing to crow about.

I suppose I, and all the rest, would have liked the new baby even if it had been another girl, but when we learned that we had another brother we were relieved and glad. Our new baby brother came two days before we got out of school for summer vacation, a very convenient time for him to be born. We could manage without a woman to help in the house, with only a friend of Mother's who stayed three days to take care of the baby until Mother came downstairs. Taking over the work and responsibility was hard for Esther and for me as her first assistant, yet it was fun in a way. Everybody helped without any quarreling or shirking of even the most tedious chores. What was more surprising, Father himself helped set the table and get the food on at mealtimes. There was such a happy atmosphere around the house it was almost like Christmas. To my four younger sisters, having a tiny baby in the house was very exciting. Ellen (she had stopped being our little Nellie after she went to school) was thrilled to share her June birthday month with the new little brother. And as for Father—at long last, after nearly twelve years and four girls in a row, Mother had produced a third son for him—he was so puffed up anybody would have thought this baby was more important than all the rest of us put together. He would have named the baby after himself but Mother, not wanting to have her little boy called Junior or Sonny, objected and they settled on Robert. A good old English name, Father said, although never used in his family as far as he knew. We immediately nicknamed our baby brother Robbie. And Robbie he stayed until he grew up and became Bob.

Robbie was a big baby, perfect in form and apparently perfectly healthy, as all Mother's babies had been, yet very soon it began to seem doubtful whether he could survive for even a few months. He couldn't, or wouldn't, eat at all well. Mother had always regretted not being able to feed any except her first three babies at the breast; still she had no reason to be apprehensive about the new baby at first. Forrest and all four little girls had thrived on the bottle. She supposed it would be the same with Robbie, but it wasn't.

I was aware that our baby brother was not doing well on the milk formula Dr. True had advised. Changes were made and I heard my parents' anxious discussions about each new formula, none better than the first. I knew Mother found it almost impossible to coax Robbie into finishing his bottle and what he did take he mostly spat up. I saw him lying in the old wicker baby carriage, sleeping too quietly, his thin little hands never curled into strong baby fists. When he was wakeful I heard his constant fretful wailing, amazingly low-pitched and so all the more pathetic to Mother's ear. I knew that her heart was wrung and her nights were many times sleepless. I didn't worry. My feelings were only slightly touched. In our family everything had always come out right in the past. Why shouldn't it now? Besides, I had much else on my mind. I was spending the summer romancing in the world of books, far away from the mundane existence of the family.

I no longer joined in childish games and was always daydreaming but was not physically absent, except when I hid away in the attic, the cupola of the barn or at the foot of the seldom-used ell stairway—safe places for concealing and reading dime novels frowned upon by Mother as too lurid for young minds. With no more than the usual amount of evasion, I picked berries, helped wash the dishes, cleaned and filled the kerosene lamps, made beds, supervised the younger sisters' laggard choring and took my turn at wheeling the baby carriage under the shade of the maple. So dreamy that I was dull-witted, I fell into each new trap schemed up by Royal and Forrest solely for the pleasure of sister-teasing. Without noticing the thin wire attached, I was forever picking up scissors or knives left lying around in odd places, then could never repress a startled, angry shriek upon receiving a rough jolt of current from the homemade "shocking machine." That reaction was most gratifying to the smirking operator who popped up mouthing devilish taunts. When my brothers sought me out, wearing bland, cat-that-licked-the-cream expressions and urged me to come see the something pretty they had found, I ought to have remembered the last time when they got me within quill-shot distance of a humped up, battle-ready porcupine they had captured. Or the time before that when they almost tricked me into stepping on a big ugly snapping turtle hitched by one hind leg to a fence post. But curiosity, way ahead of second-thought caution, propelled me out into the yard and right to an upended barrel discreetly covered with a gunny sack—to keep their little wild pets from running away in fright, they told me. With consummate showmanship the sack was whipped off. Within were two big black snakes heaving in furious coils, viciously hissing, heads rising clear up to the barrel's rim. Horrid, unblinking snake eyes glared right at me. Tongues flicked out wickedly. Shocked to a freeze, I stared back— but not for long. Shrieking loud enough to disturb the hens on their nests and the baby in his carriage, I ran for the house and Mother, leaving Royal and Forest rolling on the grass in spasms of bratty glee.

At such moments I utterly despised my brothers and their mean tricks. It wasn't that I was really afraid of any wild creature likely to be encountered in our area. Things that crawled I didn't care for one bit, but the horror part was mostly play-acting. The performance must have given me some satisfaction, otherwise I wouldn't have cooperated so heartily. Perhaps I sometimes was tired of feeling all tangled up with the high-flown personalities of romance. Maybe it was also needed relief I felt whenever my brothers' rude practical joking snatched me back to the family.

After we went back to school in September Mother became more and more distressed about Robbie. She didn't have us to wheel him when he was fussy, or to take turns beside his carriage, jogging his bottle now and then so he would stay awake and keep sucking, not doze off leaving the bottle still almost full. Then two lucky things happened.

Father took the advice of a chance acquaintance, a man who recommended for Robbie an expensive, imported-from-England baby food which was credited with saving the lives of a number of sickly babies. The new formula proved to be exactly what Robbie needed. The problem of finding enough hours to feed him his bottle was solved when Great-aunt Jessie offered to come and stay for as long as she was needed. After Robbie had grown to be a tall, husky boy Mother would often recall how, when he was little and frail, she had almost despaired of his life. Then she would remember aloud to be thankful for a stranger's interest and grateful for the tender care given by one who never knew the joy of a home and babies of her own.

Aunt Jessie stayed with us all that winter, and I got to be her friend. Not that she liked me any better than she did Esther or the baby, or my little sister Jessie who was her namesake or any of the others, but with me she had more things to talk about.

When I was younger and Aunt Jessie came for short visits, I used to think of her as just another of our relatives on Father's side—the old maid sister of Grandmother or Grandfather, I didn't remember which. She was someone very old and quite fragile, likely to have a near-fainting spell and need reviving with a spoonful of liquid from the amber-colored bottle kept on the top shelf in the back hall closet; yet when she felt like resting she didn't slump into a rocker but sat up straight in a hard-backed chair. She was forever taking off her old-fashioned steel-rimmed spectacles to wipe them with the small snowy handkerchief she kept in her apron pocket. Her teeth, uppers and lowers, were deposited every night in a glass of water kept on the stand beside her bed. (My little sisters, greatly intrigued by the novelty of removable teeth, sometimes peeked, hoping in vain to catch her in the act of putting them back in.) Aunt Jessie, so hard of hearing she would have been called "deef as a post" in earlier times, always wore a hearing aid—a thick metal disk held to her better ear by an attached band fitting over her head just in front of her grey-mixed-with-black topknot, and connected by wire to batteries placed under the front of her dress, an oddly positioned bump on her otherwise flat bosom. Even with the aid of this mechanism, Aunt Jessie couldn't follow the conversation if everybody was talking, interrupting and finishing each other's sentences —a situation very common at our house. But if you were having a private conversation with her, she could easily understand and she could hear Robbie before anyone else knew he had waked up.

When Aunt Jessie and I got better acquainted I stopped noticing only her infirmities and began to see the pleasing things about her. Although she seldom smiled on account of her false teeth, she didn't

look at all severe. She was fond of telling stories about maiden ladies
and their ridiculous ways; then she would laugh merrily, poking fun at
all old maids, herself included. Maybe she didn't feel bad about not getting married, but even if she did it hadn't made her silly or sour like
most old maids. She wasn't always going on about ailments, people
dying and funerals or about religion, although the Bible on her bedside
table was well worn. If you were the fanciful kind, you might have
supposed that Great-aunt Jessie wasn't really an old lady, but a girl
aged in a moment by an evil fairy who had waved her wand care-
lessly, leaving bits of the youngling showing through. Aunt Jessie was
quite tall but small-boned and narrow—sort of willowy (in books I read
the heroines were always "willowy"). Her rounded cheeks were firm as
a winter apple and her brown eyes were twinkly bright behind her spectacles. Her skin was wrinkled silk crepe and that was how soft her
hands felt when she soothed my headaches away. Whenever I wanted to
talk, she was always glad to listen with her whole attention, to my mind
one of the most satisfying things about her.

Of course I was obliged to listen some in return—that was only
fair. And I really didn't mind hearing. In years, Aunt Jessie was very
old—probably as much as seventy, I thought—yet she remembered just
how it felt to be fifteen like me. She had such a way of telling the small
happenings when she was young, she could make me feel, as near as
could be, that I was back there being friends with her in that long,
long ago:

We went off to school carrying books, slates and lunch pails packed
with biscuit and meat sandwiches, fat molasses cookies and rosy apples.
We did sums on our slates, chose up sides and had a spelldown. When
the master rapped smartly for attention because the big boys were
cutting up, making eyes in our direction, we blushed and giggled together behind our McGuffey readers. We dawdled our way home along
the woodsy road. A doe eyed us unafraid. We watched the busy
squirrels and heard the partridges drumming.

On a Saturday we walked across pasture and field to a big weathered-
to-silver grey house with low eaves, the home of Great-aunts Ruth and
Betsey (and their cats). Aunt Ruth and Aunt Betsey could remember
the early days when the town was being settled. While we decided on a
quilt pattern and chose pretty calicoes from their bulging scrap bag, the
aunts interspersed sewing instructions with a lesson in local history.

"Notice the shaller place in the junipers, Jessie. Jest over thar near
the buryin' groun'. Thet's the spot Pa (he wuz your great-gran'sir,
a'course) dug the cellar hole fer the log cabin. The fust winter here it
housed the hull fam'ly an' the cow, too. People say Pa wuz the one

named this place Chemung, after sum furrin place out to Noo York or down in the Jarseys, I s'pose. He wuz thar in the war. Jined up with Gen'l Washington's army when he wuz sixteen, cum hum with nothin' wuss nor a bullit hole in his leg. Times he brung us up here to settle we war little girls. We cum inter town ridin' on the oxsled, hunkered down 'mongst the household goods keepin' warm. It wuz late November, Eighty-two or Eighty-three, I fergit which. Once in, we didn't git outside the clearin' 'til spring. The wolves war here then, and lynx and b'ars aplenty, bold enuff to cum inter the pen an' carry off a squealin' shoat. Them war hard old times, but a sight better livin' in sum ways then 'tis now." The aunts gave us paper-thin, gingery molasses cookies and we drank tea from pretty pink lustre cups. As we hurried across the field trying to beat the dark home, we saw the nighthawks sweeping the sky, heard them begin their booming dives toward earth.

Aunt Jessie stayed with us until the following spring when Robbie was walking and beginning to talk. The vigorous little boy was eager to be outdoors, and Father was happy to take him all over the farm. Knowing she was no longer needed, Aunt Jessie left us in answer to an urgent call from another relative's family. For a keepsake she gave me a quilt top she had sewed when she was just my age. It was made from scraps of material left from dresses she and her sisters had sewn. She said there were also quite a few pieces from the scrap bag of her great-aunts, Ruth and Betsey Perkins. She thought I might like to finish the quilt for my own hope chest.

I put the gift away, not really believing I ever would find the time or have the skill to finish it by hand. In later years when I was rearranging shelves in a linen closet or packing for a move, I would come across Aunt Jessie's unfinished quilt and stop my work to spread the patchwork across a bed. I would count the pieces again—seven hundred and two dainty, many-patterned quadrangular bits of calico precisely sewn together. I would admire the minute stitches, so wonderfully even they made the wrong side as pretty as the face. I would put the patchwork away, thinking the time was not yet. Then at last I understood that with the unfinished quilt I had received another gift more precious by far. Aunt Jessie had given me a magic key. Because I had known her, I could open the door to many, many yesterdays ago, touch the hands of those who had lived in the days when our country began. Great-aunt Jessie's patchwork must be kept just as she had left it, unfinished but nevertheless perfect.

Some day if I live to be an old, old lady there may be a girl of fifteen, a great-granddaughter or great-great niece, who will want to be my friend. And for a keepsake I shall give her my great-aunt's patchwork.

I was then of a most uncertain age. A betwixt and between age, Aunt Jessie would have said. Sometimes I felt carefree, kin to the fledgling hawks taking off from the tall dead pine high on a blowy hilltop, gliding down the air currents in a swooping rush, then up again, wings beating strongly against the wind as they played their game of follow-the-leader. Sometimes I felt greatly put upon. Belonging to a large family was a hard lot and also a social stigma. At such moments I thought of my younger sisters as vexatious little pests forever needing their ears washed, their stockings pulled up and their slovenly manners at table corrected. Royal and Forrest I dismissed as odious clods with no higher aim in life than to hatch fiendish schemes for plaguing me and my visiting girl friends.

With Esther I seldom quarreled—perhaps we were not jealous of each other because we were so different. And never for a moment could I feel that I did not love my youngest brother Robbie. He had become such a sunny little boy, wide awake and smiling the moment he opened his eyes, just as happy to be going to bed at night. From the day he began to walk he needed hardly any tending, or rather he was no bother to us in the house because Father took him in charge. He learned to talk by saying over the names of the oxen and all the cows. The farm animals were his friends, the baby calves his playmates. His pets provided all the entertainment he needed. It was pure pleasure to see the small, chubby boy doubled up with glee over the antics of his yellow kitten ferociously attacking a ball of string or madly pursuing its own fluffy tail.

As I remember, my capricious moods were just as fleeting as the angry feelings arising from altercations among us. I have said we were a close family, but I did not mean to picture a composite, nondescript family personality or to suggest that one brother or sister was overwhelmed or even overshadowed, except perhaps momentarily, by any of the others. People might say that we stuck together against outsiders, but none could accuse us of being an everlasting mutual admiration society. We were and are, every one of us, vigorous individualists, and, when we were growing up, fully as self-centered as the general run of young people. That we came rightly by our aggressive, sharpcornered Yankee characteristics we have never denied. When we grew older it became our custom, in the heat of clashing temperaments, to administer a stinging twit, "Why keep on being a Smith all your life!"

This custom of attributing the less-attractive family traits to Father's side was perhaps rooted in Mother's outspoken dislike for the ways of Grandfather Smith and all his progenitors. Grandfather was a very overbearing man and just so had been his father before him, and before that his grandfather (according to Mother's supposition). Grandmother Smith, complaisant and yielding to Grandfather in all ways, had allowed her sons to become imbued with the idea: "A man be no man if he be not master in the house," an ancient adage brought from England by the Smiths and their fellow emigrants. Mother didn't dwell to excess on this theme, but now and then she brought it out and dusted it off as an excuse for having us kowtow to Father's notions about food and other things, or to explain why, when she allowed an expedition or some minor innovation doubtful of meeting with his approval, she tempered her permission with the admonition, "Better not let your father know about this. No need to get him all stirred up over something that doesn't amount to anything." However, except when certain of her principles were at stake, Mother customarily treated Father's wishes as rules to be followed by the family, and as children were supposed to do, we accepted his authority without questioning.

That our parents would always be there where they were supposed to be, doing what they ought to do for us, we assumed to be our natural right. Father was Father; he had his foibles and his favorites. Mother held us all in equal affection but was inclined to be indulgent toward the youngest one. Sunday night was Father's bath night. We had ours on Saturday night and were too unsophisticated to feel deprived because there was only one bathroom for the whole family. Inevitably the situation changed, until finally, Father was confronted with a full-scale teen insurrection.

The beginning, thought of at the time as no more than an isolated incident, happened the autumn after Robbie's first birthday. It was the era of the new woman. The bastion of male privilege had been breeched, the ballot secured. Some bold feminists, including a few in our insular community, had taken to wearing pants and were seen smoking cigarettes in public. All the girls—that is, quite a number of our acquaintances—were having their hair bobbed. The year before, Father had made no objection when Mother triumphantly got ready and accompanied him to the polls. He knew it would be no use to object (though it galled him, a lifelong Democrat, to know she would surely cast her vote for Warren G. Harding). When he saw a woman with rouged lips and short hair smoking a cigarette on the street, it was an interesting piece of news to be mentioned at home. It seemed to us he had a sneaking admiration for those brazen creatures. We didn't need to be told that where his own daughters were concerned,

anything even vaguely suggestive of such behavior would produce a
completely different reaction—which was why Esther went to the
barber and had her hair cut off without consulting anyone, not even
Mother (at least Mother never admitted to a foreknowledge of the rash
deed). Esther was Father's favorite daughter, the one whose good sense,
whose cleverness with animals and skill at driving an automobile he took
pride in, the one who had helped him most on the farm. His reaction
to what he considered rank ingratitude and perfidious behavior need
not be described here. The furor that ensued was a great advantage to
me. When I followed Esther's example, my shorn head was hardly
noticed. The boy friends-versus-Father struggle was still in the hatching
stage.

My youngest brother, the baby that was to be Mother's last, was
born four days after her forty-fifth birthday and a few days short of a
month before Robbie was two years old. From the moment of his birth
through the rest of her life, the tenth child held first place in Mother's
affections, a pre-eminence brothers and sisters yielded without jealousy,
for he was also his sisters' darling baby brother, the special charge of
the two older boys, and for Robbie a younger-brother companion,
someone to follow him closely and share with him all the growing-up
years. The loving attention lavished on our baby brother, more than
was always good for him, might have been compensation on the part of
some of us for the bitter resentment harbored before his birth, but I
have always believed the real reason was that when it came to babies we
were a family of natural-born push-overs.

Forrest, the younger girls and their various friends—all still attending
the rural school close to home—were a tight little group with Forrest
as the greatly admired, generally undisputed leader. He and the sisters
of his gang did not appear to be disturbed by the impending addition
to our cluttered, noisy, over-crowded and unprivate household. For so I
had come to regard my home, and anticipations of a howling infant
adding to the din, the clothesline on the front porch (exposed to public
view) draped with diapers, and pails of unwashed more of the same
smelling up the bathroom were repulsive enough to give me the
mental gags. Though it was a thing we would not have discussed openly
or ventured to whisper about on the sly, I was nevertheless well aware
that Esther and Royal were in accord with my view of Mother's unsuit-
able pregnancy. I was just as sure that they could not possibly be as
mortified as I was. It was *my* social life that was going to be ruined—
possibly forever—anyway for the coming summer; *my* romance that was
about to be nipped before it was given a chance to bud. "He" was so

wonderful! An "older" man, a college football hero (second-string but none-the-less glamorous in my eyes). I visioned his interest dissolving like the morning mist on a fine September day. What a miserable stroke of fate, or should the blame be allocated elsewhere?

Reason and emotions were confused, muddied by underneath feelings relating to sex, a subject carefully skirted in polite conversation—at least that was still the mode in our non-cosmopolitan society. The word itself, also taboo, was only a degree less shocking (and titillating) than the four-letter scrawls to be observed on rail fences and certain backhouse walls. The idea, although vague, was not exactly repugnant to me but was in no way connected with the romance of a goodnight kiss bestowed by my hero, and in that respect I assumed we were two minds with but a single thought. If it appears that I was incredibly naïve, let the reader recall that my parents had been married just as the Victorian Era was ending, and that, although I was then nearly seventeen and the year was 1922, the era of free love and the flapper was still on the far side of our horizon.

Our baby brother came on a Saturday morning in May. Breakfast, usually a little later and not quite so rushed as on school mornings, was such a hurried affair the younger children were quite bewildered. I was surprised, because I hadn't been told when the baby was coming. Perhaps Mother herself hadn't known whether it was going to be that month or some time in June, and even if she had she certainly wouldn't have believed it would happen on a Saturday morning, and anyway wouldn't have given us advance instructions about what to do; yet the way we took hold you would have thought we had been rehearsed in our parts. Father's work for the day, already planned, of course, was setting out the strawberry plants for next year's bed. He assigned Forrest, Frances and Ellen as helpers in the field, told them to hurry up and get started if they expected to have any playtime later in the day. Little Robbie went along with them, didn't even have to be told.

As soon as the children were out of the way, Mother telephoned her nurse friend and Dr. True, then went into the bathroom, locked the door and took a leisurely bath (a luxury for her) before going upstairs to the South Chamber, the room always used in sickness. Esther and I set to work clearing up the breakfast things and washing the milk pails. We complained some about the floors that would have to be swept and mopped, the chamber work and the washing and the big effort of trying to get meals for such a crew, but underneath we were excited and pleased to be at home when it was happening. Even though we wouldn't admit it, we had softened up about the new baby, were all over being angry at Mother. But it did seem strange to have her upstairs, the baby about to be born, us down there working and the house so quiet.

"Too quiet!" We suddenly thought and both remembered at the same time, "Nobody did anything about Jessie and Annie."

"They can't be still in the house."

"You don't suppose—? Those scamps, they wouldn't go upstairs, or would they?"

We stopped our work to listen: inside only a faucet dripping and the tall clock ticktocking more slowly and loudly than ever before; from somewhere outdoors the little girls' laughing shrieks. We ran out to look.

Up toward the schoolhouse an extraordinary performance was going on. Royal was riding his youngest sisters in the old wicker baby carriage. First one, then the other, he jammed in unceremoniously, leaving head rising like a turtle's, spindly legs and bare feet hanging over the front. Down the road and up again they jolted, the shaky old vehicle swaying in crazy fashion, wobbly wheels spraying gravel in all directions. While it was obvious Jessie and Annie were enjoying the untypical, mad clowning of their eldest brother, it was also quite plain to Esther and me that the game was not of their choosing. There they were, well away from the about-to-take-place event in the house and there Royal would keep them until after Dr. True had come and gone.

That was no more than a short hour later. The doctor had taken it so easy it was about twenty minutes after the baby arrived before his mud-spattered Ford rattled up to the door. Mother didn't hold it against Dr. True. After all, he had previously officiated at the births of the rest of us Smiths, nine normal uncomplicated deliveries. This time he surveyed the situation and praised the efficiency of the practical nurse. Then, congratulating Mother on her fine baby boy, he tied up the loose ends and left. (I am not making a pun, just quoting Mother's later explanation to us.)

At the dinner table the children chattered, wondering what our new baby brother looked like and what his name would be. Everybody seemed pleased with the outcome, except Royal who had retreated into glum taciturnity, the manner he had put on back in the winter. He just sat there and swallowed his food, didn't throw out one sarcastic remark about the slapdash meal Esther and I had put on the table. As soon as he had finished eating he got right up and left, letting the screen door bang behind him as much as to say, "What's so great about another boy baby! Just one more noisy little brat, as far as I'm concerned." Of course he was nowhere around when the baby was brought down for the afternoon viewing.

I wasn't much bothered by Royal's grumpy behavior, but Esther was exasperated, completely out of sympathy with him. She kept talking about it all the time we were getting supper. When she was sure Royal had brought the last pails of milk into the bottling room in the ell and was getting ready to run the separator, she suddenly dropped the bread knife and marched upstairs. I was curious about what she was up to, so when I saw her come down cradling the baby on her left arm, as easy as you please, and head for the ell, I stole out on the back porch where I could look through a window and see what went on.

The tableau inside the milk room struck me as remarkable in an odd sort of way. There were the two eldest—Royal, not yet filled out to man size but broad-shouldered, standing every inch of six feet, and Esther, a large well-coordinated young woman nearly as tall—and the third one, the tender just-born, a small blue-wrapped bundle gracefully displayed on Esther's arm. Like it or not, Royal was getting a private viewing. He stared at the crumpled-up pink features (not uncommonly pretty but very definitely male). He put out a big forefinger and poked gently at one tiny silken hand. The baby's dark blue eyes opened, his delicate fingers curled around the tip of the big, rough one, enclosed it in a miniature fist. Grinning fatuously, Royal capitulated for good. Man to man, he greeted his new brother, "Hi, Joe!" The name seemed to fit. Mother had named the baby Gardner Page, but we called him Joe.

The two little boys rounded out our family in a most satisfactory way and we were relieved to feel that the ring was closed. We couldn't have stood another addition—the last birth had been a traumatic experience for all of us (with the exception of Mother). There was an unexpected eleventh child after a time. That one, ours only by adoption, we welcomed gladly and for a summer allowed her to reign like a little queen in our household.

She joined us so secretly we only suspected she was there at first. It was when Esther, Royal and I had gone away to college, were home only for vacations and weekends. Jessie and Annie had a year or two more to attend the one-room rural school. Forrest, Frances and Ellen were going to high school or junior high in Laconia. All the neighbors were old people; in our part of town there were no little children except Robbie and Joe. In the spring after Joe was three years old, he began to feel that he had nobody to play with. Robbie wanted to spend all his waking hours away from the house, working with the baby steers he was training to the yoke or off in the woods "helping" Father, who wouldn't be bothered with more than one small boy at a time. Joe would have been content if Robbie had not been so close to Father, for although the two little boys were so different in temperament, they played well together most of the time. Robbie liked to wear a cowboy hat. Joe had fun donning a headdress with bright-colored feathers, pretending to be an Indian chief. Robbie could milk a cow before he was five years old. Joe didn't learn until Father insisted. Joe knew the ferny pool in the pasture brook where the fairies danced at midnight. Robbie saw only the minnows in the water and the place where the cows came to drink.

We were not told her name or anything else about her, but it was plain the new child was an elfin creature, too shy to give any trouble. She had to look up to Joe, she was so small. While they had long, earnest discussions—or more accurately, during his monologues—she hung on his every word, agreed with all he said, was eager to play the games he suggested. We did not know whether she had a name until someone overheard a conversation while the two were playing in the sandbox under The Big Maple. We learned then she was called Marjerie-Peegerie, a very charming name, one that ran trippingly off the tongue.

We might have had less trouble if we had left Joe's new playmate out of doors, but one of my sisters—I don't remember who—rashly invited Marjerie-Peegerie to dinner. She behaved most decorously, shared Joe's high stool, ate tiny bites from his plate and didn't delay our dishwashing more than half an hour. If only she had remained a now-and-then visitor how happy we would have been! But children are devious, very seldom what they seem—especially ethereal beings like Joe's girl friend. When Marjerie-Peegerie realized how easy it was to get the upper hand, she moved right in and began to crack the whip. She demanded and got a place of her own (with elbow room) at our crowded table. Mother was kept on the jump, making her small sandwiches without crusts, numerous special kinds of cookies and breakfast dishes not served to the rest of the family. She was careless about crumbs, refused to finish her milk and didn't allow her ears to be washed. She became a horrid little tyrant, a very bad influence on Joe, but we knew of no way to get rid of her without crushing him utterly.

She might have been with us much longer if she hadn't locked horns with Father. Up until that fatal night she kept out of his way while he ignored her presence. Whatever possessed her we couldn't imagine, but just before Father was due in to supper she plopped herself down in his rocking chair. There she sat and she wouldn't budge. We heard Joe coaxing, urging her to get up, but she sat tight. In desperation he appealed to us. What could we do! With Marjerie-Peejerie our influence was negative. When Joe saw Father come into the house he began jumping up and down, screaming hysterically. Unable to get out an intelligible word, he could only point at the seat of the old wooden

rocker. Father, appearing mildly annoyed at the fuss, glanced disin-
terestedly at his chair sitting in its usual place beside his desk, walked
over and sat down heavily right on top of Marjerie-Peejerie. Leisurely
he unlaced his shoes, placed them under the desk, put on his slippers,
arranged his spectacles well down on his nose, picked up *The Boston
Post* and began to read. Mother arrived on the tragic scene, mercifully
took Joe away. We heard his sobs diminishing to hiccups as she carried
him up the back stairs.

We walked on eggs until we realized that Joe wasn't the least upset
by the timely demise of his friend Marjerie-Peejerie. Father's old rocker
had done us a good turn, we sisters agreed.

There were plenty of times afterward when we wouldn't have said
the same. Father's favorite rocker—in fact it was about the only chair he
ever sat in—was positioned beside his roll-top desk, always left open
except on very formal occasions. The pigeonholes of the desk were
crammed with bills, tax receipts, scraps of paper covered with figures
reckoning up the tonnage of hay sold, old letters from Aunt Mary in
California and a good many other things we couldn't see the use of.
The desk was piled helter-skelter with seed catalogues (the new one
and last year's kept for purposes of comparison), bulletins from the
Department of Agriculture, the Sears Roebuck catalogue, copies of *The
Saturday Evening Post*, the *New England Homestead, The Laconia
Democrat* and the daily paper. We were strictly enjoined not to remove
a thing from Father's desk and we didn't. Yet when he wanted some
particular item he could never lay his hands on it. He would scuffle
helplessly through the clutter, glare around the room and demand,
"Who's been monkeying in my desk?" Then someone would have to
come and help him look.

It was the position of the rocker, not the messy desk, that made our
lives difficult. From where he sat, Father could keep an eye on the
progress of the meal being prepared in the kitchen and at the same
time note all the comings into and goings out from the big, family
dining-living room. The heavy front door on the other side of the house
was kept locked—everyone used the one opening onto the porch, di-
rectly behind Father's rocker. He was right there, ready to face down all
the boys who knocked on the door. If we came home later than we
should have, we could expect to find that Father, a light sleeper, had
come downstairs in his nightshirt and was sitting in his rocker reading.
Under those circumstances it was best to say a hasty goodnight on the
far end of the porch, scuttle past Father (pretending not to notice his
big silver watch so obviously displayed on the desk), forget about the

necessity of visiting the bathroom on the other side of the kitchen and hasten up the front stairs to bed.

When we talk of those crowded, happy years we laugh about every fracas. We remember how truly hospitable Father was, how kind he was to the young people who came—never really insulting any of them, even those he could hardly tolerate. We knew that our troubles were as light and transient as the down escaping from a bursting milkweed pod. We wonder when it began to end, when the strong family ties began to loosen. For Esther it was the day of her wedding; for each of the others his own memorable time.

I remember the day Royal left home to enter the University of New Hampshire. While he loaded his belongings, Robbie and Joe watched, not really understanding that their adored older brother was going away, thinking perhaps he was going to take them for a ride in his old Ford car. When he cranked up and drove away they chased after him, crying loudly, running up the road as fast as their short legs could pump. The jalopy disappeared from sight, and they threw themselves down in the road, sobbing as though their hearts would break. I went to get them, coaxed them back home, washed their faces and read them a story.

❦ 8 ❦

"...all his seed..."

OUR FAMILY had a big party for Father's eightieth birthday. The celebration was planned for the August before his November birth date so that a considerable number of our scattered family could come back to New Hampshire for the picnic-party. The Weeks' farm on Gunstock Hill in Gilford (home of our oldest sister, Esther) was the perfect place to hold a family picnic. There was plenty of room in the big farmhouse and on the back porch for the adults to sit and visit, space on the wide lawn for the younger grandchildren to rough and tumble in a game of touch football; for the great-grandchildren, fascinating visits to the calf barn and horse pasture to admire and pet the animals.

Father had looked forward to the day. He always had loved a picnic so this special birthday celebration was a wonderful treat for him. He drove himself over in his Ford car along the country roads from the old farm to Gunstock Hill, ways he had first traveled with horse and wagon more than fifty years before. He spent a good part of the day outside enjoying the August sunshine and the panorama which curved half 'round the horizon—a spectacular view of woods and fields, lakes and mountains, a view famed throughout New Hampshire.

We set his chair on the lawn beyond the wide veranda, faced to the west. Sitting there he could see the houses of Laconia clustered around Lakes Paugus and Opeechee, the green hills of Meredith beyond the city, and still farther off, the Sanbornton Mountains. This was the realm familiar in his youth. Out from the kitchen to where he sat came daughters, daughters-in-law, granddaughters, and grandsons' wives bringing offerings of his favorite foods, making sure to satisfy his hearty appetite. Below, beyond the steep slope of the hill, lay a feast for his eyes, food to nourish the spirit of one who had always loved the land of his ancestors.

When he began to be dazzled by the rays of the late summer sun and he felt a little stiff from sitting, he got up to walk about a bit, went off to pass judgment on the young stock waiting at the pasture bars, then came back again to sit on the shady veranda. Here he could get the widest view. Away to the northward beyond Lake Winnipesaukee he could see the rugged Ossipee range. Rising higher, blue wave on blue wave, the White Mountains reached, merging finally into the palest blue of the sky. Father's vision was somewhat dimmed by age, yet on a day of such crystal visibility he could clearly see Mt. Washington's peak highest of all, stark, majestic, already crowned with the glisten of early snow.

Father never did get tired of looking at the mountains, but he often said he thought the Lake with its hundreds of green islands was more sightly: Winnipesaukee, "Smile of the Great Spirit," rightly named (so legend told) by the Indians who crossed its waters in their canoes and spread their fish weirs there at the outlet, ages before our land-hungry pioneer ancestors came to spend their years wresting their farmlands from this beautiful wilderness.

It was a day of good talk, too. The menfolks shared Father's reminiscing and deferred to his opinions when local political matters were under discussion. Everyone was agreeable and all was so serene that the party scarcely seemed typical of our lively, aggressive Smith family. Even the older grandsons seemed to have an unspoken agreement to refrain from their customary brash boasts made just for the fun of "touching Grandpa Smith up a bit," so he'd get off some crusty remarks, leaving no doubt of his low opinion of today's youth and the great superiority of the days when he was young.

The day was made complete when a reporter came from Laconia to write up the event so it could come out in next day's *Evening Citizen*. Father thoroughly enjoyed being the center of attention in the family group pictures and the four-generation poses.

At the end of the day he thanked us all for his wonderful eightieth birthday celebration. We thought then that he showed his age more than usual for he broke down a bit, his voice quivered and he had to wipe his eyes, but he perked up right away—told us we'd better make plans for another party ten years from then. He was in pretty good shape for a man his age, he felt. Plenty of his family had made it beyond ninety and he believed he could, too.

After Father had left, the women washed up the dishes and talked over the party. Everyone agreed that it had been worthwhile. We all expected that he might well live to be ninety; then we'd have just such another picnic-party only by that time the family gathering would certainly be much larger.

Scarcely a year and a half later our scattered family was called back to New Hampshire. In the late afternoon of an early winter's day we gathered again at the farm on Gunstock Hill. John Weeks directed the parking of the automobiles, a solid line around his sweeping driveway.

As soon as we stepped from the warm cars we noticed how the wind had changed, beginning to blow straight out of the northeast, biting sharply at our ankles and noses. The sparkling panorama of summertime was gone. Earlier cold spells had spread an ice pall, stilling the changeable blue lake waters. We looked down across a dull white sameness splotched only by black shadows where treacherous ice reefs lay. The distant peaks of the White Mountains had disappeared, shut off from view by creeping grey clouds—tattered shrouds, already hanging far down the slopes of the Ossipees.

We hurried into the comfortable farmhouse, not staying to look longer, bent away from the icy wind. We knew well enough what all the weather signs foretold. The storm would begin about dusk and fine dry flakes would come driving down all through the night. By morning the snow would everywhere be inches deep and drifted high here on the hill, if this wind kept up.

The grey day fitted well this solemn occasion. We all felt so, but none would speak the thought for that was not our way, nor would any of us recall the plans for a summer picnic here a decade hence. There would be no more birthday celebrations for Father. He had lived less than a month past his eighty-first birthday.

Next day there would be an account of his death in *The Evening Citizen*. Two columns on the obituary page to tell the passing of a patriarch, descendant of pioneers; Samuel Smith, retired farmer, of High Maples Farm, Gilford. Six tall grandsons to bear the casket, a funeral procession stretching out a whole street long. The number of his kindred attending the funeral equal to the years of his lifetime, his direct descendants already more than half a hundred.

Our meeting, prescribed by ancient custom, was the second such gathering for our family. On the same kind of chill, dark afternoon thirteen years before we had come back to our old home after a sad trip to the family burying lot. Our family circle was broken then by Mother's death. Of that day we all remembered only the anguish, the confusion and strain of wartime emergency travel.

Those harsh memories had been softened and eased by the years. We ourselves had become the older generation, had learned to accept finality. Our grandparents used to say, "Friends and family stay to share the funeral meats." An archaic ritual for country people we once had thought; now we knew its grace and meaning. Father was gone. We felt his absence sadly, yet it was right that we should be here, all together once more in the home of the eldest one.

We helped ourselves to the food already spread out over the long dining room table. Our youngest sister-in-law, Allyn, had baked the turkey before light that morning. Gardner had wrapped it well, still hot in the big roasting pan, to bring it from their home beyond the White Mountains. There was a leg of lamb from Esther's freezer, hot rolls that Verna had made, milk from the Weeks' Dairy.

We moved about as we ate and visited, young people getting reacquainted with their New Hampshire cousins, while brothers and sisters talked of the days when we were one family living at the old farm. We laughed a little when we recalled our constant youthful escapades—how many years we had kept Father's temper on a very short fuse—yet we were proud we could feel sure none had ever given our parents cause for shame. Then we spoke of our thankfulness to "Grandma Mary," the second wife, whose affection and gentle care had made these last few years a full and happy time for Father.

Esther put her thoughts into words, "I'll miss having him drop in to eat dinner whenever he knows I'm cooking something he specially likes. He won't be here to enjoy the new maple syrup next spring nor to bring me a mess of fresh-dug dandelion greens. I've always driven him up to Sandwich Fair, you know. I doubt if I'll even go next fall. I realize that he had a long life and a good one—as much or more than any of us can expect. He never got so feeble he couldn't enjoy life; I'm glad of that. At the same time I feel that his death marks the end of an era, and I'm sad that it should be so."

After the others had gone, hurrying back to work and young families at home, my husband and I decided to stay and visit awhile with Esther and John. Now we were here, we might as well wait a day or two before flying back to Florida, at least until the weather cleared.

Right after dark it began to spit snow just as we'd known it would.

Even so the mercury was dropping, John remarked. No doubt there'd be a severe cold spell following the storm. Secretly we were glad to be secure here inside Weeks' old farmhouse while the wind grew stronger and began to howl round the corners. We heard the maples' big branches snap with cold and the rafters creaked up attic. Frost patterns were beginning to build thick on the windowpanes. Soon we'd not be able to see out where now the lights shone on the snow veils whirling in furious dance across the hillside.

Ever since the fall when we had given away our snow shovels and pulled up our Yankee roots, swearing to spend our years where we'd never need storm boots or mittens, we had sometimes felt the prick of family disapproval. So now we taunted them, quoted the old saw, "A night not fit for man or beast," told them, "For all we care, you may give New Hampshire back to the Indians." Of course it was only in fun. We could hear the big heating plant down cellar purring along efficiently. We knew the huge snowplows must already have left the town sheds. The drivers would work through the night and perhaps into the next day, keeping the roads open all over town.

Then we brought to mind the winters' storms of years before, recalled the times when often we had been snowed in for several days, how once it was almost a week before the road gang got around to our place. Sometimes the wind would blow the snow into solid drifts across the roadway. When the sun came out after such a storm, we'd look out to find the fields had become a sea of sparkling white snow waves with nothing to show where the road had been, only the stone walls barely visible on either side. Then Father would hitch four or five yoke of half-broken steers to a makeshift snowplow, put a lead pair of handy oxen ahead and break trail through the deep drifts in the road. He claimed he was making the work easier for the road gang. The snow did get pretty well flattened down, but very little was actually moved out of the roadway. Of course it was good training for the steers, great fun for the boys, too. They rode behind the teams, swinging their weight to help steady the light rig. The steers wallowed and pulled in opposite directions confused by shouted commands to "Gee" or "Haw." Father ranged alongside in vigorous good humor, yelling, prodding and wielding his goad. Only the steady old oxen ahead were calm, obeying Father's commands, keeping the unruly steers behind in some semblance of a line, apparently oblivious to all the confusion.

Talk of the years that were gone brought us back again to Esther's comment—the feeling that now an era had come to an end. Remembering then the vivid stories of Father's boyhood on his father's old farm, his intimate knowledge of the skills and customs of his pioneer ancestors, we took a different view. We began to perceive that although

Father had lived during a time of tremendous changes in farm life and progress in farm methods, and although he had adapted to the age of mechanized farming, yet at heart he had remained a man of the Nineteenth Century.

For years he had clung to old-fashioned methods of plowing the land and cultivating the crops, using his horses and oxen; he had always preferred boy-help to machines. Cleverness with hand tools he had learned very early in life. By the time he was fifteen he was swinging the scythe in pace with the best of the grown men. He was skilled with axe and adz, and he knew how to choose exactly the right piece of straight ash wood, smooth it to perfection with the drawshave, soak it to workable pliability, fashion it then into a fine new bow needed for repairing an old ox yoke.

He had reached middle age before he was able to buy his first Model T. Then he took to driving about the country roads with great enthusiasm, but he never really understood how the principle of combustion worked to make his car run. Whenever he approached a steep incline he would take a firmer grip on the wheel, stamp down hard on low and brace himself in the seat, feeling the need to urge the car up the hill. He preferred to drive about in the middle of the road, and he enjoyed looking off over the countryside as he went. Our dirt roads were not so narrow that cars had difficulty in passing, but of course both drivers had better be alert and cautious. A near-miss, with Father coming round the wrong side of a blind curve or dead center on top of a rise was enough to shake up even the rashest young driver, heading to make a call on one of us girls (might even put a permanent damper on a boy friend's enthusiasm). There was one good thing about Father's driving though—he always went along at a moderate speed and never got into any serious scrapes with his car. A few times the chickens and he misjudged each other's intentions—then the feathers flew. Once he lost control, skidded into a neighbor's wheelbarrow and flattened it out like a pancake, but the wheelbarrow had no business being out there when the road was all glare ice—even the owner admitted that. It could have happened to anyone, even the best of drivers.

Even before he was born, farming in New Hampshire had passed its peak. All of his life he saw how the woods were creeping back to take over again where well-kept farmhouses and fine barns once stood. He watched the black alders growing and the wild blackberry bushes springing up to choke the wide meadows that had been his Grandfather Sanborn's pride. There once the hand scythes had swung and oxen had hauled the wide loads up the steep hill—enough fine meadow hay to fill the mows of the hundred-foot barn.

Father himself had labored against the course, working to clear and improve his fields and pastures. He had cut down the bushes and burned the piled-up brush, drilled and blasted away the biggest boulders, put the boys and the hired men to wearisome hours of picking up the smaller rocks, loading them onto the stoneboat to be hauled off and dumped on the rock pile that was growing bigger every year.

We remembered Father's interests went beyond his own farm. He would often spend whole evenings studying over his big book of maps. He used to tell us about his experiences on a prairie farm out in Nebraska. Before he and Mother were married, he had spent a winter there visiting and working for a cousin. He would remark that he'd always wished he'd stayed longer, visited other states and seen more of the country. From the time we were little we had heard him talk of his plans to go "out West" some day to visit his sister in California. Not until he was old and had given up active farming did the right year come to realize his dream.

Right after Christmas we drove him to the Boston airport. He flew off on his first plane ride, anticipating a good long visit. At first he wrote us all about the beautiful flowers and the citrus groves, described the wonderful trips they were taking, told about the splendors of the state. Before the winter was even half over his letters began to strike a different note. The California weather wasn't what it was cracked up to be; rainy days, and the rest of the time it was too hot. The orange groves were pretty all in bloom, but the smell was too strong to suit him, sort of a sickish sweet—not like the flowers at home. He wrote again to say it was about time to get a return ticket. Spring would soon be coming in New Hampshire. Forrest would need him to help tap the maple trees. Just after March first when we were having one of the worst storms of the winter we got a final letter giving the date and hour of his arrival in Boston. He wanted to make sure we'd be on time. He said he was anxious to get back home, and the letter ended: "I'll tell you one thing. I wouldn't swap one acre of my New Hampshire farm for the whole state of California!" The truth was, we knew, that he could never be happy anywhere else. The farm had taken possession of him long before he had ever been able to pay off the mortgage and get a clear title to the land.

Father was always interested in national affairs and in local politics too, but he never was elected Selectman because he was a Democrat (there were only two others registered in town). He never missed voting in a national election, and he always voted the straight Democratic ticket except for the time he got mad at Franklin Roosevelt because he paid the farmers for not raising pigs.

Father wasn't very strong on the finer things of life; he left that to

Mother. We often said it was Mother who never let one of us think of giving up the struggle to get a good education. We had always agreed that she had done the most for us. Yet, how often, even when we were very small, Father had taken us with him to the woods and fields, up to the barn to help with the chores or down to his garden to help plant vegetable and flower seeds or to pull up weeds. We had all been inclined to think he was mostly interested in getting some work out of us. Certainly that was part of it, for every one of us had chores to do. But now we could understand that he also had wanted us to share his feeling for the land. He had succeeded. Although he had failed to hold any of his boys to his farm, he had taught all of us to love the wild life of field and wood, had educated us all in the ways of growing things.

❊ 9 ❊

Epilogue

WHEN A NEW four-lane highway to by-pass the congested traffic of Laconia was laid out, the route chosen ran through our old home farm a little distance away from the back of the buildings. Locating the highway there made necessary the cutting of a wide stretch through the property, thus destroying a large part of what had been Father's best field and pasture land. Because they weren't being worked, the state's assessors had considered those acres of little agricultural value. It was true Father had sold off his cattle and stopped plowing those fields quite a few years before he died, but just the same we were glad he hadn't lived to know how the entire grove of old pines and so many of his cherished maple trees were uprooted and burned. He would have found it hard to see the bulldozers knocking down the stone walls, those century-old boundary markers. And the fields where for so many years he had grown his crops—we doubted whether he could have borne seeing that land scraped bare, the good topsoil taken off and hauled away.

We ourselves found it very hard to accept the necessity for the new road. Of course the hilly land could not be worked profitably with modern machinery. Even if a different route had been chosen, those fields would probably never have been brought into intensive cultivation again. We realized the fact, yet we bitterly resented the destruction. We remembered with sadness the cool woods and the sweet, clean grass—how it all had been when we were children. This asphalt monster reaching across the land had gulped down our sparkling brook, stilled the living voice forever. To open a way for its stretch to the north, men with huge machines had blasted the rocky ledges to granite dust and cut an ugly gap, obliterating the slope of the shady ridge where the pink mayflowers always budded late and the foxes used to den.

How completely down-at-the-heel the buildings had become, how very much gone-to-seed everything about the grounds appeared, we had never before noticed (perhaps we hadn't wanted to see). The grapevines and cherry trees were gone. All that remained of Mother's orchard were the skeletons of a few old apple trees and one scraggly peach tree. Rampant witch grass had taken over the place where Father's vegetable garden used to be. All signs of the perennial beds around the house had disappeared. No hollyhocks nodded along the wall. Not one sunflower raised its head among the burdocks and pigweed flourishing there. The High Maples Farm we knew was gone forever. The house itself, we feared, would become a sagging eyesore, blotching the landscape. Finally, years later, the timbers would let go and the whole structure would collapse. Nothing would be left but a heap of rubble in a deserted cellar hole and all around, junipers and sumacs growing rank.

This was the sad prospect for our old homestead until Royal and Verna decided to make the place their retirement home.

The first months for Royal and Verna are a time of great discouragement. Summer is almost over before the decision is final and preparations for the move are begun. Everything must be done in a hurry or winter will be upon them before the essential repairs can be completed. An artesian well must be sunk, water pipes laid and new connections made to replace the supply of spring water cut off when the highway was built. The installation of a modern heating system is a necessity. The rusted-out old furnace wasn't adequate even forty years ago. There is so much to be done inside the house: The inconvenient old kitchen modernized, the antiquated downstairs bathroom torn out and replaced, partitions removed, repapering and painting to be done, ancient brick fireplaces to uncover and restore. Before snow flies enough has been done so they will be comfortable. They concentrate on the moving, ignoring the bleakness outside.

They are pleased with all the changes that have been made, but somehow they cannot feel at home there. The snowdrifts are no deeper; the cold is not more severe. The winter lasts no longer than winters generally do in New Hampshire, but this year the days inch by. The nights are far too long, yet no good for sleeping. Housebound, Royal chafes at the inactivity he has never before known. Everything will be better as soon as it is spring, Verna thinks.

Everything is worse. Everything is more discouraging. When the snow goes, the house and the grounds look more unkempt than before. It will take gallons of white paint and endless hours of hard work to make an impression on the great expanse of shabby, greyish clapboards. The shutters, once deep green, have faded to a nondescript drab. Some are hanging off the hinges and the rest are loose. The patches of brush growing behind the house look thicker, more impossible to clear away. That stretch of dried grass and hard ground spotted with sooty snow—how could that ever be made into a lawn again? Any perennials that may have been left are lying buried (and probably lifeless) under heaps of rubbish and dead leaves. The prospect for a vegetable garden is pretty poor. Ground that has not been touched for so long will be hard to plow, and even after that is done the newly turned sod will be almost impossible to till. The witch grass will grow back faster than it can be rooted out. The grubs and the insects are well entrenched—they will no doubt destroy what's left of the vegetable plants after the frosts have done their worst. (There are sure to be frosts later than usual this spring.)

In the warm sunshine of May the weight of worry begins to lift. Bit by bit the house has received its new coat of white. Royal has found it is indeed hard to plow and harrow a spot for a vegetable garden, but it is accomplished even if not quite to his satisfaction. He plants peas, carrots and beets, and sets out lettuce and tomato plants.

The one sad old peach tree unexpectedly bursts into lavish pink bloom. Then Royal remembers how he used to help Mother with the orchard, planting and pruning, learning the painstaking science of grafting and fruit culture. He was not more than ten years old, he tells Verna, when he acquired his first hive of honey bees and became absorbed in the study of bees and their culture. There is plenty of acreage left around the house. He recalls the many kinds of fruit that grew here when he was a boy. He believes the hardy dwarf trees developed in recent years would be just as prolific in this soil, wouldn't be as hard to prune and spray. What a pleasure it would be to have an orchard of plum and peach! To grow the old favorite apples again— yellow Transparent and Porter, the later ripening McIntosh, Cortland,

Delicious and the Northern Spy for midwinter use. Of course there should be a hive, or maybe two, of honeybees partly for their delicate apple-blossom honey but also for their very important work in pollination. While Verna and Royal are considering good locations for a strawberry bed and grape vines, Esther comes by to offer some young raspberry bushes from her patch. The place across the road where the barn used to stand should be just right for the raspberries, they agree. There is room there for a half dozen fruit trees and a row of blueberry bushes, too.

Around the house and below the maple Verna finds a multitude of slender green shoots thrusting up through wet leaves and matted grass roots. Violets, heliotrope, lily of the valley she uncovers with delight. She rakes with care and begins transplanting. She visions a rock garden below the wall where the grapevine that bore such big clusters of sweet green grapes used to climb. For now, she sets there blooming pansies and a plant of bleeding heart all in bud. Royal fertilizes the lawn, prunes the ragged forsythia bushes and nails a bluebird box at the top of a pole set up nearby. He supposes it is too late to attract nesting birds this season, but later in the day Verna spies a flash of azure in the branches of a maple tree. The shy, fastidious birds have come to investigate. Next morning the bluebirds return to set up housekeeping in earnest. Royal plants cranberry beans, sweet corn and early potatoes. Verna sows herb seeds. The seeds of contentment have also been sown.

Reminiscences Two

※

FOOD ON THE FARM

❦ 10 ❦

Breadstuff

T o our family the word "bread" used to have only one meaning—the homemade kind that was our daily fare, Mother's golden
brown, tender-crusted loaves of raised white bread made from fine
wheat flour. Even now, a mention of homemade bread will bring to
each of us the same memory picture: Home from school in the late
afternoon, the kitchen filled with the tantalizing sweet, evanescent
smell of baking bread—Mother stoops to open the oven door, tips a loaf
from the tin, presses one finger against the hot crust and sees the crust
spring back. Of course the finger test is just a habit. Long experience
tells her at a glance when the loaves are done. We say we are starving
and we wait impatiently while the loaves are taken from the tins, lined
up on the bread board and brushed with melted butter. A long ten
minutes while the loaves cool a bit. Then, thick soft slices spread
lavishly with butter, topped to suit our fancy of the day—soft maple
sugar, raspberry or strawberry jam. Never was there a more satisfying
after-school lunch.

We ate our white bread and brown bread, muffins, johnnycake and
graham gems without thought of what other children had on the table,
supposing that all mothers spent much of their time in the kitchen bak-

ing and that everybody ate only breadstuff made at home. In the pantry were two barrels sitting side by side, one of bread flour, the other of flour milled specially for the making of pastry. The flour Father brought home, whether bought at the gristmill or grocery store, was from wheat grown in the Midwest, shipped from the mills already processed. The time when New Hampshire farmers raised their own wheat was gone.

But when Grandfather was farming and for several generations before him the great stones of the many mills on the rivers and at the little falls on the swift-running brooks were kept busy grinding wheat as well as rye, barley, oats and corn raised on nearby farms. From the early years of the Nineteenth Century until after the Civil War, acreage planted to grain had continually increased. Farmers in our region counted on wheat, surpassing all other grains, as the chief crop to feed their families and to bring in cash every year. Corn was still grown extensively, but it had come to be thought of as a somewhat inferior grain, necessary for an occasional breakfast johnnycake and for the brown bread to be eaten with the Saturday pot of baked beans, but best used to feed the laying hens and fatten the hogs. Yet it was only a few decades since "Indin" corn, as the settlers called it, had literally been the sustenance of life.

When our ancestors came as frontiersmen to the lakes region of New Hampshire, the wilderness they struggled to clear was less than a hundred miles from the homes they had left in the southern part of the province, yet they had gone back a full century in time from civilization as they knew it. To keep their families from starvation until they could make a crop, they had only the little corn meal they were able to carry on their backs, such game as they could kill, and fish caught from the streams and lakes. Indian corn and beans planted between the tree stumps in the clearings were the first crops raised. The coarse meal from their corn, often pounded on a flat rock, Indian-fashion, was mixed with enough water to make a paste, then spread in small puddles on a board of green wood. Propped into a position slanting toward the fireplace heat on the baking board, the meal cooked quickly, making thin cakes. The housewife also used corn meal to make a mush stirred up with water and a little precious salt, then cooked it awhile in a kettle hung from the pothooks in the fireplace. The hot mush—dipped into wooden bowls—made a nourishing family supper. What was left could be put into an iron pan and set into the brick oven on baking day, thus making a loaf of bread. Solid and heavy it must have been, but no doubt it was exceedingly palatable to hard-working men and hungry children. When new settlers came or a man's crop failed, generous neighbors shared with those less provident or not so fortunate.

Great-great-grandmother Smith, long a widow, her baker's dozen all scattered (dead or with families grown), sat stooped close to the fireplace warmth, the woolen yarn in her needles growing into a sock with never a dropped stitch to make a pause in her rambling memories. A small grandson whittled and listened while the old woman went on:

How after the trees were cut down and burned—that was when she was a little girl—it was next to impossible to plow the land by reason of the stumps and roots. How glad they were when a gristmill was set up, and when the first grist come through all the children was so keen for the meal they could scarce wait for it to be cooked. The year when a frost in every month—in July even—killed the crops and some families near starved. People must guard their livestock night and day, for wolves, hanging near the clearing's edge, were ever on the watch for a stray lamb or calf. And how long after she was grow'd, after she was married and come to live in this house, there was always bears around. They was the most destructive of all—made havoc in the cornfields and kitchen gardens, broke down the stoutest of pens to get at the shoats.

Grandfather Smith remembered and told the stories to his boys. So it was, long after the last grists had been run through the stones and the little mills along the country streams had fallen into disrepair, the stories came down to us—not all in a piece but in bits of remembering. A casual remark as we rode with Father along the Bay Road, past the old Smith homestead, the fields where first corn, then rye and wheat, had grown to make the bread eaten by three generations of Smiths, the children no less than twelve in each generation. Or when, along a quiet dirt road, distant from any farm buildings, we happened on a falling-down building beside a brook, Father would "Whoa Up" to point out where the water wheel stood and perhaps recall some mishap on a trip to that very mill.

The gristmill in Laconia—lately torn down because of urban renewal —was operating all the time we were growing up and for some years afterward. We used sometimes to go there with Father when he carried his corn to be ground or to buy grain for the cattle. What a noisy, dusty place that old mill was! And the miller—his clothing, his hair, even his eyebrows all whited with grain dust.

Mother often used our corn meal in her cooking. She would send one of us up to the barn to fill a 2-quart pail from the meal bin. As we scooped the measure brimming full, the fresh, appetizing smell of corn rose to our nostrils. Likely as not we would take a pinch or two to roll on our tongues on the way back to the house. We liked the brown bread, a mixture of corn meal and white flour, steamed on Saturday to go with the baked beans, and we relished Mother's hot johnnycake, too (except when Father wanted it the old-fashioned way, baked with lumps of suet in it). Yet none of the breads Mother made, not even her fluffy baking powder biscuits, could compare with her white bread and raised rolls.

Making bread was the easiest kind of baking, Mother always said. Certainly the way she did it seemed so to us. She used no written directions and didn't measure, except by eye. She never took pains trying to teach us but hundreds of times we saw her scald the milk then pour it into the bread mixer to cool. We watched as she added yeast and shortening and stirred in some flour. Sometimes we turned the handle when she added flour a second time. When we were older we often helped 'make out' the loaves. We knew the right amount of rising, the hand-in-the-oven way of testing correct heat for bread and for rolls and just the shade of golden brown for perfect crust.

The art of breadmaking, learned so easily and naturally, we now value as a precious legacy. We believe Mother's old-fashioned method is still the best, even though we no longer need to test the oven heat with our hands. In place of the large bread mixer those of us who cook for small families use electric mixers plus a little arm work. The large old mixers like those owned and used by Esther and her daughter, Joann Bailey, are now fairly expensive, found only rarely in antique shops or at country auctions. But mixers which are practically the same can be purchased from a number of specialty mail order houses.

At our request, for the first time since she began cooking in her own home forty-five years ago, Esther has used a measuring cup, and with the co-operation of her daughter, has given us an exact description of the way she makes those dozens and dozens of delicious rolls and the raised bread just like Mother used to make.

❧ 11 ❧

The Spider and the Kettle

O<small>NLY WOMEN</small> who remember cooking with a wood-burning kitchen range can fully appreciate why it is ironic when "the pot calls the kettle black." Until the coming of electric power not so many years ago, farm women were never free from the bane of sooty lamp wicks and smutty pans, pots and kettles. Then the bottles of stove blacking could be thrown out. Kerosene lamps and iron cooking utensils were sold to the junkman or carried up attic and set back under the eaves. But not all housewives gave up their old reliables. In some kitchens of rural New Hampshire ancient cast iron kettles are still being used along with the newest in cooking ware. The user will tell you there is nothing quite as good for cooking a boiled dinner or simmering beef stew. No doubt she has also kept a well-seasoned spider for frying steaks and chops. And you may be sure she would never prepare corned beef hash, fried eggs and ham, liver and onions or fried pickled tripe without using that same big black spider.

We New Englanders enjoy calling an iron frying pan a "spider." Consciously or not, we are harking back to the time when meats were often cooked in shallow, bowl-shaped pots made of cast iron. These long-legged pots were made to set into the fireplace coals. When there was meat to be cooked, more hot coals might be heaped over the tight-fitting iron cover. Sitting on the hearth this frying (or roasting) pan of long ago did resemble a huge black spider.

Present-day New Englanders (including the transplanted ones) refer to many cooking utensils as "kettles." When I cook pot roast in my Florida kitchen I use a 5-quart, copper-lined kettle of stainless steel. The conveniently placed handles are of a composition which never gets more than comfortably warm to touch. I have a medium-sized aluminum kettle with a long aluminum handle and a number of pretty little kettles made of materials I can't put a name to. Some have molded handles, others are detachable. Some of my kettles I use constantly, others not so often. All are useful. Kettles, they are not. A true kettle, like a pail, has a semicircular handle of metal—a most inconvenient kind of handle for lifting a pot of hot soup from the stove, but a practical, necessary handle for the tea kettles, meat kettles and porridge kettles of our great-great-grandmothers, a long ago time when pothooks and trammels were household possessions no less valued than the pewter plates and the best featherbed of "live" goosedown.

I like electric skillets. I am on my fourth one now (or is it the fifth?), but what I really prize is my big black iron spider. It just fits the largest burner on my electric stove. It is two inches deep and has a flanged rim so the stove top doesn't get splattered. It is never washed with detergent, of course—just wiped out carefully with paper towels and a little vegetable oil before being put away.

I like washing saucepans that have been coated so the food doesn't stick, but when I make beef stew, or pea soup with ham, or veal loaf or spiced beef tongue I always wish I had a big iron kettle like the one Mother used. Perhaps one day I shall spot just the right kettle at a country auction and be able to top the bids of the ladies who crave it for a flower planter.

❄ 12 ❄

Our Forefathers'
Vegetable Fare

Almost invariably our pioneer forefathers brought their families to new homes in the wilderness after the first snow had fallen in late fall. This seemed strangely improvident to us until we understood the reasons for waiting until cold weather before the move was made. Unless the migrating families were unlucky enough to be caught in an early, heavy storm, their ox teams could travel much more easily with runners than earlier in the season with wheels. It was necessary to bring sufficient supplies from their old homes to last through the first winter. Also it was vital to be settled and to have the ground ready for planting when spring came, so they could raise and harvest crops to see their families safely through the second winter when there was greatest danger of a "hungry time." Fish caught from the streams and an occasional windfall of bear or other game meat could be counted on as supplements to the corn, beans, and pumpkins harvested from the seeds planted between tree stumps on their roughly cleared land.

Sweet corn was said to have been developed by certain Indian tribes. However, the tender sweet corn which we ate boiled on the cob, or roasted in the husks over an outdoor fire, was unknown to our great-grandparents. They used the dried Indian corn as a vegetable but first the dried kernels were put through a process to remove the coarse outer shells. When the housewife prepared "hulled" corn she made a lye solution by mixing wood ashes with cold water in an iron kettle. After the mixture was brought to a boil, several quarts of dried corn shelled from the cob were put into the black lye water and cooked until the hulls cracked. When the housewife judged the corn was ready she rinsed it in five or six cold-water baths and rubbed the kernels between her hands to remove the hulls. The corn was then returned to the kettle for more boiling and skimming until the kernels were soft and floury. Hulled corn was eaten warm with milk and sugar or molasses, or was mixed with other vegetables. It was a much-used ingredient of stews and porridges. After improved varieties of sweet corn began to be raised, housewives gave up the hard job of preparing hulled corn. But when we were young there were still many old-fashioned folk who had a fondness for hulled corn. Enterprising peddlers who went around the countryside with horse and cart selling bottled horseradish also sold this prepared corn by the quart measure. Mother always bought a bottle or two of horseradish (good but strong enough to bring tears to your eyes) and two quarts or more of the corn. Father greatly relished warm hulled corn with milk and lots of sugar, but in spite of his urging none of us would take more than a bite or two of the stuff, so Mother always had a job using it up.

The crop of dry beans, though not as essential as corn, was very important to the frontiersman. According to history, baked beans were being served in New England homes and inns a hundred years before our ancestors began planting the seeds in their central New Hampshire forest clearings. Our great-great-great-grandmothers' brick-oven beans, eaten along with her slow-baked brick-oven bread, must surely have made a very palatable meal, maybe almost as good as the beans we bake in our modern ovens.

The bean porridge we have mentioned was a long-cooked, add-to-the-kettle combination of white beans simmered for hours in corned beef (or salt pork) liquor, with or without meat pieces left in, with corn meal as a thickener, and with a quantity of hulled corn added when everything in the kettle had been cooked to mush. This bean porridge was the daily fare of the children during the winter. An early schoolmaster writing of his experiences during a winter term in our frontier town noted that his pupils' leather aprons (an article of clothing worn by those under the age of fourteen) were always plastered with rivulets of dried bean porridge. Father was not accustomed to this old-time dish. It was never served on his father's table, because Grandfather had been obliged to eat the porridge in such quantities when he was a boy (in the early 1850's) he had become surfeited with bean porridge and couldn't abide dry beans in soup or any way except baked.

According to some historians, the first crop of white (Irish) potatoes grown in the colonies was harvested at Londonderry, New Hampshire, about fifty years before our ancestors (whose homes were originally not far from Londonderry) began moving farther north to settle in the wilderness of central New Hampshire. Certainly, seed potatoes were included in the supplies our pioneers took with them. They planted potatoes along with Indian corn, beans and pumpkins the first spring after the land had been cleared. Some settlers, ill-prepared for the hardships of winter, were literally kept from starving when they raided the potato caches buried by their more prudent neighbors-to-be who were planning another summer of preparation before bringing their wives and children to settle. Irish potatoes grew very well in the newly turned soil and after awhile became a more important vegetable than Indian corn or beans on farm tables.

Pumpkin seeds planted at random among the corn hills grew vines that spread out under the shade of corn stalks and bore fruit, often of immense size, that mellowed in the autumn sunshine. Frontier women prized their pumpkin crop for the puddings and pies which gave welcome variety to the heavy diet of corn, potatoes and beans. Some varieties of early pumpkins (which later became squash) were boiled, seasoned with salt and pepper and eaten as a vegetable.

❦ 13 ❦

The Pantry Shelf

I DON'T REGRET the passing of the farmhouse pantry. It was almost always the least-convenient room in the house, yet it was where a good part of the cooking was done. Our pantry had a window, opening onto the back porch, which let in enough light so Mother could see to do her mixing easily; but when she wanted anything that was stored behind the flour barrels or in the far corners under the shelves, she must poke into the darkness and stoop down to pull out whatever she was after. In winter the casing cracks let in wind enough to make the pantry icy cold, especially when there was a northeast storm blowing, but in hot weather when we could have done with some of that airiness, never a breeze came through the open window to disturb the sticky closeness.

Sometimes when Mother's calm had been ruffled by a rare baking failure or a minor disagreement with Father she would complain about pantries in general and hers in particular. She would say they never would have been built into farmhouses if women had any say in the matter. It was her belief that pantries had been contrived by men as torture chambers for their wives. After I had spent hours teetering on top of the kitchen stool trying to clean the highest shelves of those pantry cupboards, after years of bending over Mother's low mixing board rolling out pie crust and biscuit dough, I came to sympathize with her mutterings of irritation. That is why I never regretted the lack of a pantry in my own home.

When we were children we couldn't have imagined a home without a pantry. Mother's pantry always smelled so good. It was the place where we could be pretty sure of finding her, if she wasn't in sight when we came into the kitchen. It was where we headed when we were hungry. The doughnut pail and the cookie jar sat on the long shelf between the big tin breadbox and the wooden box that held the knives and forks. We didn't take seriously what Mother said about the pantry. We knew that even while she was complaining she would go right on mixing up bread or baking pies and seeing to it that Father's dinner was ready every day—exactly when the mill whistle down in Laconia blew for noontime. And she would make sure that neither the cookie jar nor the doughnut pail would be empty for more than one day at a time.

Occasionally, Mother made molasses cookies but more often she baked the plain white rolled cookies that most of us children liked best. The cookie jar was our special preserve. Sometimes when Mother set on a plate of fresh-baked cookies at suppertime, Father would eat several and enjoy them, but doughnuts were much more important to him. Grandmother Smith had brought up her family to expect fresh hot doughnuts at every morning meal the year around, but Father wasn't set in that old-fashioned way. He was satisfied if Mother fried doughnuts three or four times a week, not necessarily for breakfast. I remember just how Mother's doughnuts looked—all cut and laid on the big mixing board ready to be fried. Rows and rows of perfectly shaped regular doughnuts, quite a number of "twisty" ones, and lots of little round doughnut holes. She would carry the board from the pantry out to the kitchen table in order to be near the kettle of fat heating on the stove.

Although I never learned to mix the dough (Mother liked to feel no one else could make doughnuts to suit Father), I often did the frying. She taught me to slide the doughnut forms gently down the inside edge of the iron kettle, letting them sink into the boiling hot lard without a spatter; to flip the doughnuts over smoothly with a long-handled fork; to recognize precisely when the doughnuts were done, ready to be lifted out and drained on brown paper.

We children liked Mother's doughnuts fresh and hot from the kettle; we liked them just as well as cookies for a cold snack with a glass of milk in the pantry or to carry in hand and munch while we played outdoors. But we took Mother's cooking for granted. To our minds,

Grammie Page's doughnuts and cookies were the extra-special ones. Grammie's cookies were rich with cream, large and crinkly-edged. Her tin cutter pressed a faint leaf design onto each sugary surface. The cookies looked so pretty, perhaps that's why they tasted so good to me.

I was always sure I liked Grammie's cookies best until she got out her lard kettle to fry up a batch of doughnuts. Although she wouldn't allow us underfoot when she was mixing the dough in the pantry, she didn't mind having us watch the frying. We sat around her cluttered kitchen, getting up our appetites and listening to her rambling talk. It was all so old-fashioned, yet so cozy: Grampa's high-backed rocking chair, the framed wall mirror with the picture of a playful kitten and a ball of yarn, the wooden sink and the low cooking range. Grammie's doughnut kettle was especially fascinating. It was a queer, sooty old iron pan with a rounding bottom, three short legs, and a long handle. Grammie used to tell us that the kettle was in the house when she married Grampa and came to live there. She supposed Grampa's grandmother must have used it back in the days when all the food had to be cooked over a fireplace. The long handle and the three legs made the kettle convenient for setting right into the fireplace coals. It was just as good to use on top of her kitchen range with the bottom set down into the firebox, Grammie said. She prized it as much as anything in the house, didn't know as she could fry doughnuts without it. By the time she had reached the end of her story, the first doughnuts would be ready to come out of the kettle. How wonderfully good they smelled! Just as fast as Grammie lifted them sizzling hot from the kettle she rolled them in sugar. We waited impatiently until we could pick up the coolest ones. Then we began to eat, and we ate and ate—as many as we could possibly stuff in. Nobody counted.

Grammie Page did enjoy seeing us children eat, so she cooked plenty of food whenever we were visiting. She saw to it that the doughnut pail and the cookie jar were full. She was very good about letting us have lunches when we were hungry, yet we didn't feel free to go to her pantry shelf without first asking. Though none of us can remember any time when Grammie Page wasn't kind to us children, we were constantly on guard against stirring her up. We were well aware of her sharp tongue for we knew how quickly her temper could flare. Frances likes to tell of one time when she felt sure Grammie's wrath would descend on the guilty grandchild.

Frances was only four years old then. It may have been the first time she had stayed away from home and Mother overnight. Even though a big sister was along to give the little girl confidence, everything was strange to her—big and exciting and sometimes frightening, especially Grammie Page herself.

Cousin Archie Page also was staying there at the time. To Frances he was part of the excitement. A big boy, ten years old, an interesting stranger to follow about and observe. He was more familiar with the place than we were, also brash enough to take liberties we wouldn't dare consider. One day Frances saw Archie come in from the barn heading for the pantry, evidently set on getting himself a lunch. She tagged after him and watched. He took the cover off Grammie's doughnut pail and reached in with both hands. Her eyes opened wide when he popped a whole doughnut into his mouth then began stuffing more down the front of his shirt. "Archie, you bad boy! You'll be sorry when Grammie catches you!"

Archie shrugged it off. "Shucks," he mumbled through a mouthful of doughnut, "Gram don't pay it no mind," and he hurried through the kitchen hunched over to conceal the telltale bulge at his front. He left the little girl puzzling: if it was all right for Archie to take so many doughnuts all at once, without even asking, then why did he make sure to hide them? And why did he run out the back door so fast?

All day long she followed Grammie about her work: into the pantry to skim the cream from the milk pans; to the garden to pick some peas then shell them, sitting on the old school bench beside the kitchen door; into the pantry and out again several times while Grammie got supper on the table; finally to the cow tie-up in the barn, watching while Grammie and Grampa did the milking; back once more to the house where Grammie poured the warm milk into clean pans set on the wide pantry shelf. The doughnut pail was right at hand there on the shelf. A dozen times Frances thought Grammie was about to lift the cover and discover the shameful plundering. She never did. The visit ended and the little girl was carried home. Archie stayed on at Grammie Page's, unrepentant and smug.

❄ 14 ❄

Molasses

WHEN OUR FAMILY was young Father used to drive into Laconia
at least once a week to do the grocery trading. The custom of exchang-
ing farm produce for seeds and foodstuff at the grocery stores had remained almost unchanged since the days when Grandfather Smith was
farming the old place in Meredith, back in the 1800's. But marketing
was easier for Father because our farm was nearer to town and there
was a constant demand for our maple syrup and sugar, eggs, fresh
fruits, berries, and vegetables. The money from these crops was a good
addition to the income from the dairy cows yet Mother's list was a long
one so Father almost always had to put out money to boot when he
went to the grocery store. He bought in large quantities, of course—
flour by the barrel, sugar in twenty-five-pound cloth sacks, five-pound
sacks of table salt, and molasses by the gallon.

The molasses jug was kept under the kitchen sink. Beside it sat an
identical stone jug that held vinegar. When the vinegar jug was empty
we had only to go down cellar, turn the spigot on the particular cider
barrel (marked by Father) that had aged to full-strength vinegar, and
draw off a pailful to refill the jug. Whenever the molasses supply was
getting low, Mother drained that jug and set it out for Father to take

along on his next trip into Laconia. Every storekeeper sold molasses from a barrel or hogshead which was laid on wooden horses in the back room. A spigot was inserted in the bunghole so the molasses could conveniently be drawn off into stone jugs or glass jars. I remember one winter's day when Mother was so busy that she forgot about draining the jug until after Father had gone out to hitch up the team for the trip into Laconia. I offered to help and she let me although she was afraid I was too little to manage that heavy stoneware jug. I tipped the jug up against the side of the iron sink, steadied it with one hand and set a pint glass jar under the small mouth. I had to wait so long for the molasses to start that my arm began to hurt. Finally it started to come out in slow hollow-sounding gasps. *Glub-Glub-Glub!* A long pause while I suffered from the cramps in my fingers. Two more big *Glub-Glubs* and then nothing at all. I thought there must be more because the glass jar wasn't even three-fourths full. I grasped the bottom of the jug with spread fingers. Held it upside down high over the jar as my arms could reach. One last great Gl-u-u-b came plopping out. The jar was overflowing and a sticky pool was spreading in the sink! I had made the mess so I had to clean it up. Right then I would have been pleased to shake hands with whoever coined the familiar expression, "Slower'n cold m'lasses in January." Only I would have put the word *eg-zaspera-tin'* in there somewhere.

Mother's molasses jug needed refilling about once a month; it takes longer to use up the small size bottle I buy at the supermarket. Although a gallon of molasses now seems like a great quantity, I am sure many families who ate the tangy, brown liquid as a table syrup used much more than we did. We children spread our bread and butter with maple sugar (molasses was for 'poor' people), and there was always either maple syrup or honey on our table. Father had such a great sweet tooth he spooned white sugar over his food in a prodigal manner. We never heard him complain about the pounds of sugar he had to buy for Mother's preserving either. Although he didn't consider it fit to eat on the table he enjoyed the flavor of molasses in Mother's cooking. He was especially fond of "ginger cake" as he called it, and when Mother made hot gingerbread for supper he would often finish off his meal with as many as four big pieces.

Now that it is too late by many years I constantly regret not learning more about farm life in the time of our parents' youth. A few relatives and friends remain of the generation that considers me a young-timer, and it is their recollections which have proved the most valuable source in my search for old-time foods and eating habits. I made occasion to visit Uncle Otis Smith with the idea of pursuing the subject of molasses, and after a preliminary conversational exchange we got around to the point I had in mind.

"Yes, we surely did use a quantity of molasses," he began. "In the house, that was. We couldn't afford to feed it to cattle as farmers do nowadays. Never heard of such a thing, anyway. Of course, there was a time when molasses was a whole lot more necessary than it was when I was young. Two hundred years ago, when your ancestors first came to these parts, any food they couldn't raise or get from the streams and woods had to be brought up from the seacoast towns by ox cart, or lugged up on their own backs. Of course they made maple syrup and once in a while they got a windfall of honey from a wild bee tree. But all told, their chief sweetening was molasses. A good many families didn't see white sugar from one year's end to another. Fact was, white sugar was still somewhat of a luxury in the 1850's when my father was growing up. I suppose that was why he always had such a craving for sweets. Never could seem to get enough. He expected hot doughnuts fresh made every morning and he got them—sometimes pie, too. When he was old and had diabetes, going without sweets was a wicked hardship on him. Mother had to hide the sugar bowl."

This reminiscing was taking us astray so I reminded him, "You didn't tell me anything about Grandmother's cooking with molasses. Didn't she used to make gingerbread?" A little smile quirked his mouth but the corners turned right down again and his old eyes snapped. Was it remembered indignation I saw there?

"Well, I should say she did make gingerbread! A real treat it was, too! There was one time I have good reason never to forget. I guess I was about seven years old then. Big enough to do my share of the chores and run errands, but Father didn't expect me to work in the fields with my older brothers. Let's see—I'm eighty-three now—so that would have been in the summer of 1892.

"We were having a spell of good hay weather—late in July, as I recall. Our old farm on Meredith Hill was pretty steep and rocky, you know. There was a good deal of hand mowing to be done. That time, the grass in the big back field was still standing and Father was anxious to get it down and drying. Farmers planned to get at the mowing about as soon as the dew was off in the morning. Then if the weather held they could 'turn' the hay around midday. It would be raked by late afternoon and they'd have a good part into the barn before it got so dark they had to give up. I've seen the time when we would be driving in with the last load after the moon was up. We'd just unhitch and leave the hayrack standing on the barn floor and the hay to be pitched off next morning.

"My brothers, Charles and Sam (Sam was your father, of course), were pretty near grown and able to do a man's work. This time Father had hired an extra hand. That made four to mow with the hand scythes. Brother Wallace—he was almost five years older than I—could go behind with a fork to do what spreading was needed. As I was finishing up my chores in the barn I heard them sharpening their scythes out under the corn house where the grindstone was set up. There was the squeak as the wheel was turned, and the gritty, monotonous complaint of steel blades on the wet, stone wheel. It's been a good many years since I've heard that sound but it's just as plain in my mind as if 'twas yesterday. That's a queer thing when you stop to think about it—I can't recall a good many things that have happened in recent years, but the sights and sounds, the way things smelled when I was a boy, they're still as clear as can be.

"When there was a piece of work to be done in the fields the men wouldn't come up to the house until it was finished even if it got to be past noon, so sometimes Mother would send them down a hot lunch. That day she called me into the house in the middle of the morning. I could tell right away that she had made gingerbread, for the kitchen was full of the good smell of hot molasses baking with ginger and spices. She took that gingerbread out of the oven, cut it into squares, quick as a wink—packed it into a basket and covered it with a linen napkin to keep it hot. Told me to hurry down to the further end of the back field where the men were working. I took the basket and started off.

"Whenever I think about haying season on the old farm I always remember the bobolinks. It used to seem to me they had taken possession of the fields. The air was filled with their singing. Bobolinks nest on the ground, you know. The male bird sits and swings on the tall grass somewhere near the nest—watching for bugs, I guess. But when he sings, he flies high above the field. It's just as if he was so full of happy song he's pouring it all out, fast as he can. Kind of a bubbling out, so the notes tumble, all mixed together. That's a fine time in a boy's life— when you don't have any worries, and you feel things so keenly. The birds' songs, the sun so bright and hot, the gingerbread smelling so good your mouth waters, the grass just cut (that's wonderfully fragrant too).

"As I came down over the brow of the hill I saw the men had about half of the hay down. Really a pretty sight. The men swinging their scythes—all spread out across the field—the swaths of cut grass lying smooth and even. I guess *you* can't picture that. Your father's farm in Gilford was most all machine mowing. Only the roadsides and the runs, and a few places along the stonewalls had to be mowed with the hand scythe. But in my father's time, when there was a big piece—like a meadow—to be cut, it was common to see four or five, even half a dozen men swinging the scythes at one time. Handling the scythe well is a fine skill. Father taught his boys young, and he was particular about how it was done. He always told us 'Stand straight. Pull back your shoulders. Swing with your arms and keep the point and heel of your scythe down.' Father himself could mow an extra wide swath so he always led off. After he had made a few sweeps with his scythe, the next man would start—then the next, and so on. That way, the mowers were staggered, each at a safe distance from the lead and the one following.

"They were glad enough to lay down their scythes in the swaths when they saw me coming down over the hill for they were hungry and thirsty, too. Father had wrapped a stone jug full of water in a wet gunny sack, set it where it would catch the breeze over on the stone wall under an apple tree. They unwrapped that jug of cold spring water and passed it around—took my basket and gobbled up that warm gingerbread to the last crumb! Never even offered *me* a bite!"

His story ended abruptly. That didn't seem right—to leave the small boy standing there dejected, not saying a word of protest while those hardhearted older ones ate up all that delicious gingerbread. So I asked him, "Why didn't you just take a piece and eat it on the way down?"

"I don't know. Too dumb, I guess."

A typical Yankee answer to a foolish question! I should have known better than to ask. He had given me my gingerbread story—the story of a farm boy with a task to perform and that's all there was to it. Afterward I looked through Aunt Mary's Cookbook and found these directions for making gingerbread: *1 cup molasses, 1 cup sour milk, 2½ cups flour, ½ tspn nutmeg, ½ cup sugar, 1 egg beaten, ½ scant cup shortening, 1 teaspoon ginger, 1 rounding tspn soda.* And that's all there was to Grandmother Smith's 'receipt.' Sufficient for any good Yankee cook, no doubt.

❧ 15 ❧

Making Boiled Cider

NEW ENGLAND COOKBOOKS, old and new, make mention of boiled cider used in applesauce, mincemeat, and in old-fashioned beverages like switchel, but there are never any directions for boiling down sweet cider to the proper consistency. Perhaps there were no printed directions because in former times when this concentrate was made on many farms in our area the process was so familiar there was no need for writing anything down. Mother always put boiled cider in her mincemeat, and of course she used quantities in the cider applesauce we ate every fall and winter. Cider wasn't boiled every season because the finished product, stored in stone jugs, would keep perfectly until it was used up. Every second or third autumn after the cider was made, Father used to set up a simple outdoor arch where he could build a fire and boil cider in the ancient brass kettle. At the time, none of us paid particular attention to the boiling except for helping tend the fire, a pleasant enough after-school task. In later years when cider apples were no longer plentiful and cider was more expensive to make, Father gave up the boiling. Then one autumn, the next to last year of his life, he got the notion of making boiled cider again. He felt it would do him a world of good, he told Esther plaintively, if he could get outdoors and tend a fire, but the job of boiling cider was really too much for him to undertake without some help. To humor him (and because she could use some of the boiling) Esther agreed to help. That was how she became our authority on the making of boiled cider. The old brass kettle wasn't used again for many years until, after a bit of persuasion, Royal and Verna took on a one-year-only project so that we could once more enjoy the flavor of boiled cider applesauce like Mother used to make. Verna kept a record of the experiment in her garden diary.

Oct. 2.
Brisk, bright day. Colors beginning to creep in on nearby hills. Went to mill in Meredith to observe and arrange for having cider made.

Oct. 3–5.
To orchard on Marsh Hill where we picked up "drops." Brought home ten bushels of good Macs. Cleaned the old brass kettle and had tiny hole in bottom mended. Went for wood—had to settle for softwood slabs. Scrounged for containers to hold cider. Cleaned and painted an old ten-gallon keg, borrowed another (five-gallon) from Forrest. Made new spigots for both kegs. Found some one-gallon glass jugs in ell chamber.

Oct. 6.
Took apples to cider mill. Enjoyed view of distant White Mountains. Nearer Ossipee Range in full color. Stayed while apples went through the press. Wanted to make sure of taking home juice from our own apples. Cider very clear and clean tasting. Good to know there's not one rotten or wormy apple in the thirty gallons. Cold tonight. Freeze probable.

Oct. 7–9.
Escaped freeze after all, here on the hill. Got the new sign put up "High Maples, 1805" just before Barbara and Allan and children arrived for a visit. Grandsons much interested in cider boiling project. Outdoor fireplace grill removed and cross piece set up for hanging kettle. Got cider to boiling. Started with five gallons (kettle half full) and kept adding as boiling progressed. After three hours, had to cover. Rain coming on.

Oct. 11.
Sunny and cool after a day of rain. Maples around the house now wearing red and gold. Meadow larks piping again in the lower field. Boiled for two-three hours. Called in Esther to advise on cider. Verdict—too thin!

Oct. 12.
Boiled again about four hours. Big afternoon for Smith and Turner grandsons, helping Grampa and drinking lots of sweet cider. Trips to cider keg and cute spigot followed by numerous trips to bathroom. Mothers disapproved!

Oct. 14.

Project completed. Thirty gallons of sweet cider reduced to two of boiled cider. Strained through cheesecloth and stored in stone jugs.

Royal's summary: "The project was a success, I would say. It provided entertainment for my grandsons, and I had quite a lot of fun, too. I spent the best part of three days on the boiling, but at the same time I was able to get some work done cleaning up the garden. I took pains to see the cider didn't burn at any stage. The taste is as good as what Father used to make, I believe. The amount of time and effort involved amazed the young people. I told them it was a good example of the way things were done years ago when people expected to work for the food they ate."

❈ 16 ❈

The Fruits of Our Earth

WHAT A WONDERFUL PLACE our cellar was in late fall. How well we remember the great hoard of foodstuff there. The shelves and the cupboards, the crocks, the boxes, barrels and bins packed full, heaped up—every year there was more than our family could possibly have used through the longest New Hampshire winter.

Harvest time was always a great satisfaction to Father, and rightly so, for there was never a year when his land failed to produce abundant crops of corn and potatoes and beans. His vegetable garden was his special pride. From the day the first radishes were pulled and the first leaf lettuce was big enough to pick until the last of the tomatoes were gathered in ahead of a killing frost, we were never without several kinds of fresh vegetables on the table. In those days wild apple trees, come up from seeds scattered by the birds, grew everywhere in New Hampshire fields and pastures. These "cider apple" trees (as we called them)—grafted with scions from cultivated varieties—flourished along with the trees that had been planted. Both kinds bore fair, large fruit year after year without requiring much care. We had other kinds of fruit trees, too, almost all that would grow in New Hampshire, even peaches which wouldn't do well that far north except where the frosts came late, as they did on our farm.

February was the month when the garden was planned and it was decided whether to plant some new fruit trees. As soon as the mailman brought the new seed catalogues, Father would leaf them through to admire the glossy, colored pictures, then put the books aside. On a stormy, cold day that kept him indoors he would ask Mother to sit down with him and study over the seed catalogues. Mother would read some parts aloud, especially the glowing descriptions of newly developed plant varieties. She and Father would decide to try several of the most appealing new kinds, but for the most part they stuck to those which had proved their worth in past years. After the vegetables were chosen, they added some flowers to the list—asters and petunias, some fancy new gladiola and dahlia bulbs to increase last year's, which were dug and stored in the cellar during the winter.

Although she dearly loved to work out in the sunshine, Mother never had much time to help with the planting and cultivating after the family began to grow. She tended her flower beds and once in a while she managed to get out of the house long enough to pick some berries or fruit. She would steal away to the raspberry patch, planning to stay while the baby was napping, just long enough to get some of the ripest berries before they were pecked off by the blackbirds or spoiled by a sudden rain shower. Never could she stay long enough to fill her pail, for even if the baby slept on so we didn't have to call her, the little ones would find out where she had gone and be out there right away, getting scratched with briars, pestering until she gave up and came out from the middle of the patch to give them the attention they were bound to have. Hasty and frustrating though it might be, Mother's berry picking was relaxation from the regular household chores and the canning and preserving. She used to say there weren't half enough hours in the long summer days to get it all done. The remark wasn't a complaint. She really enjoyed all kinds of food preparation. She was greatly concerned with keeping us as well fed and healthy in winter as in summer. A well-stocked cellar was truly vital, she believed, and Father was of the same mind. He scorned those tight-fisted Yankee farmers whose custom it was to sell off the best part of all their crops, thus running the chance of leaving their families scraping the bottom of the barrel a long time before dandelion-green time. In fact, Father was inclined to go to the opposite extreme. He usually stored such quantities of potatoes and root vegetables there were bushels left to spoil and be thrown out when the cellar was cleaned in early summer. The reason he was extravagant in this respect, Mother used to say, was because life had been harder on Grandfather Smith's old farm. When Father was a boy, they had known what it was to be pretty short-rationed. He was determined that no child of his should ever go hungry to bed.

We never did, not even for a punishment. Or perhaps it would be more accurate to say *especially* not as a punishment, because the crops that were raised on our farm were family property. The vegetables in the garden, all the fruits and the berries were first of all food for our table. Whenever there was more than we needed to eat or to store for winter use, it was sold and we children had some share of the profits. That was considered right, the same as it was taken for granted we all must do our share of the work.

Small hands could drop seeds along the rows marked in the smoothed garden earth. They could help keep the rows of beets and carrots and parsnips free from weeds after the seeds had sprouted and grown. Small children could move quickly along the rows of potato vines to spy out and pick off the sticky, hard-shelled potato beetles chewing away at the tender leaves. (It was always pay-on-the-spot for that miserable job. A nickel for each quart Mason jar filled with the crawling pests.) Children a little older could ride and guide the horse hitched to the cultivator, thus freeing Father to manage the machine as it was pulled along the corn rows. (A two-hour turn in the broiling sun, perched up on the back of a sweaty work horse plodding across the field and back, over and over again, cultivating acres of corn rows—that was no joy ride!) There were numerous jobs that had to be done every day: Chickens to feed and water, barn chores and house chores, wood to carry. For half-grown boys, and sometimes for their sisters, there was work in the hay fields. Everybody but the baby helped pick berries. Sometimes the work was fun; much was plain drudgery. We knew it all had to be done, so we worked—not always willingly but certainly without shirking. We had no reason to complain for there were also hours and hours of play time.

Harvesting was over and the hogs had been butchered by the time the ground was frozen deep. The field corn was husked and the popcorn ears were hung high in the shed, out of the way of mice and squirrels. The best of the pumpkins and squash had been gathered and put under cover where they wouldn't rot or freeze. The stacks of dry beans were stored in the barn, ready for threshing.

The bins and the boxes in the dark root cellar were full. The winter apples had been packed in barrels and brought into the main cellar. Greening and Russet, Baldwin, Northern Spy, Nodhead, Blue Pearmain and Sheepnose—there were apples for lunch boxes, apples for pies and for sauce. Some kinds were ripe for eating right then. Others wouldn't be at their best until January or even March. On a rack near the low opening into the root cellar were barrels of cider making into next year's good strong vinegar. A keg of sweet cider was propped up against the wall. A turn or two of the spigot driven into the bunghole would bring a rush of tingly-cold, amber liquid foaming out to fill Father's big pitcher (and run it over if you didn't look sharp). How we did enjoy that cider on stormy Sunday afternoons when Father built up a roaring fire in the kitchen range and fixed us a bucket of hot buttered popcorn.

Mother's shelves and jam cupboards, stretching the length of one cellar wall, couldn't possibly have held one more jar. There were quarts and quarts of tempting vegetables and just as many of fruit. Gleaming rosy strawberries, cherries and raspberries were set off by the dark richness of blueberries, plums and grape juice. The delicate pastel of peaches and pears contrasted prettily with the spiced whole crabapples and chili sauce. The treasure of jars filled with jams and jellies of various flavors was reckoned by the dozen. Two-gallon stone crocks sitting on the floor were filled with spicy piccalilli, dill pickles and mustard pickles. Big ten-gallon crocks sitting alongside were packed with slabs of pork laid down in salt brine after the pigs were butchered. The door leading to outside was shut and barred by an inner door nailed in place. The cracks were stuffed to help keep out the cold.

We were ready for winter.

❧ 17 ❧

Thanksgiving Day

EVERYBODY KNOWS THE story of how the Pilgrim Fathers set aside a day for feasting, a thanks-giving for the first harvest in the New World. If the traditional account is historically correct, then Father's family must have missed the first Thanksgiving dinner by eight or nine years. As late-comers they did not experience the devastating period of starvation suffered by the Pilgrims, yet they were not much better prepared for their new life in the young colony. Our ancestors were craftsmen, at home in English villages, therefore completely ignorant of the harsh wilderness of New England, where each man must clear land and make a living for his family from the rocky soil or subsist entirely on food taken from the forest and the sea. During early years the constant shadow of threatening starvation lay over the settlers' homes. Hunger was a familiar enemy forever to be kept at bay. Each year with the harvesting completed and a surety of food for the winter ahead, the guard could be lowered for one day of gaiety and feasting. One among those who lived to prosper was our ancestor Robert Smith. When he died in 1706 full of years (and after having enjoyed many, many Thanksgiving dinners, we suppose), he left wide sea-grass meadows and well-tilled acres to be divided among his numerous descendants.

In Grandfather Smith's home Thanksgiving was just as important a holiday as it had been two centuries earlier in the time of the first New England Smiths. Although religious customs and ways of eating had changed and the fear of starvation had faded with the passing generations, those who continued to make their living by cultivating the soil never forgot to be grateful at the harvest season. For Grandfather and the boys it was a day of rest and relaxation, a holiday from all but the necessary barn chores. For Grandmother and her daughter it meant a busy week beforehand preparing for the feast. So much was served at that one meal—heaping dishes of various kinds of vegetables raised on the farm, great platters of roasted fowl with dressing and rich gravy, all the extravagant once-a-year desserts they were so fond of—such an overabundance of food the family could never consume even half at one sitting. That was Thanksgiving when Father was a boy.

We carried on the tradition.

The ritual in our home was exactly suited to Father's pleasure. His harvests were his greatest pride, and at Thanksgiving time he thoroughly enjoyed his role of good provider. In a sense he was an epicure; he loved good eating for its own sake. "What you put in your mouth oughtn't to be the most important thing in life," Mother sometimes told us. "But your father's folks were all the same. Their stomachs always came first!" Her irritation was only surface deep. She appreciated not having to stint on any food produced at home. She never had to worry that her children would be undernourished. She did her part by cooking to please Father always, and at Thanksgiving she made a special point of serving all the old-fashioned dishes he liked so well. At this time of year Father spent lavishly for foods which many farmers considered too dear. Regardless of the price he always brought home several pounds of mixed nuts in the shell and grapes—the sweet seedless green and the large meaty pink and purple clusters; raisins too, and cheese—a thick wedge cut from the big wheel on the grocer's counter and a smaller slice of the kind marbled with sage (the herby flavor was good but so strong a bite or two was enough).

Preparation for the dinner began with Father's annual turkey hunt, which always took place some time before any marketing was done. Since we never raised turkeys and because he didn't trust the quality of the dressed fowl sold in the stores, Father felt obliged to take time for a good deal of telephoning and visiting around town in search of a live bird that would meet his standards. Nobody was fooled. We knew this yearly excursion was a satisfaction he wouldn't have missed for the world. When he came home in triumph, bringing his trophy caged up in a chicken crate, he called Mother (and as many of us as he could scare up) to come out and admire. He liked to point out the broad breast and the bright red wattles, the proudly held head, all characteristics which proved the excellence of the young tom turkey he had chosen. Then the unsuspecting bird was established in a vacant hen house with a roost all to himself. There he was pampered with a diet tempting enough to make him stuff himself for a week or so and thus insure his end as the most tender, best-flavored roast turkey ever served up on our table.

If it had been possible we would have avoided any further meeting with the turkey until that time, but of course we had to help with his care. We were not in the least fearful of becoming sentimentally attached to the vainglorious strutting creature but treating him so royally just to fatten him up for such an ignoble end did seem rather an underhanded trick.

We knew all too well how it would be. When the day of execution came, the surprised turkey, gobbling indignantly, would be rudely captured, lifted by his stout legs and carried away to the chopping block hanging upside-down, dizzy and deflated. A final squawk of protest, a single stroke of Father's sharp axe and the once arrogant head would lie in a puddle of blood on the frozen ground. The muscles would jerk and the witless body would leap and rush about briefly in a grotesque parody of life before flopping over. A hot redness brighter than the wattles would stain the glossy feathers and trickle onto the withered grass. Without ado the twitching carcass would be grasped by the feet and plunged into a bucket of scalding water, hung up and defeathered, dressed off neatly, then carried into the house for a singeing over the open flame and a final pinfeathering. There it would hang in the cool cellarway, waiting to be stuffed and trussed up for the roasting.

From Father's point of view there was nothing repulsive about the slaughtering. It was simply a necessary part of food preparation which didn't in the least affect his gustatory anticipation. He couldn't understand why we all seemed to be out of earshot just when he needed to impress some helpers. We had our reasons. A closer acquaintance with bloody feathers and stinky innards would have spoiled the dinner for us. Better to shirk the job and preserve the appetite.

Some years Thanksgiving Day was quite mild, with the sun slanting a mellow light across the brown fields; but more often, as we remember, it was chilly with maybe a spit of snow at times. Then it seemed that the grey countryside was just waiting quietly with nothing much to disturb the stillness except the lively conversations of little black-capped chickadees hunting everywhere for seeds, or perhaps a downy woodpecker's intermittent hammering, or the sound of a hunter's gun from off in the distant fields where a cock pheasant had been flushed. The pattern of our day was always the same, whatever the weather might be.

We ate at half past seven in the morning, a little later than usual because it was a holiday. Mother cooked special dishes never served at breakfast except on Thanksgiving Day, so the huge morning meal was something of an occasion in itself. Before any of us could remember this family custom had been established as a kind of getting-in-practice-session for the feasting later in the day. The food was always the same. There were platters of oysters that Mother had dipped in beaten egg, then rolled in cracker crumbs and pan-fried until they were crispy on the outside, sweet and juicy to bite into. There were heaped dishes of boiled potatoes diced and browned to a crust in bacon fat, hot muffins to eat with the sparkling red sauce of whole cranberries heavily sweet-ened yet sharp on the tongue. To finish off the meal in the old-fash-ioned way, we went back to the every-morning custom of Father's boyhood: We ate pie for breakfast. Big slices of spicy homemade mince-meat pies just baked in Mother's oven. Mince pie in the morning! And on top of all that hearty food. It required a heroic effort but we made it. The last crumb disappeared. We were crammed to the ears but nobody was worried. Dinner time was hours away.

After breakfast Father and the boys went out to finish the barn chores. Then the boys yoked the steers to the oxcart and made a trip to the pasture woods for a load of pine boughs. Father always liked to have a covering to hide the low banking of clean dry sawdust held in place against the house sills by boards staked into position around the sides of the building. After the snow came and drifted into the branches there was added insulation from the bitter winds. Against our green-shuttered white farmhouse the border of darker green boughs filled with snow gave a cheerful, snug appearance. Cutting and hauling home the pine branches was work but at the same time it was fun for the boys—good exercise and training for them and for the steers—the kind of job that was suitable for Thanksgiving morning.

Mother's day had begun long before light, even earlier than usual because so much had to be done before half-past one, the hour ap-pointed by long custom for our Thanksgiving dinner. While we cleared the breakfast table and washed up the dishes, she finished getting the turkey ready for the oven. Trimmed and clean, stuffed to a pleasing roundness with delicately seasoned oyster dressing, stitched up in a pattern of neat crisscrossing, with legs tied down and wings tucked demurely under, the bird was a fair promise of good things to come. Mother's skill had exorcised the spectre of the chopping block.

By the time the dining room clock struck half-past twelve the turkey was beautifully brown. Kettles of vegetables were bubbling on top of the stove; pies sitting on its back shelf were warming up slowly. The table was set with Mother's best linen cloth and the real silverware. We had not arrived at this stage without concerted effort. Mother hadn't once sat down since breakfast. The place had been in a flurry of activity inside and outside. Without being reminded and without any of the usual bickering over whose turn it might be, the younger children had set about bringing in firewood. When they were finished, the kitchen woodbox was so full the hinged cover wouldn't go down, and beside the stove was a neat pile of special sticks for Mother to use first. After being properly praised they had gone off to play in the barn. The baby (if there happened to be one of the age to keep getting under Mother's feet) had been given a bottle and rocked to sleep. A big pan of potatoes and a smaller pan of onions brought up from the cellar had been washed and peeled. The Hubbard squash especially saved for the dinner had been split open and the seeds taken out (if the squash turned out to be extra good, the seeds would be dried and saved for next spring's planting).

In the middle of the morning Father had come in bringing the bunches of celery he had pulled and packed, roots and all, in sand just before the first hard freeze took everything left in the garden. After sampling the grapes and cracking a few nuts to take in his pocket he had helped Mother turn the turkey so the underside would brown. He had exchanged his work gloves for a pair of woolen mittens lying on the drying shelf up by the stovepipe, then gone back out to help the boys. A dozen times or more the storm door had burst open, letting in a blast of cold air and closing with a bang on the children's comings and goings. No emergencies—just ordinary hurry-up calls to the bathroom, or fingers and toes to be warmed, or a spat resulting in angry feelings best soothed by withdrawing from the others for a spell to the cheerful bustle of the kitchen.

All of a sudden it was one o'clock. The noise and activity multiplied twice over. The turkey came out of the oven. The vegetables were done. Mother was at the stove holding the fussing baby on one hip while she stirred up the gravy. The whole family was back inside, congregating in the kitchen. Boots and rubbers, mittens, caps, and coats were being pulled off and thrown helter-skelter. Appetites had revived and grown to tremendous proportions. We were beseiged by a ravenous troop.

"When do we eat?"

"I'm so hungry I'm *starving!*"

"I want something to eat. *Right now!*"

"Can I have a sandwich? Well, can't I even have a *doughnut?*"

The troop was reassured and re-formed into helpers, boys and little ones and all. Wraps were put away in the kitchen closet, boots lined up behind the stove. Everybody got washed up. Somebody volunteered to amuse the baby. Bread and pickles and celery and cranberry sauce went on the table. Father got out his whetstone and sharpened up the big butcher knife, then began to carve the turkey. His helper scooped out the stuffing and arranged the sliced meat on two big platters (there always had to be two dishes of everything on our long table). The vegetables were drained, riced or mashed, buttered and seasoned. The plum pudding was brought in from the cold ell kitchen. Everything was dished up and we gathered around the table. Just as we were sitting down the dining room clock went half-past.

Mother's happiest moment came when she lifted her head after saying the blessing and looked around the table at the faces of her healthy, well-fed children. On special occasions such as Thanksgiving Father didn't mind waiting for a reasonably short blessing to be said. He was proud that his children never had to go hungry and pleased with Mother's cooking, but he believed in claiming the credit that was his just due. His hand had been in the preparation of the dinner from start to finish. The food on his table, he wanted it clearly understood, was certainly not manna fallen from heaven.

There was never a year when Thanksgiving dinner failed to come up to our expectations. The vegetables were invariably better than last year's. The turkey *did* always turn out to be the most tender, best-flavored ever served on our table. The mince pie tasted fully as good as it had at breakfast (most everyone took *both* mince and pumpkin). Father ate immensely, savouring every dish and urging everybody else to have some more. He always finished with a big dish of the old-fashioned plum pudding that was his favorite.

Afterward it was pleasant to sit for awhile around the table, feeling comfortable and lackadaisical. While we nibbled at the grapes Father cracked nuts. Each chose a favorite kind—walnut, almond, Brazil nut, cashew, or filbert. As he cracked and passed the nuts around, Father told us where he supposed each kind was grown and we speculated about those faraway places.

That was one night in the year when Mother didn't get any hot supper. Anybody who felt up to it could have a sandwich or a piece of pie. When Father came in from doing the evening milking Mother made him a cup of hot tea and he picked the bones of the turkey in the privacy of the pantry.

❧ 18 ❧

The Christmas Tree

Our Christmas Tree was always a spruce or fir balsam, tall enough so the tip, which had to be a perfect spire, just grazed the sitting room ceiling. There it stood—every year in the very same corner —a glorious magnet for the eyes and noses of children indoors, a token of joy winking merrily through the frosty windowpanes at passersby riding along the snowy road.

Christmas dinner, like our Thanksgiving meal, followed the traditions of Father's family. At this lesser feast we ate the same kinds of homegrown vegetables, but the meat was roast pork or a baked ham from the pigs slaughtered earlier in the fall. There was cranberry sauce and pickles. For dessert, mince pie and a steamed pudding, rich with raisins and spices, served hot—drenched with Grandmother's pudding sauce. The decorated tree was not part of family custom, for our grandparents didn't have Christmas trees and didn't exchange gifts in the family. As a holy day, Christmas was observed in churches but was not made much of in farmers' homes, at least not in our area.

Our family Christmas traditions may have had their beginnings in the years just before Father and Mother were married, when she was teaching school. In that long ago time, one-room country schoolhouses were community centers where neighbors often gathered for evening sings and spelling bees. On Friday afternoons before the school term ended, school board members, friends and relatives from babies to grandfathers were invited to a program of songs, recitations and other displays of the pupils' talents and learning. For the Christmas program it became the custom to set up an evergreen tree cut down and brought in from the nearby woods by the older boys. All the children, even the littlest ones who sat at the small desks in the front row, helped decorate the tree with garlands of strung popcorn and colored paper loops, perhaps a few shining glass ornaments from the store. The teacher sewed colored netting material into small sacks with drawstrings of yarn at the top. These netting bags, one for each pupil and a few extra for younger children certain to attend the exercises, were filled with good things to eat. When hung from the tree's branches, the treasures of oranges, nuts, and candies, seen through the colored netting, added to the splendor of the tree. After the exercises the treats were distributed to the eager children.

Mother was an enthusiastic teacher. She loved the Christmas celebrations with her children in school, so of course she began the custom of the tree for her own children. We chose the tree in the woods and helped bring it home the day before Christmas. We strung the popcorn and hung the tinseled cardboard angel near the top of the tree. We took down the treasured glass ornaments from their place in the cupboard, handling them ever so carefully. Gently we hung the shining globes on the green boughs. We set new red candles into the metal holders and clipped the holders to branches, making sure none of the candles was tilting. (We weren't allowed to light them, for fear of fire, until Father came in from the evening milking.) We helped Mother fill the bright net bags, stuffed full as could be—at the bottom an orange; next the sugared popcorn and all the kinds of candy we had helped Mother make; at the very top, the thin, thin Christmas ribbon candy from Keller's store in Laconia. Last of all, each secretly put on a gift for sister or brother (we drew names like the children in school). When we came downstairs before light on Christmas morning, we found our presents from Father and Mother heaped around the tree.

When we recall Christmas at home and remember the joy of receiving some toy we had longed for, we wonder how Mother managed to buy for us all with the little money she had to spend. We think of the lighted candles, the smell of warm evergreen needles, the good things to eat in Mother's pantry, on the table, and on our Christmas tree. Then we always remember Mother herself with special tenderness. Christmas was her time.

❦ 19 ❦

The Sugar House

T<small>HIS</small> <small>YEAR</small> when it is time to think about tapping the maple trees, Forrest will tell everyone, "I don't know as I'll make any syrup this season. Seems as if the rheumatism in my back always gets me just when it's about time for the sap to start running. With Sam and Nathan away, I won't have any help from my boys. I don't see how I can undertake so much hard work by myself. Don't know as I even want to try."

But several of Sam's friends will offer to help with the tapping. Bob Weeks will stop by one evening to talk about the boiling. "You remember I learned to run the evaporator by myself last year, Uncle Forrest," he will say. "I can handle the boiling evenings so you won't have to stay late at the sugar house when there has been a good run. You know that Sheila always likes to help with the sugaring-off parties for the children. My five—all the cousins, for that matter—will feel pretty bad if they miss out on the good times at the sugar house."

Letters will come from distant families. "It's been a long time since we were in New Hampshire during sapping season. Perhaps this year we can make it. Be sure to let us know when you start boiling."

Then Forrest remembers the high pile of slabwood stacked beside the sugar house, handy to the firebox of the big evaporator inside. The job of getting the wood ready was done last fall, same as always. He thinks of the big pans scoured clean, overturned to keep out squirrels and mice. In no time at all the rig could be set up, ready to go. On the other hand, he recalls the tedious business of cleaning up after the sap has stopped running. Every year hundreds of spiles to gather up, to wash and let dry in the sun. Then the equipment all to be stored, ready for starting the whole business over again another year. When cleanup time comes, the young helpers will have gone, their enthusiasm evaporated along with the last of the snowbanks. The thought amuses more than it irritates him. The cleanup chores can be done in a leisurely fashion. Working in the warm sunshine is good for rheumatism. Thus he weighs the pros and cons, still not making up his mind.

As the pale winter sun begins to brighten and the days lengthen Forrest feels the stirring deep within the maples. After fifty seasons in the sugar orchard, his familiarity with the stimuli of nature is rooted deep as the rock maple itself. The pull of long habit is strong. He can't give up. Not this year, anyhow. The word goes out to all the family, "Uncle Forrest has had a bulldozer come to clear paths through the deep snow in his maple orchard. He's getting ready to tap the trees."

There was a time when the cans of maple syrup and boxes of candy labeled HIGH MAPLES FARM were shipped all over the nation, sometimes to foreign countries as well. In Father's orchard, the largest in the county, fifteen hundred buckets were hung every year. Seasons when the weather was right and the sap ran well we could make nearly a thousand gallons of fine-quality maple syrup. From other producers we always bought an equal amount of syrup to make the soft sugar, maple butter and candies to supply the summer trade and fill the Christmas orders. That was in the years after the big new sugar house was built and equipped with the most efficient evaporator of the time. Located about midway between Father's first orchard to the west (now a part of Forrest's land) and the younger, greater number of maples growing on the high slopes of the cow pasture east of the farm buildings, the place was in plain view of passersby on the main road from Laconia.

On Sunday afternoons when the boiling down was in process, a constant stream of visitors crossed the field to the Smith "sugar camp" as they called it. They came to enjoy a sugaring-off, the traditional outing of early spring, and perhaps to carry home a gallon can of warm, first-run syrup. Others came to take pictures. Sometimes a professional photographer would arrive with his crew to record the colorful activities, the rustic scene. In the foreground was the sugar house with clouds of steam rising through the vented roof. In the background were ancient maples, buckets hanging from their great trunks, in the distance a glimpse of snowy hillside and evergreen trees. At intervals the gathering crews came in from the orchard to empty their loads into the big holding tank at the back of the sugar house. The horses standing at rest in their harnesses, reins hanging loose on drooping heads, were the picture of weariness. And the yoked oxen as they approached up the gully, pulling the loaded sled across the rocky brook, responding in perfect unison as the teamster used his goad—a tiny prick at the near ox, a flick against the nose of the off ox—they were the picture of harnessed power, old-fashioned style.

When our youngest brother, Joe, recalls those years on the farm, he thinks of sapping as the hardest work of all. "Yet I really enjoyed it the most," he says. "Forrest usually did the boiling, but sometimes I took over after I got home from school, so he could leave to have supper and do his own barn chores. It was a big responsibility—tending the fires, taking care not to let the sap in the holding tank get so low the pans would be in danger of burning on. Still, I liked being there alone, working in the early evening. After awhile someone would come down from the house to bring my supper and stay awhile to keep me company. Mother always sent down fresh rolls or biscuits. We'd keep the food hot back by the smokestack. With a pot of coffee and some eggs hard-boiled in the sap, nothing could have tasted better."

The older grandchildren share Joe's happy memories of those years at the big sugar house. The smallest ones came just for the fun. They tumbled about in the snow outside and got underfoot inside. They stickied fingers and faces and snow suits with "leather aprons" and then were shepherded away home by their parents. Oldest grandson David remembers how young he was when his grandfather taught him to drive the big white-faced oxen, Zeke and Ezra. Wielding the goad expertly, he made numerous trips over rough terrain bringing in loads of sap. Exhausting work even for a man, it took plenty of grit for a boy to keep going all day long. Joann and Jeanne filled pans with clean snow scooped from under the pine trees and helped set the long tables. Jack and Bob ran errands back and forth from the farmhouse and rode the big sleds "helping" to gather sap from the buckets. They played around the brook (invariably one or the other fell in and had to suffer the indignity of being carried off dripping and shivering).

Many Laconians who were youngsters then remember coming with a church group or Scout troop for an evening sugaring-off party. The lantern-lit interior of the sugar house seemed a place touched with magic. The cold sap, running through a pipe into the biggest pan back next to the smokestack, immediately began to bubble, threatening to foam high over the sides onto the floor. A quick dash of some mysterious substance made the roiling subside at once to a gentle even boil. The clear liquid moving through conduits from one pan to the next gradually thickened and became a lovely amber color. While the visitors watched and asked questions, the man at the evaporator moved through clouds of sweet steam, laboring in rhythmic ritual. Donning asbestos gloves, he swung wide the iron doors to thrust huge sticks of cordwood into the gaping, red hot maw, then back again to the side of the evaporator to study the strange instruments standing in the bursting bubbles of the pan nearest the front. Came the peremptory call: "Time to syrup off. Hurry with the buckets." A thick hot stream poured from the opened faucet. One bucket was filled and replaced by a second, perhaps a third before the master at the faucet shut off the flow with a sudden downward jerk. The steaming buckets were carried away to the canning table where the syrup was filtered through felt "hats" to remove any traces of sediment before it was funneled into tin cans. At once the wizard of the evaporator was back at his work, checking the quantity of cold sap remaining in the huge tank outside, feeding the voracious fire, peering through the steam—flashlight in hand—to note the readings of hydrometer and thermometer.

Meantime, the kettle of syrup boiling away on the small stove over in one corner had reached the sugar stage. The food in the kitchen lean-to was ready. There were plates stacked with plain doughnuts, sliced sour pickles, a pot full of strong black coffee (made with sap instead of water). There were pans packed with snow. There were spoons and new wooden skewers. We set on the bowls of unstirred sugar. Guests gathered around the long table and set to. Spooning the hot liquid onto snow, they made "leather aprons" to pick up with the skewers and eat like lollipops; or if they pleased, they stirred until they had bowls of creamy warm sugar to eat along with the doughnuts and sour pickles. When the food had all disappeared, our guests went off across the field to the road, leaving us with the job of cleaning up for next time. The sap in the pans stopped bubbling as the fire was left to burn low for the night.

We locked up the sugar house and headed for home, glad the distance up across the field was no farther. As soon as we stepped outside, we could tell it had started to freeze even before the sun went down. Patches of old snow crunched under our feet. The voice of the brook, only recently freed from winter's silence, was muted to a whisper. The sap in the bottoms of the buckets hanging on nearby maples had already frozen solid, and the March sky was without a cloud. The Big

Dipper shone clear, Orion's belt sparkled, the sliver of moon curved right side up. Tomorrow would be another good sap day for sure.

Esther and Royal remember a much earlier time when there was no sugar house and no evaporator. They were old enough then to help gather sap and tend the fire under the pan set up on a crude brick arch out in the open, near the maple trees in Father's first orchard. Father was still using some of the equipment brought from Grandfather Smith's old home in Meredith. The shoulder yoke, carved from basswood and marked with deep knife cuts, W. SMITH, 1880, was a convenient device for carrying two full pails without any spillage. The wooden buckets—they always had to be soaked in the watering trough ahead of time so they wouldn't leak—must have been made in a cooper's shop perhaps a hundred years earlier.

A dozen years had passed. Forrest was fifteen years old before the first sugar house was built. Really only a converted shed with a brick arch for an evaporator and outside chimney added, the building (always called the "little sugar house") stood close to the farmhouse dooryard. Two men with some boy-help and one team could do the work of gathering and hauling in the sap, and get the boiling down accomplished late in the afternoon or evenings without much trouble. Robert's earliest memories are of the spring after the little sap house had been built. He was our little brother Robbie then, a merry, sturdy three-year-old just emerged from a sickly babyhood.

"I was eager to be outside. Father and the big boys were glad to take me everywhere with them," Robert recalls. "But I was too small to get very far on my own in the deep snow, so I rode in a box attached to the sled in front of the sap tank, right behind the oxen. The box was so big I could just peer over the edge. I remember the red knitted mittens I wore and the woolen cap pulled down over my ears. I can see now the buckets attached to the big maple tree that stood at the pasture gate. On the way home we always went down the steep bank, across the brook and through the gate to gather the sap from a certain tree and others that were scattered along the road back to the sap house. It was Royal who usually teamed the oxen. I suppose I knew he could handle those big white-faced cattle, yet I couldn't help feeling pretty worried every time we came to that place. Those oxen looked awfully big to me. Royal would use the goad, urging them on. I would brace myself in the box and hang on while we plunged into the water and went bumping and grinding up the other bank."

Two springs later Robbie was training his own little steers, twin brockle-faced calves coupled in a small old yoke handed down from Grandfather Smith's time. The little steers learned how to pull together, answer the goad signals and respond to Robbie's commands. Their names, Hokum and Hooey, had been picked up from the slangy conversation of older sisters. The little boy had no idea of belittling his pets; the words were good-sounding and short—appropriate names for steers, he thought. As we look back now, it seems no time at all before Hokum and Hooey were big oxen, drawing loads of sap to the new sugar house, and their tall young master was preparing to enter college the next fall. Our youngest brother, Joe, Mother's last baby, was in high school and there were grandchildren old enough to help in maple syrup season.

Now that time too is a part of the long-ago past. The sugar house is gone and the pines grow thick in the paths where the horses and oxen used to draw the sleds. Some years ago Forrest built a snug sap house in his own orchard and installed an evaporator to boil the sap, which is gathered by tractor power.

One day next spring when the weather is right (old hand though he is, Forrest cannot explain exactly how he knows), the volunteer crew will go out to tap the maples. Among Forrest's trees a few ancient maples (some of Father's original orchard) are still standing, their trunks ringed with scars from the bite of many drills. It is hard to find another good spot to set a spile and hang the bucket.

"Don't tap that one," Forrest will tell the boys. "That's a tree so old it won't run much sap anyway. Let it rest this year." He will go on through the orchard pointing out the younger trees, showing his helpers how to handle bit and bitstock. "Tap away from the scars of old holes," he will explain. "Choose a spot about waist high, beneath a good-sized branch, if you can. Bore straight in to the new wood, far enough so a space will be left after the spile is driven in. That way you make a well where a reservoir of sap can build up—it causes pressure and makes the sap run faster."

So Forrest will begin another season in the maple orchard. The family will come to visit. Old customers will put in their orders early to be sure of getting the best syrup. Perhaps this will be a very good year, or maybe the sap "runs" will not be up to those of other seasons. No one can foretell, for it is a matter of chance, depending on the vagaries of weather.

I have become only a recipient, so I will also write a letter asking for a share of the first run. When the shipment arrives, my grandchildren will eat pancakes swimming in delicious New Hampshire maple syrup. My grandchildren have never walked in the snow, never have watched a maple tree being tapped and then put their tongues to the rough bark to taste the first sweet drops oozing out as the bit is withdrawn and the curls of new wood fall to the ground.

Youngest granddaughter, Ann Elizabeth, feels she has been cheated. "Some time you've got to take me up North when it's maple syrup time," she tells me. "I want to drink cold sap from the buckets (like you used to when you were little). I want to go to Uncle Forrest's sugar house and have "leather aprons" on snow with all my cousins (I don't even know all their names) who live up there."

I have to promise that we will go—some year very soon!

RECIPES

Old "receipts," whether adapted for today's use or given in the original as items of historical interest, are identified in relationship to my generation as: Grandmother Smith's Johnnycake, Mother's Piccalilli, Aunt Mary's Spiced Beef Tongue, *etc.*

Recipes from the kitchens of my sisters or sisters-in-law are indicated in the following manner: Frances' Doughnuts, Ellen's Lemon Sponge Pie, Verna's Spiced Cider Jelly, *etc.*

Recipes furnished by members of younger generations are identified in relationship to my parents as: Apple Cream Muffins, *Granddaughter Joann Bailey's recipe;* Young Homemaker's Basic Mix, *Granddaughter Jeanne Eddinger's recipe;* Pineapple Squares, *Granddaughter-in-law Sheila Weeks' recipe.*

Recipes used with the permission of friends are designated "From the kitchen of . . . ."

❧ 20 ❧

Breads

Yeast breads, brown bread, fruit breads,

johnnycake, muffins, biscuits, coffee cake,

pancakes, waffles, and homemade mixes

ESTHER'S WHITE BREAD

MADE LIKE MOTHER'S

Scald
6 cups milk

Combine in a small bowl
2 packages dry yeast
¾ cup lukewarm water

Turn the hot milk into a bread-mixer pail. Add
½ cup butter
1 cup sugar
2 teaspoons salt

Cool to lukewarm. Add
The yeast mixture

Stir in, using a large spoon,
4 cups bread flour

Mix well, stirring until batter is smooth. Set the pail in a warm place (75-80°) for 60 minutes or until batter has become light and spongy.

Stir in thoroughly, a little at a time,
About 9 cups bread flour

Attach the kneader. Turn the handle (this motion kneads the dough). Continue to knead for 3 minutes. At this stage the dough should form into a ball around the kneader. If the dough seems too soft, a little more flour may be added, but care must be taken not to make too stiff a dough or the bread will be hard and dry. Set breadmixer in a warm place (75-80°) until dough has doubled in bulk. Stir down thoroughly. Let rise again until double in bulk (second rising will be quicker). Stir down and turn dough out onto a floured board. Form two loaves (each half-loaf should be about the size of a grapefruit). Place two half-loaves side by side in greased bread tins. Form remainder of dough into rolls and place in greased tins. Let rise until doubled in bulk. Place loaves and pans of rolls in a preheated oven as ready. Bake at 375° for 35 to 45 minutes or until done. Rolls will be done when they are lightly browned on all sides. Loaves will need the longer baking time. MAKES 2 DOUBLE LOAVES AND APPROXIMATELY 36 ROLLS.

Note: All-purpose flour may be used but a little more may need to be added in order to make the dough stiff enough to form a ball.

BASIC DOUGH FOR BREAD AND ROLLS
MADE WITHOUT USING A BREAD MIXER

Scald
   3 cups milk

Dissolve
   1½ packages dry yeast and
   1 tablespoon sugar in
   ¼ cup lukewarm water

Add to hot milk
   ½ stick butter (¼ cup)
   ⅓ cup sugar
   1 teaspoon salt

Place mixture in a large bowl or kettle and let cool to lukewarm. Add the yeast mixture.

Add and beat until smooth, using an electric mixer or rotary beater,
   3 cups sifted all-purpose flour

Cover with a towel and set in a warm place (80°) for 40 minutes or until batter is spongy and light.

Stir in very thoroughly
   5-5½ cups sifted all-purpose flour

At this point the dough should be just stiff enough to stir into a ball. Place dough in a greased bowl large enough to allow room for rising. Cover with a towel. Let dough rise until doubled in bulk. Punch down and let rise a second time. After second rising, punch and stir down. Make into loaves or rolls in shapes as desired. Arrange in greased tins.

Brush with
 Melted butter

Let rise until doubled in bulk. Bake rolls in preheated oven at 425° for 20-25 minutes or until done. Bake bread at 375° for 40-45 minutes or until loaves test done. MAKES ONE LOAF AND TWO DOZEN OR MORE ROLLS.

VARIATION: CINNAMON ROLLS

Prepare dough as in basic recipe (*see p. 152*). Roll into a rectangle about ¼ inch thick. Brush generously with melted butter. Sprinkle with ¼ cup sugar mixed with 1 teaspoon cinnamon. Roll up and cut into ¾-inch slices. Place in greased pan, cut side down. Brush with more melted butter. Let rise until doubled in bulk. Bake at 375° for 25 minutes or until done.

VARIATION: ORANGE ROLLS

Proceed as for Cinnamon Rolls. After spreading with melted butter, sprinkle with ⅓ cup sugar mixed with 2 tablespoons grated fresh orange peel. Shape and place in greased pan. Let rise until doubled in bulk. Bake as for Cinnamon Rolls. Remove from pan and let cool a little. Ice with confectioners' sugar frosting, using fresh orange juice instead of water.

VARIATION: MAPLE PECAN ROLLS I

Proceed as for Cinnamon Rolls. Cream ¾ cup butter with ½ cup soft maple sugar (packed). The mixture may be warmed over hot water to make creaming easier. Spread part of the sugar-butter mixture on the rectangle of dough. Sprinkle with ¼ cup finely chopped pecans. Spread remainder in a shallow, 9-inch round pan. Roll up dough and cut in ¾-inch slices. Place cut side down in the pan. Press a pecan half into the top of each roll. Brush with melted butter. Let rise until doubled in bulk. Bake as for Cinnamon Rolls. Remove from pan immediately before syrup hardens.

VARIATION: MAPLE PECAN ROLLS II

Spread the maple sugar-butter mixture in the bottom of individual muffin pans. Place a pecan half upside down in each pan. Form rolls with a small biscuit cutter and place in muffin pans. Bake as for Cinnamon Rolls. Remove from pans as soon as baked. Serve pecan side up.

TWO EGG ROLLS

Scald
   3 cups rich milk

Dissolve
   1½ packages dry yeast in
   ⅓ cup lukewarm water

Add to the hot milk
   ½ stick butter (¼ cup)
   ⅓ cup sugar
   1 teaspoon salt

Pour the mixture into a large bowl or kettle (6-quart size). Let cool to lukewarm.

Beat in, using an electric mixer,
   2 large eggs

Stir in
   The yeast mixture

Add and beat until smooth, using an electric mixer,
   3 cups sifted all-purpose flour

Cover with a clean towel and set in a warm place (80°) for 40 minutes or until the batter is light and spongy.

Stir in thoroughly
   5-5½ cups sifted all-purpose flour

Place dough in a greased bowl large enough to allow for rising. Allow dough to rise until doubled in bulk. Punch down and let rise a second time. After the second rising, punch down and shape into rolls as desired. Arrange in greased tins.

Brush with
Melted butter

Let rise until doubled in bulk. Bake in preheated oven at 425° for 25 minutes or until done.

MRS. JOHNSON'S OATMEAL BREAD

ADAPTED FROM AN 1898 "RECEIPT"

Mrs. Johnson was the wife of an old-time New Hampshire rural mail carrier, one of the first in the nation. All the folks along his route considered Mailman Johnson a friend. They could depend on his coming every day, even in the most severe winter weather. He was so obliging, always ready to carry medicine to any family where the children were down sick, or to take messages from one neighbor to another along the route. If requested, he would even deliver one of his wife's famous "receipts" along with the mail. That is how it happened that Mrs. Johnson's Oatmeal Bread, a favorite for two generations of the Bailey family, is now baked in Granddaughter Joann Weeks Bailey's kitchen for the enjoyment of a third generation.

Place in a bowl
1 cup quick-cooking oats

Pour over the oats and allow to cool to lukewarm
2 cups boiling water

Combine in a small bowl
1 package dry yeast
¼ cup lukewarm water
1 teaspoon sugar

Mix in a large bowl or bread-mixer pail
  1 cup scalding-hot milk
  ⅓ cup molasses
  ½ cup butter or vegetable shortening
  1 teaspoon salt

Cool to lukewarm. Stir in
  The oatmeal mixture
  The yeast mixture

Add and beat until smooth
  2 cups sifted all-purpose flour

Cover and set in a warm place (75-80°) for 45 minutes or until batter has become light and spongy.

Stir in thoroughly, a little at a time,
  6 cups sifted all-purpose flour

Place dough in a greased bowl large enough to allow room for rising. Allow to rise until doubled in bulk. Punch down and let rise again. Turn dough onto a floured board and knead lightly until smooth and free of air bubbles. Form into 3 loaves and place in buttered bread tins. Let rise until barely doubled in bulk. Bake in a preheated oven at 375° for 45-50 minutes or until loaves are done. Turn loaves out on a wire rack and brush with melted butter.

GREAT-AUNT JESSIE SANBORN'S GRAHAM BREAD

ADAPTED FROM AN 1890 "RECEIPT"

Scald
  2 cups milk with
  ½ cup light cream

Combine in a small bowl
  1 package dry yeast
  ½ teaspoon sugar
  ½ cup lukewarm water

Add to the hot milk
  ½ cup butter
  1 teaspoon salt
  ½ cup dark molasses

Cool to lukewarm. Add
  The yeast mixture

Beat in, using an electric mixer or rotary beater,
  2 cups all-purpose flour

Add and continue to beat until batter is smooth
  1 cup graham (whole wheat) flour, measured before sifting

Cover with a cloth and set in a warm place (80°) for an hour or until the batter is light and spongy. Stir in thoroughly, then knead lightly to make a smooth dough,
  4½ cups graham flour, measured before sifting

Place dough in a greased bowl large enough to allow rising. Set in a warm place and let rise until doubled in bulk. Punch or stir down and make into loaves. Place loaves in greased bread tins. Brush with melted butter. Let rise until doubled in bulk. Bake in a preheated oven at 375° for 45-50 minutes or until done. Turn out on a wire rack and brush with butter. MAKES 2 LOAVES.

SWEDISH LIMPA BREAD

ADAPTED FROM A BERQUIST FAMILY RECIPE

Scald
  3 cups milk

Add to hot milk
  1 teaspoon salt
  ½ cup butter
  ½ cup brown sugar
  ½ cup molasses

Turn into a large bowl or 6-quart kettle and let cool to lukewarm.

Stir in
  2 packages dry yeast dissolved in
  ½ cup warm water

Beat in thoroughly, using an electric mixer,
  2 cups all-purpose flour

Add and continue to beat until batter is completely free of lumps
  1 cup light rye flour, measured before sifting

Cover with a cloth and set in a warm place for 40 minutes or until the batter is very light and spongy.

Stir in vigorously
  3 cups sifted all-purpose flour

Add and continue to stir until dough is smooth and light
  3 cups rye flour, measured before sifting

Place dough in a greased bowl large enough to allow room for rising. Set aside in a warm place and let rise until doubled in bulk. Punch or stir down with a large spoon, and let rise again. Repeat this process (second rising will not take as long). Punch down and make into three or four round loaves. Place loaves in greased pie pans or round cake tins. Let rise until doubled in bulk. Bake in a preheated oven at 375° for 45 to 60 minutes or until done.

SWEDISH BREAD BRAIDS

GRANDDAUGHTER JEANNE EDDINGER'S RECIPE

Heat to the boiling point
  3 cups milk

Stir into hot milk
  ½ cup butter
  ⅓ cup sugar
  1 teaspoon salt

Cool to lukewarm.

Mix in
>2 packages dry yeast dissolved in
>½ cup lukewarm water

Add and beat with an electric mixer until batter is smooth
>2 eggs
>3 cups all-purpose flour

Cover and set in a warm place (80°) for 40 minutes or until the batter is light and spongy.

Stir in very thoroughly
>6 cups all-purpose flour

At this point the dough should be firm enough to form a ball when stirred. Place dough in a greased bowl large enough to allow rising. Set aside and let rise until doubled in bulk. Punch or stir down with a large spoon and let rise again. After the second rising, punch down and divide dough into three parts. Divide each part again into thirds. Roll between your hands into long, thin ropes. Braid and place on a greased cookie sheet (three braids). Brush with melted butter. Allow to rise until doubled in bulk. Bake in preheated oven at 425° for 10 minutes, then at 375° until bread is done. Time will vary according to thickness of braids. Brush the hot bread braids with melted butter. Drizzle on a thin white icing and sprinkle with chopped pecans.

Note: Swedish Bread Braids should be served warm from the oven. Do not cut. Allow your guests to tear off portions as desired.

FRANCES' CHRISTMAS BREAD

Scald
>2 cups milk

Add to hot milk, then allow to cool until lukewarm
>½ cup butter
>1 teaspoon salt
>1 teaspoon cinnamon
>¼ teaspoon cardamom seeds, crushed
>½ cup sugar

Stir in
   2 packages dry yeast dissolved in
   ½ cup lukewarm water

Beat in, using an electric mixer,
   2 medium eggs

Add and continue to beat until batter is smooth
   2 cups all-purpose flour

Stir in
   2 cups mixed candied fruits

Stir in and mix thoroughly
   4 cups all-purpose flour

Place dough in a greased bowl large enough to allow rising. Cover and set in a warm place (about 80°). Let rise until doubled in bulk. Punch down. Turn out onto a floured board and knead lightly. Form into two braids. Place braids on greased cookie sheets. Let rise until doubled in bulk. Bake in a preheated oven at 375° for 45 minutes. Brush warm bread all over with butter.

Variation: Form into two loaves and bake in bread tins. Ice top with thin white frosting.

GRANDMOTHER SMITH'S BROWN BREAD
ADAPTED FROM AUNT MARY'S COOKBOOK

Sift together
   2 cups all-purpose flour
   2 cups yellow corn meal
   2 teaspoons baking soda
   1 teaspoon salt

Mix
   1⅓ cups milk
   1⅓ cups buttermilk
   ¾ cup dark molasses

Add and mix well
The flour–corn meal mixture

Pour mixture into two greased 1-pound coffee cans, filling each about two-thirds full. Tie over the cans a tight cover made of heavy aluminum foil. Place filled cans on a rack in a deep kettle. Add boiling water to come halfway up around the cans. Cover the kettle. Add more boiling water as needed to maintain the level. Steam 2½-3 hours. Remove the loaves from cans. Place in a preheated 300° oven to dry out for 15 minutes.

FRANCES' COLONIAL BREAD

Mix in a bowl
½ cup light molasses
1 teaspoon salt
1 teaspoon baking soda
2 cups buttermilk (room temperature)

Let stand 10 minutes. Stir in
2½ cups graham flour (unsifted)
1 cup sifted all-purpose flour

Add and mix to a smooth batter
1 tablespoon melted butter

Pour batter into a greased 9 × 5-inch loaf tin. Bake at 350° for 70 minutes or until bread is done. Turn bread out on a wire rack and brush with melted butter.

JESSIE'S APPLE BREAD

Sift together
2 cups all-purpose flour
1 teaspoon baking powder
1 teaspoon baking soda

Cream together
> ¼ *cup softened vegetable shortening*
> ⅔ *cup sugar*

Stir in
> *2 medium eggs, beaten*

Mix in alternately
> *2 cups coarsely grated, hard apples*
> *The flour mixture*

Stir in
> *1 tablespoon grated lemon peel*
> ⅔ *cup chopped nutmeats (pecans or walnuts)*

Bake in a large, greased, loaf tin in preheated oven at 350° for 50 minutes or until done. Brush loaf with melted butter. Allow to cool in tin.

Suggestion: Apple bread will slice more easily if, after cooling, it is stored overnight in the refrigerator, but if any of the younger members of the family happen to get a sniff of this bread while it's baking, no doubt you'll have to serve it at once. No one will mind if it crumbles a bit.

HICKORY NUT BREAD

FROM THE KITCHEN OF LOIS NELSON

Sift together
> *2½ cups all-purpose flour*
> *1 teaspoon salt*
> *2 teaspoons baking powder*

Cream
> ¾ *cup sugar*
> ¼ *cup melted butter*

Beat in
> *1 large egg*

Add alternately, stirring to make a smooth batter,
   1 cup milk
   The flour mixture

Stir in
   1 cup chopped hickory nutmeats

Pour batter into a greased bread tin. Let stand for 25 minutes. Bake in preheated oven at 325° for 60 minutes or until bread is done. Allow to cool slightly, then turn out on a wire rack.

Note: Substitute pecan nutmeats, if hickory nuts are not available.

DATE BREAD

Combine in a mixing bowl and allow to cool
   3 cups dates, cut in quarters
   1½ cups boiling water

Sift together
   3 cups all-purpose flour
   2 teaspoons baking soda
   ½ teaspoon salt

Cream
   2 tablespoons softened butter
   1 tablespoon vanilla
   1 cup sugar

Beat in, one at a time,
   2 large eggs

Add alternately to the creamed mixture
   The flour mixture
   The water drained from dates

Mix in
   The date pieces
   1 cup broken nutmeats (walnuts or pecans)

Turn batter into 2 greased loaf pans. Bake in preheated oven at 325° for 60 minutes or until done. Test by inserting a wooden toothpick into bread; tooth pick will come out clean when bread is done. Turn bread out onto wire racks and brush with melted butter.

JESSIE'S BANANA BREAD

Sift together
  2 cups all-purpose flour
  ½ teaspoon baking soda
  ½ teaspoon salt
  1½ teaspoons baking powder

Cream together
  ¼ cup softened butter
  ¾ cup sugar

Blend at high speed in an electric blender
  3 medium-size bananas
  1 large egg
  ⅓ cup buttermilk

Mix well together
  The blended ingredients
  The creamed mixture

Stir in
  The flour mixture
  1 cup chopped pecans

Turn the batter into a large greased loaf tin. Now turn oven to 350°. Let batter sit in the pan until oven is hot. Bake 60 minutes or until done. Allow bread to cool in the pan for 15 minutes, then invert pan on a wire rack.

APRICOT-ORANGE BREAD

Cut into small pieces and place in a bowl
1 7½-ounce package moist-pack apricots

Cover with
1 cup boiling water
½ cup fresh orange juice

Set aside to cool.

Sift together
2½ cups all-purpose flour
1 teaspoon baking soda
2 teaspoons baking powder

Cream together
1 cup sugar
2 tablespoons softened butter
¼ teaspoon salt

Beat in one at a time
2 large eggs

Stir in alternately
The flour mixture
The liquid drained from apricots

Mix in
The apricot pieces
1 cup chopped blanched almonds

Pour batter into 2 greased loaf tins. Bake in preheated oven at 325°
for 60 minutes or until bread is done. Allow bread to cool in tins for
15 minutes then invert on a wire rack.

GRANDMOTHER SMITH'S JOHNNYCAKE

Sift together
  ½ cup all-purpose flour
  1 cup yellow corn meal

Cream together
  2 tablespoons softened butter
  ¼ cup sugar

Dissolve
  1 teaspoon baking soda in
  1½ cups buttermilk

Stir into creamed mixture alternately
  The flour–corn meal mixture
  The buttermilk mixture

Mix in
  1 cup finely cut beef suet (optional)*

Spread the batter thin in a greased 9 × 13-inch baking pan. Bake in a preheated oven at 425° for 20 minutes or until done.

  *Suggestion: Beef suet adds true, old-fashioned New Hampshire touch.

UNCLE CHARLIE'S LUMBERMILL JOHNNYCAKE

ADAPTED BY COUSIN PEARL SMITH YORK

Sift together
  ¾ cup all-purpose flour
  ¾ cup yellow corn meal
  ⅓ cup sugar
  1 teaspoon salt
  ½ teaspoon baking soda

Mix in well a little at a time
  2 cups buttermilk
  2 tablespoons vegetable oil

Pour batter into 2 greased 8-inch cake pans. Bake in a preheated oven at 375° for 25-30 minutes or until lightly browned.

ELLEN'S CUSTARD CORNCAKE

When Ellen was a bride living in West Virginia, she eased her home-sickness by trying out recipes from home, learning to cook the familiar New Hampshire way. When she wrote asking directions for making corn bread, Mother sent this recipe, the creation of her old school friend—a lady as elegant as this corncake. We believe this recipe is a delicate descendant of the ancient "Spider Cake" made by our pioneer grandmothers in the days of open fireplace cooking.

Sift together
  1 cup yellow corn meal
  ½ cup all-purpose flour
  ⅓ cup sugar
  ½ teaspoon salt
  3 teaspoons baking powder

Stir together to make a smooth batter
  The corn meal–flour mixture
  1⅓ cups milk
  2 tablespoons melted butter

Pour batter into a greased 9 × 13-inch pan (layer must be thin). Allow to stand for 15 minutes.

Mix custard layer:

Beat together in a bowl
  1 egg
  1⅓ cups light cream

Pour the egg-cream mixture in a thin stream over the batter in the tin. Allow time for the liquid to soak in. Bake in a preheated oven at 450° for 10 minutes, then at 350° for 40 minutes.

Note: Use stone-ground corn meal if available.

Suggestion: Serve Custard Corncake hot from the oven and eat it with a fork. This corncake is also excellent warmed up.

MAPLE CORN MUFFINS

Sift together
> 1 cup flour
> ¾ cup yellow corn meal
> ½ teaspoon baking soda
> ½ teaspoon salt

Mix together to make a batter (this will not be smooth)
> ¾ cup buttermilk
> ¼ cup commercial sour cream
> ⅓ cup maple syrup

Stir in
> 2 lightly beaten eggs

Stir into batter
> The flour–corn meal mixture

Bake in a heated, greased, iron muffin tin in oven preheated to 450° for 15 minutes or until slightly browned.

APPLE CREAM MUFFINS

GRANDDAUGHTER JOANN BAILEY'S RECIPE

Sift together
> 1¾ cups all-purpose flour
> ½ cup sugar
> ¾ teaspoon cream of tartar
> ½ teaspoon baking soda
> ½ teaspoon salt

Beat together
> 1 large egg
> ¼ cup salad oil
> ½ cup heavy cream

Add and stir just enough to blend
> The flour mixture

Stir in gently
   1 cup peeled and diced apples

Fill greased muffin tins two-thirds full. Sprinkle lightly with
   Sugar and cinnamon

Bake in preheated oven at 425° for 15 minutes or until muffins are done. MAKES 12 MUFFINS.

ANNE'S BLUEBERRY MUFFINS

Sift together
   1¾ cups all-purpose flour
   ¾ teaspoon cream of tartar
   ½ teaspoon salt
   ½ teaspoon baking soda

Beat together
   1 large egg
   ½ cup sugar
   ¼ cup salad oil
   ½ cup milk

Stir together lightly
   The flour mixture
   The beaten ingredients

Stir in
   1 cup fresh blueberries, floured

Fill greased muffin tins two-thirds full. Bake in a preheated oven at 450° for 15 minutes or until muffins are done. MAKES 12 MUFFINS.

AUNT MARY'S CORN GEMS

AN OLD-FASHIONED "RECEIPT"

Sift together
  1 cup yellow corn meal
  1 cup flour
  ½ teaspoon salt
  1 teaspoon baking soda

Beat together
  6 mixing spoons* buttermilk
  6 mixing spoons commercial sour cream
  2 mixing spoons molasses

Stir in
  The flour–corn meal mixture

Pour into a sizzling-hot, greased, old-fashioned iron gem pan (or use a muffin pan). Bake in a preheated oven at 375° for 12 minutes or until done.

  * Although "mixing spoon" was used in original "receipt," a standard tablespoon can be used.

ESTHER'S OLD-FASHIONED GRAHAM GEMS

Sift together
  ½ cup all-purpose flour
  1 teaspoon baking soda
  ½ teaspoon salt

Add
  1 cup unsifted graham flour

Beat together
  1 large egg
  1 cup sugar

Add alternately, stirring until ingredients are just blended
  The flour mixture
  1 cup buttermilk, warmed to room temperature

Stir in
  6 tablespoons melted butter

Bake in greased, old-fashioned gem pans or use muffin pans in a pre-heated oven at 400° for 18 minutes.

Variation: We like these gems made with light rye flour fully as well as the whole-wheat kind.

Note: Esther serves Graham Gems hot for breakfast. They are also good warmed up.

BUTTERMILK BISCUITS

ADAPTED FROM GRANDMOTHER SMITH'S "RECEIPT"

Sift together
  2½ cups all-purpose flour
  1 teaspoon baking soda
  2 teaspoons cream of tartar
  ½ teaspoon salt

Mix in, using a pastry blender,
  ½ cup cold, heavy cream, well soured

Stir in lightly and quickly
  1 cup cold buttermilk

Turn the dough onto a floured board. Pat into a rectangle about ¾-inch thick. Cut with a small biscuit cutter. Place biscuits close together in a greased 9-inch square baking pan. Dot with cold butter. Bake in a preheated oven at 475° for 12-15 minutes or until biscuits are lightly browned. MAKES 16 BISCUITS.

Suggestion: To avoid last-minute rush, mix and shape the dough several hours before serving time. Refrigerate in the pan. Bake and serve piping hot. Wrap leftovers in aluminum foil and reheat for breakfast. Delicious when spread with lots of butter and homemade strawberry jam!

ALLYN'S BAKING POWDER BISCUITS

ADAPTED FROM MOTHER'S "RECEIPT"

Sift together
 4 cups all-purpose flour
 6 teaspoons baking powder
 ½ teaspoon salt

Stir in to make a soft dough
 1½ cups milk
 ¾ cup light cream

Roll or pat dough into a thick rectangle. Use a large biscuit cutter. Spread butter over bottom of a preheated 9 × 13-inch baking pan. Place biscuits close together. Dot each biscuit with a small piece of cold butter. Bake in a preheated oven at 450° for 15 minutes or until biscuits are lightly browned on top.

ANNE'S TEA BISCUITS

Sift together twice
 2 cups all-purpose flour
 3 teaspoons baking powder
 1 tablespoon sugar
 ½ teaspoon salt

Work in with a knife or pastry blender
 4 tablespoons cold butter

Add gradually, cutting in to make a dough,
 1 scant cup milk

Roll out the dough into a ½-inch thick rectangle. Spread with softened butter. Flour your hands and roll dough as for a jelly roll with butter inside. Roll out again into a rectangle and spread with softened butter. Roll up. Repeat this process of rolling out and spreading with butter a third time. Roll up jelly-roll fashion and then roll out into a rectangle.

Cut with a 2-inch biscuit cutter. Place bicuits on a greased cookie sheet spaced so they do not touch.

Bake in a preheated oven at 450° for 12 minutes, or until biscuits are lightly browned.

CREAM BISCUITS

Sift together
 2 *cups all-purpose flour*
 1 *teaspoon baking soda*
 2 *teaspoons cream of tartar*
 ¼ *teaspoon salt*

Work in with a pastry blender or knife
 1 *cup commercial sour cream*

Mix to make a soft dough

Cut into very small pieces
 ½ *stick cold butter*

Turn dough out onto a floured board. Roll into a rectangle. Beat with a rolling pin to a flat, thin sheet. Dot with one third of the butter pieces. Roll up the dough and repeat the beating process twice, dotting each time with butter. Roll into a thick rectangle and cut with a small biscuit cutter. Place biscuits close together in a greased 9-inch square baking pan. Prick tops with a silver fork. Bake in a preheated oven at 475° for 12 minutes or until biscuits are lightly browned.

Variation: Roll dough into an oblong, ¼-inch thick. Spread the center with strawberry jam. Roll up like a jelly roll. Cut off pieces ¾-inch thick. Set on a greased baking sheet, cut side down. Bake in a preheated oven at 450° for 15 minutes.

YOUNG HOMEMAKER'S QUICK MIX

GRANDDAUGHTER JEANNE EDDINGER'S RECIPE

Sift together
   4 cups all-purpose flour
   1 teaspoon salt
   4 teaspoons baking powder

Cut in, using a pastry blender,
   1 cup Crisco (or other vegetable shortening)

Mixture will be the consistency of coarse meal. Store tightly covered. MAKES 6 CUPS.

Jeanne's suggestion: Use Quick Mix for all baking-in-a-hurry—for plain or fancy drop biscuits, drop cookies, muffins, and waffles. (Recipes follow).

QUICK MIX MUFFINS

Stir together to make a dough
   2 cups Quick Mix (see above)
   1 tablespoon sugar
   1 egg, slightly beaten
   About ½ cup milk

Do not overmix. Dough will be somewhat lumpy. Spoon into greased muffin pans, filling two-thirds full. Bake in a preheated oven at 400° for 15 minutes or until done. MAKES 8 MUFFINS.

QUICK MIX WAFFLES

Beat together until light and foamy
   2 egg yolks
   2 tablespoons sugar
   1 cup milk

Mix in
  2 cups Quick Mix (see opposite)

Fold in
  2 egg whites, beaten until stiff

For baking waffles, follow manufacturer's directions which come with your waffle iron.
MAKES WAFFLES TO SERVE 2 TO 4.

VERNA'S BLUEBERRY COFFEE CAKE

Sift together twice
  2 cups all-purpose flour
  2 teaspoons baking powder
  ½ teaspoon salt

Cream together
  ¾ cup sugar
  ¼ cup softened butter

Beat in
  1 large egg

Stir in alternately
  The flour mixture
  ½ cup milk

Fold in
  1½ cups fresh blueberries, lightly floured

Spread in a greased 9-inch square baking tin.

Mix, using a pastry blender,
  ½ cup sugar
  ⅓ cup sifted flour
  ¼ cup cold butter
  ¼ teaspoon allspice
  ¼ teaspoon cinnamon

Spread crumbed mixture on cake. Sprinkle with
  ½ cup finely chopped pecan meats

Bake in a preheated oven at 350° for 45 minutes. Cut into squares and serve warm.

MAPLE COFFEE CAKE

Sift together
  2 cups all-purpose flour
  ½ teaspoon salt
  2 teaspoons baking powder
  ¼ teaspoon nutmeg
  ¼ teaspoon cinnamon

Cream thoroughly
  ½ cup soft maple sugar
  ½ cup softened butter

Add
  1 large egg, beaten

Stir in alternately
  The flour mixture
  ½ cup milk

Add
  ½ cup broken nutmeats

Spread dough in a greased 9-inch square baking pan. Make a topping: Rub together
  3 tablespoons soft maple sugar
  3 tablespoons flour
  ¼ cup cold butter, cut into bits
  ¼ teaspoon cinnamon
  ¼ teaspoon nutmeg

Spread this mixture in dabs over batter. Sprinkle on
  ¼ cup broken nutmeats

Bake in preheated oven at 350° for 45 minutes. Mark into squares at once. Serve warm.

BUTTERMILK PANCAKE MIX

On Sunday nights Mother often mixed up a batter and fried pancakes in her big iron spider. We called them griddlecakes or flapjacks, and we ate them doused with so much maple syrup we had to finish off with a spoon. Mother mixed her batter with sweet milk or sour, whichever she had on hand, and her griddle cakes were always good. Grammie Page used buttermilk because she churned every week. When we were visiting there in wintertime Grammie would sometimes heat up her old black griddle and fry us small round cakes for supper. We slathered on fresh-churned butter and poured the maple syrup from a pretty, pressed-glass pitcher. Grammie stood at the stove frying while we sat around the kitchen table eating and eating until not one of us could stuff in another tender little griddlecake. Then we would sit there in the warm kitchen, content—too sleepy and sluggish to start upstairs to bed until Grampa lit a lamp and led the way up the "ell chamber" stairs. Unfortunately none of us ever wrote down directions for mixing griddlecake batter (of course Mother and Grammie Page didn't use a "receipt" for anything so simple!). Our pancakes were sometimes tender and good but more often they were tough as shoe leather until we acquired and adapted a recipe used by the chef at a famous Swedish-American restaurant. This pancake mix, now used often in our family kitchens, will never fail to produce delicious tender griddlecakes—little or big, whichever your family prefers.

Sift together
>   *4 cups all-purpose flour*
>   *2 tablespoons baking powder*
>   *1 teaspoon salt*

Mix in a large bowl
>   *1 quart buttermilk (room temperature)*
>   *2 tablespoons sugar*
>   *2 teaspoons baking soda*

Stir into the buttermilk
>   *The flour mixture*
>   *¼ cup vegetable oil*
>   *½ package dry yeast*

Add and mix well
   6 eggs, beaten until light
   1½ cups light cream

Store the mixture in the refrigerator until a half hour before pancakes are to be cooked. MAKES 10 CUPS, ENOUGH TO SERVE 8 TO 12, DEPENDING ON SIZE OF APPETITES.

Note: This pancake mix keeps well for several days if refrigerated.

Suggestion: Serve Buttermilk Pancakes and maple syrup with baked sausages, bacon, or ham as a luncheon dish.

BUCKWHEAT PANCAKES

ADAPTED FROM AN 1897 "RECEIPT"

Place in a large deep bowl
   2 cups buttermilk

Stir in
   1 cup buckwheat flour (unsifted)
   1 cup sifted all-purpose flour

Add
   1 tablespoon sugar
   2 tablespoons melted butter

Sprinkle over the mixture
   ½ package dry yeast

Stir in
   2 large eggs, beaten until light

Cover bowl with a towel and let stand at room temperature for several hours or leave overnight in a cool place if you will serve for breakfast.

Stir in
   1 teaspoon baking soda
   ¼ cup heavy cream (optional)

Note: Buttermilk and eggs should be at room temperature.

Suggestion: Serve Buckwheat Pancakes with warm maple syrup accompanied by country sausage.

SWEDISH PANCAKES WITH MAPLE SYRUP

FROM THE KITCHEN OF LOIS NELSON

The mothers of our Swedish-American relatives and friends very often served the special dishes of their home country in combination with native American foods. We think real Swedish pancakes united with pure maple syrup are especially delightful.

෴

Put in a bowl
  3 large eggs, beaten until light

Add and continue to beat, using an electric mixer or rotary beater,
  ½ teaspoon salt
  3 tablespoons sugar

Add alternately, a little at a time, beating after each addition until the mixture is very smooth (about 10 minutes beating time),
  1 cup all-purpose flour
  3 cups milk

Heat in an electric skillet or heavy frying pan
  About ½ tablespoon vegetable shortening

Tilt the pan to spread the hot shortening. Start cooking pancakes with electric skillet temperature at 380°. Test heat of other frying pan as for any pancakes.

Pour into the center of the skillet
⅓ cup of batter

Cook until the edges of the pancakes turn brown and the center is not runny. Slip a spatula under edges of the pancake to loosen, turn and brown (2-3 minutes on each side). Fold pancake twice, or roll. Place on a platter in a warming oven. Continue to cook until all the batter is used. Serve with whipped butter and warm maple syrup. SERVES 4 OR MORE.

Note: To serve Swedish pancakes for a crowd, double or treble the recipe and use two electric skillets.

FRENCH TOAST WITH MAPLE SYRUP

GRANDDAUGHTER SUSAN WOOLDRIDGE'S RECIPE

Use
16 slices soft white bread
1 pint maple syrup, warmed

Beat together in an electric blender
8 large eggs
¼ cup light cream or milk
½ teaspoon sugar
1 grind of pepper from a mill

Grease very lightly and heat a large frying pan. Pan should be hot enough so a drop of water sizzles. Pour about one fourth of the egg mixture at a time into a pie plate or pan with raised edges. Dip slices of bread into the egg mixture. Turn to coat. (Do not allow bread to soak through.) Brown the dipped bread on one side. Turn. Sprinkle generously with

Cinnamon

Brown the other side. Turn and transfer to a warm platter, again sprinkling with cinnamon. Continue to cook and keep the French Toast warm until all the egg mixture and bread slices have been used. SERVES 4 TO 6, DEPENDING ON SIZE OF APPETITES.

Suggestion: Susan serves her French Toast with whipped butter and Canadian bacon slices.

❊ 21 ❊

Fish and Seafood

Freshwater and saltwater fish, chowders

and sauces, oysters, and shellfish

LAKE TROUT

On Lake Winnipesaukee and the smaller lakes of New Hampshire, fishing is a popular sport both summer and winter. These lakes—well stocked with cusk, bass, shad, smelt, salmon, and lake trout—attract many sportsmen from distant cities as well as the local fishermen. Of course these waters are no longer important as a general source of food supply, but the fish caught there and in the streams and ponds are just as good eating as any taken in the olden days. Lake trout, always very much prized by our family, is good served in a variety of ways. We were especially fond of lake trout baked and stuffed the way Mother used to cook it. Uncle Otis Smith prefers his cut into steaks, rolled in flour and pan-fried. Small trout, weighing a pound or so, are good for broiling. These lake fish must be properly prepared before cooking or the finished product will be too oily—of such strong flavor it may be unappetizing. Experienced fishermen always remove the oil glands (see directions below) when dressing the trout. The fish may be cooked whole or skinned and filleted, as preferred.

❦

The following method of dressing and cooking lake trout comes from a fisherman who has been catching Lake Winnipesaukee trout ever since he was a small boy more than fifty years ago.

Dress fish when freshly caught. Holding fish by gills pour over it a stream of hot water. Keep rotating fish and continue the even hot water bath until beads of oil appear on skin. With a thin-bladed, sharp knife, cut through skin around fish just below head and down the back to tail. Peel off skin in two sections (as you would peel a peach). Remove fins and carefully cut out dark oily strip of flesh (oil glands) running along backbone. Cut off head. Slit belly and remove viscera. Fillet fish. Wash. Dip in egg and roll in crumbs. Brown in butter and oven-fry until fish flakes.

A 4-5 POUND TROUT MAKES 4 SERVINGS.

FRIED SMELT

As soon as the water is clear of ice in early spring, lake smelt travel up the brooks to spawn. At that time these small fish are very good eating and may be taken with dip nets; five pounds per fisherman is the limit now set by New Hampshire law.

The length of time a smelt-run will last and the hour when it will begin in some one of the numerous brooks emptying into the lakes are completely unpredictable. Perhaps a few dozen smelt may appear and that will be all for a day or for several days, or a big run may start in the small hours of the morning. When that happens, the electric torches of patient watchers pick out a shadowy mass of swiftly moving smelt, crowding each other in the cold, dark water. As if by magic, excitement spreads and shortly the bank becomes so crowded with eager fishermen they elbow each other for dipping space. In no time at all a five-pound pailful of the lively little fish can be scooped out of the water with a net. Night and day during the season, conservation officers are on the watch for those greedy souls who attempt to make off with more smelt than they are allowed.

There are several schools of thought on the proper method of cleaning and frying smelt. We consulted Forrest, who has had long experience. Forrest cleans five pounds of smelt in less than an hour, pan-fries them to perfection. Following are his directions:

Plan to cook smelt as soon as possible after they are caught. Keep them in ice water until dressed. Using a long, thin-bladed, sharp knife, make a slit from the head down the belly. Make one quick scrape with the knife to remove viscera. In a frying pan heat fresh vegetable oil to 475°. Oil should be 1 inch deep. Wash the cleaned smelt under cold running water. Drain. Roll in a mixture of 2 parts flour to 1 part corn meal. Cook in small quantities. Do not allow smelt to touch in the hot oil. Fry quickly until crisp and slightly browned.
You will need 5 pounds of smelt to feed 6 people.

FISH CAKES

OLD-FASHIONED NEW HAMPSHIRE STYLE

We never agreed with "Down Country" people who thought fish cakes must always be eaten with baked beans. In New Hampshire we generally served this dish as a main course, along with ketchup and piccalilli, mustard pickles, or salad greens in season.

Soak overnight in cold water to cover
   1 pound salt codfish

Drain. Cover with cold water again and cook over low heat for 60 minutes. Drain. Cover again with cold water and cook for 60 minutes. Drain well and cool. Set aside.

Boil until just barely soft but not falling apart
   8 medium potatoes, peeled

Prepare
   4 tablespoons very thick white sauce

Add
   Salt and pepper to taste

Grind, using medium blade of food chopper,
   The codfish
   The cooled potatoes

Mix with
   The white sauce

Form into flat cakes. Dip into
   2 small eggs, beaten

Roll in
   Seasoned cracker meal

Pan-fry cakes in a small amount of hot fat or oil until crusty on one side. Turn and brown other side until crusty. SERVES 6 TO 8.

ELLEN'S CREAMED SALT CODFISH

Cover with cold water and let soak overnight
  ½ pound salt codfish

Drain codfish and cut into bite-sized cubes.

Scald in a double boiler
  2 cups milk

Stir into milk
  4 tablespoons flour mixed with
  ½ cup cold water

Cook, stirring constantly until sauce is thick and smooth. Add
  1 egg, slightly beaten

Add codfish pieces and heat thoroughly. Serve over toast or with new potatoes boiled in their jackets. Serves 2 to 4.

Note: Salt codfish is often sold in unwrapped pieces. Ellen says this is satisfactory, but she prefers the codfish packed in wooden boxes, the old New England type, when it is available.

HALIBUT LOAF

FROM A NEW ENGLAND KITCHEN

Grind, using medium blade of food chopper,
  1½ pounds halibut fillets

Crumb the inside and discard brown crust of
  ½ loaf of soft white bread

Mix in a saucepan
  The bread crumbs
  1½ cups light cream

Cook over low heat, stirring until the mixture resembles a smooth, thick paste.

Add
> *The ground fish*
> *2 tablespoons grated onion*
> *1 teaspoon salt*
> *½ teaspoon white pepper*

Fold in
> *3 egg whites, beaten until stiff*

Put the mixture into a bread pan lined with brown paper. Set the pan into a second pan containing hot water. Bake in a preheated oven at 350° for 60 minutes. SERVES 4 TO 6.

Suggestion: Serve with a cream sauce, plain or with lobster or shrimp bits added.

ANNE'S BAKED FRESH SALMON

Place in a shallow baking pan
> *A thick slice (3 pounds or more) boned fresh salmon*

Season with
> *2 tablespoons salt*
> *1 teaspoon pepper*
> *Sprinkling of fresh lemon juice*

Spoon over the fish
> *1 cup commercial sour cream*

Sprinkle on
> *1 teaspoon grated onion*

Bake in a preheated oven at 375° for 45 minutes or until fish is tender and sour cream topping is lightly browned. SERVES 4.

FISH SOUFFLÉ
FROM THE KITCHEN OF GRETA HANSON

Scald
  2 cups milk

Melt in a double boiler
  2 tablespoons butter

Add and stir until smooth
  3 tablespoons flour
  ½ teaspoon salt
  ½ teaspoon white pepper
  ⅛ teaspoon nutmeg

Add a little at a time, stirring constantly,
  The hot milk

Cook over low heat, stirring until sauce is smooth. Remove from heat.

Stir in
  3 egg yolks slightly beaten

Return to heat and cook for 2 minutes, stirring.

Mix in gently
  2 cups cooked, flaked halibut

Fold in
  3 egg whites beaten until stiff

Spoon mixture into a buttered 2-quart soufflé dish or casserole.

Cover with
  ½ cup soft bread crumbs

Dot with
  Cold butter

Bake in a preheated oven at 350° for 30 minutes. SERVES 6.

Note: Other non-oily fish may be substituted for halibut.

OVEN-FRIED BLUEFISH FILLETS

Split and bone
 2 fresh-caught bluefish (1½-2 pounds each)

Brown in a frying pan
 4 tablespoons butter

Spread on a sheet of aluminum foil
 1 cup cracker meal mixed with
 ½ teaspoon salt
 ¼ teaspoon freshly ground pepper

Beat well and pour into a shallow dish
 1 large egg

Wash and dry fillets with a paper towel. Dip into beaten egg. Roll in seasoned cracker meal, coating well. Brown, skin side down in the hot butter. Turn and brown other side. Place fillets skin side down in a baking pan.

Pour over the fish
 Remaining browned butter

Sprinkle on
 1 tablespoon dry white wine

Bake in preheated oven at 375° for 35 minutes. Slide fillets onto a heated platter. Garnish with parsley and lemon wedges. SERVES 4.

FILLETS OF SEA BASS WITH SHRIMP STUFFING

Use
A fresh-caught 8-10-pound sea bass

Fillet the fish and cut into 6 or 8 serving pieces. Place in a shallow baking pan, skin side down.

Tuck under each fillet
  A thin slice of salt pork

Prepare in an electric blender
  2 cups soft bread crumbs

Mix in a bowl
  The bread crumbs
  1½ cups fresh shrimp, cooked and cut into pieces
  ½ cup fresh mushroom pieces, sautéed
  1 teaspoon salt
  ½ teaspoon white pepper
  4 tablespoons melted butter
  2 egg yolks, beaten
  ½ cup dry white wine

Spread stuffing on top of fish fillets, dividing it evenly. Bake in preheated oven at 375° for 30 minutes. Remove to a hot serving platter. Garnish with parsley and lemon wedges. SERVES 6 TO 8.

Note: The best way to procure fresh sea bass is to have a husband who is an enthusiastic surf fisherman, like mine; otherwise buy the bass fillets, or if this is impossible, halibut will make a very good substitute.

FISH FILLETS WITH CRABMEAT STUFFING

Use
  3-4 pounds lean fish fillets

Wash and dry fish with a paper towel. Cut into 6 servings.

Pick over and flake
  ½ pound fresh claw crabmeat

Crumb in an electric blender
  2 slices soft white bread

Heat in a saucepan
  2 tablespoons butter
  1 teaspoon paprika
  1 teaspoon salt
  ½ teaspoon pepper

Add and heat
  The crabmeat

Combine
  The bread crumbs
  1 beaten egg
  1 tablespoon sherry
  The crabmeat mixture

Place the fish fillets, skin side down, in a shallow baking pan lined with aluminum foil.

Tuck under each fillet
  A very thin slice of salt pork

Top each serving with a mound of stuffing. Bake in a preheated oven at 400° for 35 minutes. Serves 6.

FISH CHOWDER

A fish chowder such as we always used to make in New Hampshire began with a whole fresh fish which had to be cleaned and skinned, head and tail cut off, and the meat separated from the backbone. The head, tail, and broken bones were made into stock. Then the preparation of the chowder began. With apologies to old-fashioned cooks who are purists, we offer this simplified recipe which eliminates much of the work but none of the ingredients that make a real New England fish chowder.

Put in a Dutch oven or heavy kettle
  A 1½-inch cube of fat salt pork, diced

Cook and stir over low heat until pork bits are lightly browned.

Add
  1 onion, diced

Cook over very low heat until onion pieces are soft.

Add
  4 or 5 potatoes, peeled and diced
  1½ teaspoons salt
  1 large bay leaf, broken
  Cold water to cover

Cook for 20 minutes or until potatoes are soft. Discard bay leaf.

Add
  1-1½ pounds haddock fillets, cut in pieces

Add a small amount of water if needed. Cook over low heat for 10 minutes.

Heat
  1 cup milk
  1 cup cream

Combine hot milk-cream mixture with chowder. Heat but do not allow to boil. Add
  1 teaspoon white pepper
  2 tablespoons dry white wine (optional)

Serve over "common" crackers which have been split and toasted. SERVES 6.

Note: Either fresh or frozen fish fillets may be used. Saltines, oysterettes or other crackers may be used if the old-fashioned "common" crackers are not available.

ELLEN'S CLAM CHOWDER

Put in a Dutch oven or heavy saucepan
  A 1½-inch cube of fat salt pork, diced

Cook and stir over low heat until pork is crisp and brown.

Add
  4 onions, diced
  6 large potatoes, diced
  2 teaspoons salt
  1 bay leaf
  Cold water to cover

Bring to a boil. Simmer until vegetables are soft and well blended. The water should be nearly all absorbed. Discard bay leaf.

Add
  5 8-ounce cans minced clams and juice
  1 cup light cream or milk

Heat just to the boiling point. Add
  One dash of Tabasco

Ladle into heated bowls. Serve with "common" crackers and dill pickle strips. Serves 8.

Note: Ellen uses fresh-steamed clams when available. She says clam chowder is best when made a day beforehand and reheated.

FRESH SHRIMP BISQUE

FROM THE KITCHEN OF MARTHA BOHGREN

Place in a kettle
  2 pounds fresh shrimp
  ½ lemon
  Cold water to cover

Bring to a full rolling boil. Turn off heat and leave shrimp to cool in liquid. Drain and reserve liquid. Shell and devein shrimp and set aside. Crush shells with a wooden mallet or rolling pin to loosen meat particles and release flavors.

Combine in a kettle
   The reserved liquid
   The crushed shells
   1 small onion
   8 peppercorns, crushed
   1 teaspoon salt
   1 whole clove
   1 bay leaf
   Several sprigs parsley
   4 stalks celery with leaves

Bring to a boil and simmer for 20 minutes to make a broth.
Strain through cheesecloth or a very fine wire strainer. Reheat.

Melt in a double boiler
   4 tablespoons butter

Stir in
   6 tablespoons flour
   1 teaspoon paprika

Add a little at a time, stirring constantly,
   The hot broth (there should be about 4 cups)
   1 cup light cream, heated
   2 tablespoons sherry
   The shrimp, ground or chopped very fine

Correct seasoning to taste. Serve with oyster crackers or breadsticks.
SERVES 4 GENEROUSLY.

RICH OYSTER STEW

NEW HAMPSHIRE STYLE

Heat in a double boiler
  3 cups milk
  1 cup light cream

Melt in a heavy frying pan
  1 tablespoon butter

Add
  2 pints medium oysters with juice

Heat slowly until the oyster edges start to curl. Shake the pan or stir oysters gently. Do not overcook. Add to the hot milk
  The oysters and juice
  1 tablespoon butter
  Salt and pepper to taste
  1 tablespoon sherry wine

Serve with oyster crackers, adding 1 cup crackers to hot stew before serving. SERVES 4 AS A MAIN COURSE.

PAN-FRIED OYSTERS

Use
  32 large, fresh, raw oysters

Drain off liquor and pat oysters dry with a paper towel.

Mix and spread on a sheet of aluminum foil
  1½ cups "common" cracker crumbs
  ½ teaspoon salt
  ½ teaspoon white pepper
  ⅛ teaspoon celery salt (optional)

Beat slightly
  1 large egg

Melt in an electric skillet or heavy frying pan
  4 tablespoons butter

Roll oysters in the cracker crumbs. Dip in the beaten egg and roll again in crumbs. Fry in the hot butter until browned on one side. Turn and brown other side. Serve with lemon wedges or with cranberry sauce, as Mother used to do. SERVES 4 GENEROUSLY.

SCALLOPED OYSTERS

Clean, reserving all of the liquor,
  1½ pints fresh, medium-sized oysters

Crush with a rolling pin
  Unsalted crackers to make
  3 cups medium-coarse crumbs

Cut into bits
  4 tablespoons cold butter

Butter a large shallow oven-to-table casserole.

Spread over the bottom
  1 cup cracker crumbs

Cover with
  One half of the oysters

Add
  One half of the liquid
  Salt and pepper as desired
  1 teaspoon sherry

Dot with
  About one third of the butter pieces

Make a second layer, using
  The remaining oysters and liquid

1 cup crumbs
Seasoning as before

Cover with the
Remaining crumbs and butter pieces

Bake in a preheated oven at 450° for 25 minutes. SERVES 4 TO 6.

Note: The natural oyster liquid seems to bring out the flavor of the oysters hidden in a crisp, buttery blanket of crumbs.

CORN-OYSTER CASSEROLE

FROM THE KITCHEN OF GRACE MUNGER

Mix together
    2 cups cream-style canned corn
    1 cup medium-coarse cracker crumbs
    1 egg, beaten
    ½ cup milk
    ¼ cup melted butter (½ stick)
    1 teaspoon salt
    1 teaspoon sugar
    ⅛ teaspoon pepper
    1 pint small fresh oysters
    2 tablespoons finely chopped green pepper

Pour into a buttered casserole. Bake in a preheated oven at 375° for 30 minutes or until set. SERVES 4 TO 6.

LITTLE SHRIMPBURGERS

Put through food chopper, using medium blade,
    2 pounds raw shrimp, shelled and deveined

Mix thoroughly
  The ground shrimp
  1 cup soft bread crumbs
  1 teaspoon white pepper
  1 teaspoon salt
  1 tablespoon scraped onion

Form into 18 small patties. Sauté in hot butter or vegetable oil until pink and lightly browned (about 5 minutes on each side). Serve with Hot Seafood Sauce (*see below*).
SERVES 6.

HOT SEAFOOD SAUCE

Combine in a large saucepan
  1 large can tomato sauce (approximately 2 cups)
  2 cups tomato juice
  ½ cup lemon juice
  8 whole cloves
  1 large onion
  2 stalks celery with leaves
  2 bay leaves, broken
  1 teaspoon dried parsley (or sprigs fresh parsley)
  1 teaspoon dry mustard
  1 teaspoon salt
  1 tablespoon brown sugar
  1 small, dried, hot red pepper

Simmer mixture, stirring occasionally, for 60 minutes.

Remove from heat. Add
  2 tablespoons horseradish

Strain sauce. Reheat.

Melt in a double boiler
  2 tablespoons butter

Stir in
> *1 tablespoon flour*

Add the hot sauce a little at a time. Continue to cook and stir for ten minutes. Serve hot with oysters, shrimp, or clams, any style. MAKES 2½ CUPS.

Note: Hot Seafood Sauce can be refrigerated and reheated as needed.

BAKED CRAB-STUFFED SHRIMP

Shell and devein, leaving tails on,
> *24 fresh-caught jumbo shrimp*

Split lengthwise along the deveined edge but not far enough to separate halves.

Flake
> *1 cup fresh claw crabmeat*

Heat in a saucepan
> *2 tablespoons butter*
> *1 teaspoon paprika*
> *½ teaspoon salt*

Add and mix
> *The crabmeat*
> *1 cup soft bread crumbs*
> *4 tablespoons mayonnaise*
> *2 tablespoons sherry*

Lay the shrimp flat in a baking pan with tails fanned out. Place a mound of crabmeat filling on each shrimp. Bake in a preheated oven at 425° for 20 minutes. SERVES 4.

SHRIMP-CRABMEAT CASSEROLE

Shell, devein, and cut up
    2½ cups fresh, cooked shrimp

Pick over and flake
    1½ cups fresh claw crabmeat

Combine in a casserole.

Prepare a sauce:

Melt in a double boiler
    3 tablespoons butter

Mix in
    3 tablespoons flour
    1 teaspoon salt
    ½ teaspoon pepper

Heat and add a little at a time, stirring until smooth,
    1 cup light cream
    2 cups milk

Cook over low heat for 15 minutes, stirring occasionally.

Add
    2 tablespoons sherry

Pour sauce over the shrimp-crabmeat casserole.

Cover with
    Fine bread crumbs

Dot with
    Cold butter

Heat in a preheated oven at 425° until bubbling hot and browned on top. SERVES 6.

CRAB BAKE

FROM THE KITCHEN OF MERRY LOU PESSAS

Pick over and flake coarsely
  1 pound fresh claw crabmeat

Heat in a frying pan
  2 tablespoons butter

Sauté in the hot butter
  1 onion, sliced

Wipe with a damp towel and chop fine
  8 fresh mushrooms, caps and stems

Discard onion pieces. Add chopped mushrooms. Cook and shake over low heat until mushrooms are tender. Add
  The crabmeat
  1 teaspoon salt
  ½ teaspoon pepper

Cook until crabmeat is heated. Stir gently in order not to break up crabmeat. Remove from heat.

Mix with
  4 tablespoons mayonnaise

Spoon mixture into cleaned crab shells or ramekins.

Garnish each filled shell or ramekin with
  2 thin pimento strips, crossed

Bake in preheated oven at 375° for 15 minutes or until crabmeat is hot and slightly browned. SERVES 6 TO 8.

ANNE'S CRAB-OYSTER LOAF

Cut the top from
  A small loaf French-style bread

Reserve top. Scoop out inside, leaving a shell ½-inch thick. Break the removed bread pieces into bite size.

Pick over and flake
  ½ pound fresh claw crabmeat

Heat in a saucepan
  ½ cup butter

Add and sauté
  The crabmeat

Remove crabmeat and reserve butter.

Place in a small saucepan
  ½ pint medium oysters with juice

Cook over low heat until edges are curled.

Mix in a bowl
  The bread pieces
  The oysters, chopped
  Oyster liquid
  The crabmeat
  ½ teaspoon ground seafood seasoning
  1 teaspoon salt
  Half of reserved butter

Pile mixture lightly into bread shell. Replace top. Brush all over with remaining butter (add more if needed). Wrap bread in aluminum foil. Bake in preheated oven at 350° until hot and crisp. SERVES 4.

Suggestion: Serve as a luncheon dish accompanied by a crisp green salad.

Note: If commercial seafood seasoning is not available substitute ½ teaspoon white pepper.

LOBSTER NEWBURG

BOSTON STYLE

Melt in a chafing dish or double boiler
  2 tablespoons butter

Add
  2 cups cooked, fresh lobster pieces

Cook for 3 minutes, stirring constantly.

Add
  A *pinch of nutmeg*
  1 teaspoon salt
  ½ teaspoon pepper

Beat together and stir in
  2 egg yolks
  1 cup whipping cream

Add
  1 tablespoon sherry

Cook and stir until mixture is thickened. Serve at once on toast points or tiny hot biscuits. SERVES 4.

Note: Substitute frozen or canned lobster if necessary.

Variation: Use fresh or canned shrimp instead of lobster.

❧ 22 ❧

Meat and Poultry

*Some New England country dishes, beef
and pork, lamb, chicken, turkey
and stuffings*

CORNED BEEF

TO CORN BEEF AT HOME

Use a 4- or 5-pound piece of choice lean brisket. Prepare a salt brine heavy enough to float a potato. (Use 4 quarts of water and 3 pints or more of pure salt [not iodized].) Submerge meat completely in the cold brine. Turn several times during the corning process. Some consider 48 hours sufficient time for corning. Others leave meat in brine as long as a week.

TO BOIL CORNED BEEF

Wash under cold running water or if meat seems very salty, soak for half an hour in cold water. Place meat in a heavy saucepan or Dutch oven. Cover with cold water. Bring slowly to the boiling point and cook for a few minutes. Remove scum. Cover and simmer until tender (3-4 hours). Drain and serve hot, or if meat is to be pressed let stand in cooking water until cool. Place in a dish. Cover with a cloth and put a weight on top. Serve cold, sliced.

Note: Old-fashioned New Englanders do not like the flavor and texture of red beef (that which has been corned using saltpeter in the brine).

BOILED DINNER

OLD-TIME NEW HAMPSHIRE STYLE

The boiled dinners we Smiths ate were prepared the same and cooked nearly as long as in the days of our great-great-grandmothers, when cooking was done in a kettle hung in the fireplace. Although Mother herself didn't approve of overcooking vegetables, she never varied the time-honored ritual of the boiled dinner because any innovations would have ruined the meal for Father. She put the corned beef and salt pork (about a half a pound of pork to a six-pound piece of beef) into her largest kettle and got it to boiling right after breakfast. Next into the kettle went a large head of cabbage cut into quarters. (Two hours was thought none too long for the proper cooking of boiled cabbage.) At eleven o'clock or thereabouts a dozen or more whole, peeled potatoes and as many scraped carrots were added. The same quantity of beets, scrubbed but not peeled, was set to cooking in a saucepan. When it was time to eat at noon, the meat was so tender it fell to pieces at the touch of a knife. The carrots, potatoes, and the cabbage (pretty well disintegrated) were skimmed from the hot broth and dished up together. The skins were slipped from the beets and they were added to the platter. It was (in the opinion of Father and his contemporaries) a very satisfactory medley of odors and tastes needing only a dash or two of strong cider vinegar to make it perfection.

Note: In some sections of New England the salt pork was omitted or different vegetables might be included, but, as far as New Hampshire people were concerned, only the ingredients and cooking method given here would produce an honest-to-goodness boiled dinner.

RED FLANNEL HASH

Housewives in our town always used to serve corned beef hash with vegetables, the next day after having a boiled dinner. Whatever was left over was chopped fine and mixed up to make Red Flannel Hash, a meal just as good as the day before's—better, some thought. Once a bad thunderstorm came up just as a neighbor woman started to warm up some Red Flannel Hash in her iron frying pan. A bolt of lightning came down the kitchen chimney, rattled off the stove covers and ripped around the room. It didn't set anything afire, but it flattened the frying pan, took every bit of that hash and pasted it all over the kitchen ceiling. Mother pitied the poor woman, having all that mess to clean. Father said it was a worse pity to waste all that good Red Flannel Hash.

Mother never measured amounts for the ingredients of her hash, just put together all that was left. The amounts given here are approximate. Do not skimp on the amount of corned beef. Chop all ingredients separately.

Mix in a large bowl
2 cups chopped cooked corned beef
3 or 4 cups chopped boiled potatoes
2 cups chopped cooked beets
2 cups chopped cooked carrots
Salt and pepper to taste

Heat in a heavy iron frying pan
4 tablespoons butter
1 medium onion, sliced

Sauté onion slices until yellow; remove and discard. Turn hash into the hot pan. Heat slowly. Keep loosening around the edges with a spatula to prevent burning. If the hash seems dry, add a little cream. When a good brown crust is formed, turn the hash out onto a hot serving dish. Serve accompanied by hot biscuits or johnnycake. Set on the chili sauce and the shaker of cayenne pepper.
SERVES 6 GENEROUSLY.

HOG'S HEAD CHEESE

These directions for making Hog's Head Cheese in the old-fashioned New Hampshire way have been furnished from memory by my brother-in-law, John F. Weeks, Sr.

❧

Wash and scrub a hog's head. Using a meat saw cut head into sections. Place meat in a large kettle (copper or iron kettles were formerly used). Cover with cold water. Add seasonings (salt, pepper, and a little sage, if desired). Bring to a boil and cook slowly for about three hours or until meat is ready to fall from bones. Remove meat from liquid and let cool until it can be handled. Pick over, discarding all pieces of gristle, fat, and skin. Pack meat pieces into loaf tins or a large deep dish. Cover with cheesecloth and lay a weight on top. Leave for 24 hours or more. Slice in the dish. Arrange slices on a serving dish. Quantity depends on size of hog's head.

MILK GRAVY

AS MADE BY ELLEN

This very old-fashioned dish, one of Father's favorites, was often served when fresh meat was scarce.

❧

Cut into small pieces
  A 1½-inch cube of salt pork

Heat in a heavy iron spider. Fry the salt pork bits until crisp.

Stir into the hot fat (do not remove salt pork pieces)
  2 tablespoons flour

Continue to stir until mixture is well blended. Add very slowly, stirring constantly
  1 cup heated milk

Cook over low heat, stirring until the gravy is thick and smooth. Serve over toasted bread or with hot boiled potatoes (the way Father ate it). SERVES 2 TO 4.

BEEF STEW WITH DUMPLINGS

When Mother made beef stew, she stirred up some dumplings and cooked them right on top of the boiling stew—with the cover off, of course. Her stews were rich and hearty, and her dumplings were always just right—not heavy but with enough substance to stick to a man's ribs through a cold afternoon in the woodlot. Mother's beef stew, embellished with a little wine and a bit of seasoning, makes a popular buffet supper dish.

❧

Wipe with a paper towel and trim fat off
   A 5-pound piece of beef chuck

Fry out in a heavy kettle
   The fat pieces

Sear the beef in the hot fat.

Add
   A beef soupbone or veal knuckle
   1 large onion
   Several celery stalks with leaves
   2 large carrots, washed but not scraped
   1 small dried red pepper
   2 teaspoons salt
   6 whole peppercorns
   4 whole allspice
   Cold water to cover

Cook over low heat until vegetables are soft and meat will fall from the bones. Skim out meat and vegetables. Strain hot broth (there should be about a quart) and set aside. Discard cooked vegetables, bones, fat and gristle. Cut meat into small chunks. Store meat and broth in refrigerator overnight.

When you are ready to complete the stew, skim the broth and discard most of the solidified fat.

Place in a large heavy kettle
   The broth
   2 cups diced carrots
   1 medium onion, sliced thin
   2 cups diced celery
   4 cups potatoes, sliced thin
   1 teaspoon salt
   4 cups cold water

Heat and simmer until vegetables are soft.

Add and heat to the boiling point
   The meat pieces
   1 cup Burgundy wine (or any red wine)

Stir in and simmer until blended
¼ cup flour mixed to a paste with
Cold water

SERVES 10 TO 12.

Suggestion: For a real old-fashioned touch, serve homemade dumplings.

VERNA'S DUMPLINGS
MADE LIKE MOTHER'S

Sift together
2 cups all-purpose flour
4 teaspoons baking powder
½ teaspoon salt

Stir together to make a soft dough
The flour mixture
½ cup milk (about)

Roll out on a floured board. Shape with a small biscuit cutter. Dip cutter into flour to keep edges of dumplings lightly dusted. Keep the stew at a gentle boil. Drop dumplings into hot liquid. (Do not allow them to touch.) Cook about 10 minutes. Turn and cook until done.

Note: Verna advises beginning cooks to leave dumplings uncovered for 10 minutes, then cover (without turning) and continue to cook for 10 minutes.

ROAST BEEF WITH BURGUNDY WINE

Use either a whole tenderloin or an eye of round weighing 5-6 pounds. Roll the meat in seasoned flour. Lard by laying thin strips of salt pork in the roasting pan and over the top of the meat.

Pour over meat
½ cup Burgundy wine

Roast in an open pan in preheated oven at 450° for 20 minutes. Turn meat and replace pork strips. Add
½ cup Burgundy wine

Roast 20 minutes more. Meat will be well browned on the outside, bright pink all the way through. Serve cold, sliced very thin, accompanied by horseradish sauce. SERVES 12.

BEEF ROLL WITH MUSHROOM GRAVY

Mix well
2 pounds top round beef, double ground
1 teaspoon salt
1 teaspoon pepper
1 teaspoon liquid from bottled horseradish sauce
2 teaspoons scraped onion
Pinch of allspice

Shape into a thick 8-inch cylinder.

Roll in
Seasoned cracker meal

Put on a rack in a baking pan.

Lay over the top
6 very thin slices salt pork

Bake in a preheated oven at 350° for 60 minutes.

MUSHROOM GRAVY

Wipe with a damp paper towel and slice
12 or more fresh mushrooms (keep stems and caps separated)

Combine in a saucepan and bring to a boil
2 cups brown beef stock
The mushroom stems
1 medium onion

Strain and discard mushroom pieces and onion.

Add
   ¼ cup heavy cream

Reheat and keep hot.

Sauté in a heavy saucepan or frying pan
   The sliced mushrooms caps in
   3 tablespoons butter

Remove and reserve mushroom caps.

Stir into the melted butter
   3 tablespoons flour

Add a little at a time, stirring constantly
   The hot liquid

Cook and stir until gravy is smooth.

Add
   The reserved mushrooms
   1 teaspoon brandy
   Pinch of nutmeg

Place the hot meat on a heated platter. Cover with the gravy. Decorate with sprigs of fresh parsley. SERVES 6.

ANNE'S BEEF CASSEROLE

Cut into 1½-inch cubes, discarding gristle and fat
   3 pounds beef (round steak)

Cook in vegetable oil until tender and golden
   4 small onions, cut medium-fine
   2 cups diced celery

Toss in a paper bag
> *The beef cubes*
> *⅓ cup flour*
> *1 teaspoon salt*
> *½ teaspoon pepper*
> *1 teaspoon dried herbs for seasoning beef**

Combine in mixed layers in a large oven-to-table casserole
> *The beef cubes*
> *10 small new potatoes, peeled*
> *12 large fresh mushrooms halved*
> *1 cup fresh green beans (optional)*
> *The partially cooked celery-onion pieces*

Pour on
> *1 cup hot beef stock*
> *1 cup rosé wine*

Bake in a preheated oven at 350° for 2½ hours, tightly covered.
SERVES 4 GENEROUSLY.

* Dried herbs for seasoning beef are sold under the name Bouquet Garni For Beef. If this commercially prepared mixture is not available, substitute the same amount of a combination of dried herbs such as savory, basil, thyme, oregano, and sage.

LITTLE MEAT LOAVES IN TOMATO SAUCE

GRANDDAUGHTER JEANNE EDDINGER'S RECIPE

Prepare tomato sauce:

Melt in a heavy saucepan
> *2 tablespoons butter*

Add
> *3 tablespoons minced onion*
> *3 tablespoons minced green, sweet peppers*
> *3 tablespoons finely chopped celery*

Cook over low heat, stirring occasionally until vegetables are soft. Add and simmer while meat loaves are baking
>A *1-pound can tomatoes, strained*
>1 *6-ounce can tomato paste*
>2 *tablespoons brown sugar*
>1 *teaspoon salt*
>½ *teaspoon pepper*
>½ *cup cold water*

Season as desired
>2 *pounds ground round steak*

Pack the meat into muffin pans (twelve little meat loaves). Bake in a preheated oven at 375° for 15 minutes. Turn out meat loaves onto a serving platter or into a shallow casserole and cover with hot tomato sauce. SERVES 6.

MARY'S MEATBALLS WITH SPAGHETTI SAUCE

Chop fine
>3 *large onions*
>1 *clove garlic*
>4 *large stalks celery*
>½ *large green pepper*

Place chopped vegetables in a large saucepan. Add and mix well
>1½ *teaspoons hot red pepper, seeded and diced*
>2 *20-oz. cans tomatoes*
>2 *6-ounce cans tomato paste*
>2 *6-ounce cans water*
>1 *tablespoon salt*
>2 *teaspoons pepper*
>1 *tablespoon paprika*
>2 *tablespoons sugar*

Simmer sauce for 3 hours, stirring occasionally.

Mix and form into small balls
>3 *pounds ground round steak*
>1 *large egg*

1 *clove garlic, minced*
1 *cup bread crumbs*
1 *teaspoon salt*
½ *teaspoon pepper*

Heat in a frying pan
4 *tablespoons olive oil*

Brown meatballs in the hot oil a few at a time. Add them to the sauce as ready. Simmer meatballs in sauce for 2 hours. Serve over thin spaghetti, cooked according to package directions. Top with a generous sprinkling of grated Parmesan cheese.

Note: This recipe yields enough sauce to be used with spaghetti to serve 15 to 18.

SWEDISH MEATBALLS

FROM THE KITCHEN OF ELSIE NILSSON, SWEDEN

Have butcher grind together three times
1½ *pounds beef, top or bottom round*
½ *pound lean, fresh pork*

Mix well together in a large bowl
The ground meat
2 *eggs*
1 *teaspoon salt*
½ *teaspoon white pepper*
2 *teaspoons sugar*
2 *tablespoons fine bread crumbs*
2 *tablespoons scraped onion*
2 *pinches of allspice*
3 *tablespoons carbonated soda water (club soda)*

Form into small (about 2-inch) balls.

Brown meatballs a few at a time in
3 *tablespoons melted butter*

Make
  Brown gravy

Reheat meatballs in gravy. SERVES 6 TO 8.

Variation: Place meatballs on a broiler pan. Broil, turning once, until lightly browned on all sides.

Suggestion: Make meatballs very small and serve on toothpicks as a hot hors d'oeuvre.

AUNT MARY'S SPICED BEEF TONGUE

Wash and place in a large kettle
  A smoked beef tongue

Cover with cold water and bring to a boil. Drain. Add
  Cold water to cover
  ⅓ cup cider vinegar
  1½ teaspoons salt
  3 bay leaves, broken
  10 whole peppercorns
  6 whole allspice
  1 large onion, sliced
  2 tablespoons finely cut lemon peel

Bring to a boil. Simmer 3 hours or until meat is tender. Cool in liquid, then remove and drain tongue. Discard skin and root. Chill. Slice thin. Serve with Sweet Mustard Sauce or snappy old-fashioned "Made" Mustard (*recipes follow*).

"MADE" MUSTARD

Mix
  3 teaspoons dry mustard
  3 teaspoons flour

3 teaspoons sugar
¼ teaspoon salt

Stir in to make a smooth paste
2 tablespoons cider vinegar

SWEET MUSTARD SAUCE

FROM THE KITCHEN OF GRACE MUNGER

Mix in a double boiler
1 cup brown sugar
4 teaspoons dry mustard
3 teaspoons all-purpose flour
½ teaspoon salt

Stir in gradually
1 cup light cream

Cook slowly for 60 minutes stirring constantly until sauce is smooth, then occasionally. Remove from heat. Stir in
4 tablespoons cider vinegar

MAKES 2 CUPS.

Suggestion: Use as a dressing for cole slaw. Serve hot with hot meats. Store in refrigerator and use with cold sliced meats.

ESTHER'S BEEF HEART–MASHED POTATO PIE

With very short notice, Esther can always prepare a well-balanced, completely home-cooked meal for ten, two dozen, or thirty-five. The huge freezer in the cellar at the Weeks' home is kept packed with various cuts of meat, vegetables, loaves of bread and dozens of rolls, frozen blueberries and other fruits; also, of course, at least half a dozen pies ready to bake. If she knows a day ahead that some of the family may be dropping in for a midday meal she sometimes gets out a beef heart from the freezer and makes up this casserole. Esther's grandchildren have never found out the source of this good-tasting ground meat, so they try the dish without question and pass their plates for more.

❧

Place in a large heavy kettle
  A beef heart
  Cold water to cover
  1 teaspoon salt
  2 bay leaves, crumbled

Bring to a boil. Simmer 3 hours or until meat tests very tender when tried with a fork. Cool meat in the broth. Skim off fat from liquid and discard. Save some broth. Trim and skin beef heart. Discard every bit of fat and gristle. Put meat pieces through food chopper, using medium blade.

Mix in a large oven-to-table casserole
  The ground meat
  Broth enough to moisten
  1 tablespoon grated onion
  Salt and pepper to taste

Heat the meat in the casserole. Boil
  12 medium potatoes, peeled

Mash, moisten with hot milk, and season. Spread a thick layer of mashed potato over the meat. Dot top with butter. Return casserole to oven to heat until potato is slightly browned. SERVES 8 OR MORE.

PRESSED VEAL LOAF
ADAPTED FROM THE SWEDISH RECIPE FOR KALVSYLTA

Use
  A 4-5-pound piece of veal shoulder
  1½-2 pounds of pigs' knuckles or pigs' feet, split

Wash and dry the meat with paper towels. Place in a large kettle. Cover with cold water and bring to a boil. Drain and rinse meat under the cold water tap and remove scum.

Put into a heavy kettle or Dutch oven
   The meat
   3 bay leaves, crushed
   1 onion, cut in half
   1 large, unpeeled carrot
   1 large lemon, quartered
   1 tablespoon salt
   12 peppercorns
   1 teaspoon dried marjoram

Simmer until meat is ready to fall from the bones (2 hours or more). Strain the broth and reserve. Remove meat from bones, discarding all fat pieces and gristle. Grind, using the coarse knife of the food chopper. Boil the reserved broth until it is reduced to about 1 cup of liquid.

Press into a loaf pan
   The ground meat

Pour on
   The hot broth

Set a weight on top of the meat. Refrigerate for 24 hours. Slice, and arrange on a platter garnished with parsley and spiced crab apples or apple rings.

Suggestion: Flatirons were once commonly used as weights for pressing meat as well as for the weekly ironing. I don't own an antique flatiron, so I substitute a brick, wrapped in aluminum foil.

VEAL ROAST IN ROSÉ WINE
(With glazed vegetables)

Wash and roll in seasoned flour
   A boneless veal rump roast, 4 pounds or more

Lard the roast by using very thin slices of fat salt pork tucked under the roast, in meat pockets and laid over the top.

Pour on
>   *1 cup rosé wine*

Roast in a preheated oven at 375° for 30 minutes per pound or until veal is done as desired. Baste occasionally, adding more wine as needed.

Prepared for cooking, quantities as needed,
>   *Small new potatoes*
>   *Carrots*
>   *Small onions*

Precook vegetables in salted water until just beginning to soften. Drain, drench with melted butter, sprinkle with light brown sugar. Cook vegetables around meat in roasting pan for at least 30 minutes. Remove vegetables and meat to warming oven. Add ½ cup wine to juice in pan. Stir, strain and serve as pan gravy.

Suggestion: Serve meat slices on platter surrounded by vegetables. Garnish with parsley.

VEAL CUTLETS IN BURGUNDY SAUCE

Wipe with a paper towel and cut into 2½-inch pieces, discarding skin and bones (which may be used to make veal stock),
>   *4 large slices veal leg, cut ½ inch thick*

Heat slowly, stirring occasionally, in an electric or heavy iron frying pan
>   *6 tablespoons butter*
>   *1 medium onion, sliced*

Mix
>   *½ cup flour*
>   *2 teaspoons salt*
>   *1 teaspoon white pepper*

Toss in a clean paper bag
>   *The flour mixture*
>   *The veal pieces*

Discard cooked onion pieces. Brown the meat quickly in the hot butter, turning once. As meat pieces are browned, place them in a large shallow oven-to-table casserole (one layer of meat).

Brown lightly in the remaining butter
12 fresh mushrooms, sliced

Turn mushrooms and remaining butter over the meat.

Add
½ cup hot veal or chicken stock
½ cup Burgundy wine

Cover tightly and bake in a preheated oven 40 minutes at 325°. SERVES 4.

Variation: Omit mushrooms and include onions, or use both mushrooms and onions.

ROAST FRESH HAM WITH HERB STUFFING

Use
An 8-10-pound fresh ham, boned

Make stuffing. Mix
½ teaspoon sage
1½ teaspoons salt
½ teaspoon pepper
¼ teaspoon allspice
Pinch of dried thyme
Pinch of dried marjoram

Prepare, using an electric blender,
4 cups soft white bread crumbs

Mix in a large bowl
The bread crumbs
The seasoning mixture
1 tablespoon scraped onion

Stir in
  2 eggs
  ¼ cup butter melted in
  ¼ cup hot water
  ¼ cup dry white wine

Wash and dry meat. Fill opening with stuffing. Sew or skewer to close opening. Place meat, skin side up, on a rack in an open roasting pan. Sear for 10 minutes in a preheated 500° oven. Reduce heat to 325°. Turn meat skin side down.

Pour on
  2 cups dry white wine

Cover and roast for 4 hours or until a meat thermometer registers done for pork. Uncover for about the last 30 minutes to brown the meat. Make gravy from pan drippings if desired. SERVES 8 TO 10.

BAKED HAM WITH MAPLE GLAZE

Use
  Half of a tenderized ham (8-10 pounds)

Wash ham under cold water faucet. Dry with paper towels. Place in a covered roasting pan. Bake in a preheated oven at 300° for 2 hours. Allow ham to cool. Remove the rind. Score the fat in diamond shapes.

Mix to make a paste
  ½ cup soft maple sugar
  3 teaspoons dry mustard

Spread this mixture in a thick coating over the entire surface of the ham.

Pour on
  ½ cup brandy

Bake in a preheated oven at 325° for 60 minutes. Baste every 10 minutes, using liquid in the pan. SERVES 16.

Suggestion: Serve hot with Maple Candied Sweet Potatoes (*see p. 247*) and Spiced Cranberry Sauce (*see p. 392*) or cold applesauce.

ANNE'S COUNTRY-STYLE RIBS

Use 4-5 pounds of fresh pork loin ribs. Have the ribs cracked to make serving easier. Wipe with a paper towel and place in a roasting pan. Brush with Sauce (*recipe follows*). Bake in a preheated oven at 325° for 2 hours. Baste with Sauce every 30 minutes.

SAUCE

Heat in a heavy saucepan
  6 tablespoons butter

Add and sauté until very soft
  1 medium onion, chopped

Mix and add
  1 small bottle ketchup
  1 equal bottle of water
  ½ cup cider vinegar
  1 tablespoon dry mustard
  1 teaspoon salt

Cook over low heat, stirring until well blended. SERVES 6 TO 8.

ESTHER'S PRESSED PORK LUNCHEON LOAF

Wash and dry with paper towels a fresh pork shoulder, 5 pounds or more. Place in a heavy kettle. Add

  1 tablespoon salt
  1 large or 2 small whole onions
  12 peppercorns
  8 whole allspice
  2 bay leaves, crushed
  ½ cup cider vinegar
  Hot water to cover

Bring to a boil. Cook over low heat at simmering point for 3 hours or until meat is ready to fall from the bones. Cool in liquid to room temperature. Discard liquid. Separate meat from bones, discarding all fat and gristle. Pack meat pieces into a loaf pan. Cut aluminum foil to cover the meat. Set an old-fashioned flatiron (or brick) on top of the meat loaf. Refrigerate.

Suggestion: Serve sliced thin with horseradish or Mustard Sauce (*see p. 221*).

ROAST OF CANADIAN BACON IN RED WINE

Use
  A 3-4-pound piece of Canadian bacon, unsliced

Remove paper or plastic wrapping from meat. Wash and dry with paper towels.

Marinate for an hour or longer in
  1 cup dry red wine

Place meat in a roasting pan lined with aluminum foil. Pour the wine marinade over the meat. Cover and bake in a preheated oven at 325° for 2 hours. Serve hot or cold, sliced thin.

Suggestion: Combine slices of Roast of Canadian bacon with slices of Veal Loaf (*see p. 222*) to make an attractive cold meat platter.

ROAST LEG OF LAMB
ESTHER'S METHOD

Wash and dry with paper towels
  An 8-10-pound leg of lamb

Rub all over with
  2 teaspoons salt

Sift onto the meat
  Flour to coat

Place meat on a rack in a roasting pan. Insert a meat thermometer into the thick part of leg (it should not touch a bone). Roast in a preheated oven at 300° for 3 hours or until meat thermometer registers done for lamb. Serve hot or cold. SERVES 12.

Note: Esther serves cold roast lamb with mashed potatoes smothered in hot gravy, accompanied by her Spiced Grape Sauce (*see p. 385*).

ROAST LAMB, SWEDISH-AMERICAN STYLE

FROM THE KITCHEN OF IDA BERQUIST

Use
  4-5-pound leg of lamb

Wipe meat with a damp paper towel. Remove sinewy pieces. Sprinkle with
  Salt
  Pepper
  Flour

Make several shallow gashes in fatty side. Insert
  Thin slices of onion

Place meat, fat side up, on a rack in an open roasting pan. Insert a meat thermometer (it should not touch a bone). Roast in a preheated oven at 325° for 40 minutes.

Pour over meat
  1 cup hot black coffee

Continue to roast, basting every 20 minutes with pan drippings until thermometer registers done for lamb.

Make gravy using
  2 cups pan drippings, strained
  1 cup light cream, heated
  1 teaspoon red currant jelly (or any tart jelly)

SERVES 4 TO 6.

Note: The coffee gives a rich brown color to the gravy and helps remove any strong "mutton" taste.

Suggestion: To serve leftover lamb, reheat sliced meat for 10 minutes in a preheated 300° oven. Reheat gravy and add a little more currant jelly.

JESSIE'S BRAISED LAMB SHANKS WITH VEGETABLES

Use
   4 lamb shanks, cut into chunks

Trim fat off meat. Wipe with a damp paper towel.

Roll in
   2 tablespoons flour seasoned with
   ½ teaspoon salt
   ¼ teaspoon freshly ground pepper

Heat in a frying pan
   ¼ cup vegetable oil

Brown the meat pieces in the hot oil, turning several times (about 15 minutes cooking time). Remove meat pieces to a heavy kettle.

Add
   1 cup hot water
   ½ cup red wine

Simmer for 1½ hours or until meat is almost ready to fall away from the bones. Remove meat.

Add to the broth and cook until soft
   2 celery stalks
   12 small new potatoes, scrubbed
   6 small white onions, peeled
   8 new carrots, scraped

½ bay leaf
½ teaspoon dried marjoram
½ teaspoon dried thyme

Discard celery stalks and bay leaf. Return meat to kettle and reheat. Arrange vegetables around meat on a hot platter. Garnish with parsley. SERVES 4.

Suggestion: Serve broth as pot gravy, or thicken if desired.

OLD-FASHIONED CHICKEN IN GRAVY

THE WAY MOTHER MADE IT

Place in a large kettle (Mother always used her big, black, iron kettle which she set right into the fire)

2 large stewing chickens, cut into pieces
1 large whole onion
1 washed, unscraped carrot
Several celery stalks with leaves
2 teaspoons poultry seasoning
2 teaspoons salt
1 teaspoon black pepper
Enough hot water to cover

Bring to a boil quickly, then stew at a low temperature until meat can easily be separated from the bones. Strain the broth. Discard skin and bones. Cut chicken into good-sized pieces. Store meat and broth separately overnight in refrigerator.

Make plenty of gravy from the broth, using flour to thicken. Season to taste. Combine chicken pieces with gravy and heat. SERVES 8 TO 10.

Note: Mother always baked a big pan of baking powder biscuits to go with the Chicken in Gravy.

MOTHER'S TWO-CRUST CHICKEN PIE WITH GRAVY

Prepare and cook two frying-size chickens as for Old-fashioned Chicken in Gravy (*see p. 231*). Cool. Remove meat from bones and strain stock. Store meat and stock separately in refrigerator until ready to use.

Mix
>   *3 cups Family Pastry Mix (see p. 331)*
>   *½ cup cold water (or less)*

Divide dough in half. Roll one piece to line a large deep-dish pie plate with a flaring rim.

Pack with
>   *Chicken cut into bite-size pieces*

Add
>   *Seasoning to taste*

Make an extra-flaky top crust using following method: Roll out remaining dough; spread with softened butter; fold dough with butter inside; form into a ball and roll out again. Repeat the process, adding more softened butter. Place top crust over chicken. No broth or liquid is added to chicken before baking pie. Crimp edges and spread crust with cream. Prick to allow steam to escape. Bake in a preheated oven at 450° for 45 minutes. If crust browns too rapidly, lay a piece of aluminum foil over the pie during last 15 minutes. Cut the pie into 6 very generous, or 8 smaller servings. Serve smothered with gravy made from stock.

BAKED CHICKEN FOR A CROWD

GRANDDAUGHTER JOANN BAILEY'S RECIPE

Use fryer breasts, legs and thighs. Plan amounts according to ages and appetites of family and guests to be served. Wash, dry, and brush cut-up chicken pieces with Basting Sauce (*recipe follows*). Arrange chicken, skin side down, in shallow baking dishes. Bake in a preheated oven at 350° for 30 minutes, brushing twice with sauce. Turn chicken pieces. Brush well using all remaining sauce. Bake for 30 minutes more.

BASTING SAUCE

Mix in a saucepan and warm
 ⅓ *cup tomato ketchup*
 ½ *cup melted butter (1 stick)*
 ⅓ *cup cider vinegar*
 1 *teaspoon celery seed*
 2 *teaspoons salt*
 ½ *teaspoon white pepper*

ALMOND CHICKEN AND MUSHROOM CASSEROLE

Cut up
 2 *3-pound stewing chickens*

Wash and place in a large heavy kettle.

Add
 2 *celery stalks with leaves*
 2 *medium onions*
 1 *large carrot*
 2 *teaspoons salt*
 2 *teaspoons poultry seasoning*
 1 *teaspoon white pepper*
 Hot water to cover

Cook slowly until chicken is just soft enough to be separated from the bones. Strain broth and separate meat from bones. Discard vegetables, skin, bones and gristle. Store meat and broth separately in refrigerator overnight.

Prepare casserole.

Skim fat from broth. Heat
 3 *cups broth*

Wipe with paper towel dipped in water (do not wash) and slice
   24 fresh mushrooms (2 6-ounce packages)

Heat in a double boiler or in a saucepan
   4 tablespoons butter

Add the mushroom pieces. Sauté for 3 minutes or until mushrooms are tender. Remove and drain. Reheat butter (add more if necessary).

Stir in
   ½ cup flour

Add the hot broth a little at a time. Cook slowly for 15 minutes stirring often enough to keep the sauce smooth.

Add
   ½ cup light cream, heated

Cook and stir for at least 15 minutes. Sauce should be very smooth and well blended but not thick.

Combine in a 2½-quart oven-to-table casserole
   Chicken pieces, cut into chunks
   Mushroom pieces
   ½ cup thin-sliced, blanched almonds
   The hot sauce
   1 tablespoon sherry

Crumb in an electric blender
   3 slices soft white bread

Toss with
   4 tablespoons melted butter

Spread crumbs over the casserole. Sprinkle on
   ¼ cup thin-sliced, blanched almonds

Heat casserole in a preheated oven at 375° until bubbling hot and browned. Serve with rice or mashed potatoes.
Serves 6.

Suggestion: Serve Almond Chicken and Mushroom Casserole as the main dish for a buffet dinner. Prepare completely the day before and reheat.

CHICKEN BREASTS WITH BELGIAN ENDIVE

Granddaughter Mary Ellen Naylor became familiar with French cuisine when she spent a year studying in Paris. This recipe is her Americanized version of one of her favorites.

❧

Simmer in a saucepan until reduced one half
    2 cups chicken stock or broth (homemade or canned)

Wash and skin
    4 whole chicken breasts

Split breasts and pound to flatten them slightly. Roll in flour seasoned with salt and pepper.

Heat in an electric skillet or frying pan
    4 tablespoons butter

Add and cook until soft
    1 large onion, sliced

Remove and discard onion pieces. Brown chicken.

As chicken is browned, place it in a roasting pan or large shallow casserole. Add the chicken stock to the butter remaining in the skillet. Scrape up all brown particles and pour over the chicken. Add
    ½ cup dry white wine

Cover and bake in a preheated oven at 350° for 50 minutes.

Use
    1 large head Belgian endive for each 2 persons to be served

Slice endive heads crosswise in sections. Separate leaves. Wash in cold water. Drain and place in a saucepan.

Add
    1 teaspoon salt
    ¼ cup lemon juice
    ½ cup hot chicken stock

Simmer until tender. Drain.

Place chicken pieces on a platter and keep warm.

Add to the juices in roasting pan
  ¼ cup cream

Pour over the chicken or serve separately as gravy. Add endive to the platter. SERVES 4 TO 6.

ROAST TURKEY WITH OLD-FASHIONED CRACKER STUFFING

ESTHER'S METHOD

Prepare for stuffing
  A 15-18-pound turkey

Make stuffing. Mix
  8 cups cracker crumbs, rolled medium-coarse
  A 2½-inch cube of fat salt pork, ground
  1 medium onion, ground
  2 eggs
  1 teaspoon salt
  ½ teaspoon pepper
  1 teaspoon poultry seasoning
  1½ cups milk (about)

(Mixture should stick together when rolled into a ball).

Preheat oven to 300°. Melt for basting
  ½ cup butter (1 stick)

Stuff and truss turkey. Place, breast side up, on a rack in an open roasting pan. Baste with melted butter. Roast for 2½ hours, basting every 30 minutes with the melted butter and pan drippings. Turn the bird breast side down. Roast for 1 hour, basting as before. Turn bird, breast side up, and roast for 30 minutes or until done.

ROAST TURKEY WITH OYSTER STUFFING

Prepare for stuffing
  A 10-12-pound turkey

Make a basting broth. Combine in a saucepan
  The giblets
  1 carrot
  1 medium onion
  1 teaspoon salt
  6 peppercorns, crushed
  1 teaspoon poultry seasoning
  2 cups hot water

Simmer until meat and vegetables are soft. Strain. Discard solid parts.

Combine in a saucepan and heat
  The liquid
  ½ cup butter
  ½ cup rosé wine

Mix to make the stuffing
  6 cups soft white bread crumbs
  1 pint fresh oysters, ground or chopped fine
  The oyster liquid
  ½ teaspoon pepper
  1 teaspoon salt
  4 tablespoons melted butter
  About 4 tablespoons basting broth

Stuff and truss the turkey. Place, breast side up, on a rack in a roasting pan.

Lay over breast and legs
  4 thin strips fat salt pork

Roast uncovered in a preheated oven at 350° for 3 hours or until turkey is done. Baste every 15 minutes with hot basting broth and pan drippings until breast is browned. Turn breast side down. Continue to baste every 15 minutes. Reverse position to breast side up about a half hour before roasting time is up. Make gravy from pan drippings if desired. SERVES 12.

Note: It is important to baste continuously as suggested when roasting uncovered at 350°. Turning the bird is an old-fashioned trick which improves flavor and retains moistness.

ROAST TURKEY WITH ALMOND STUFFING

Prepare for stuffing
  A 10-12-pound turkey

Make a basting broth. Combine in a saucepan
  The giblets, neck, and wing tips
  2 stalks celery with leaves
  1 small whole onion
  Several fresh parsley sprigs
  6 peppercorns
  2 whole allspice
  1 teaspoon salt
  ½ teaspoon poultry seasoning
  2 cups hot water

Simmer until meat and vegetables are tender. Strain. Discard solid parts. (There should be about 2 cups liquid.)

Combine and heat
  The liquid
  ½ cup melted butter (1 stick)
  ½ cup dry white wine

Mix to make the stuffing
  5 cups soft white bread crumbs
  1 cup ground blanched almonds
  1 large egg, beaten
  ½ teaspoon white pepper
  1 teaspoon salt
  A 1-inch cube of fat salt pork, ground
  About ¾ cup hot basting broth

Stuff and truss the turkey. Place, breast side up, on a rack in an open roasting pan.

Lay over breast and legs
    4 thin slices salt pork

Roast uncovered in a preheated oven at 350° for 3 hours or until turkey is done. Baste every 15 minutes with hot basting broth and pan drippings. When bird is well browned, turn breast side down. Rearrange pork slices. Continue to baste. Reverse position again when turkey is nearly done. Make gravy from pan drippings if desired.
SERVES 12.

❧ 23 ❧

Vegetables

SMITH FAMIILY BAKED BEANS

Many New Hampshire farmers didn't bother to raise beans for baking, but Father always planted both the white pea beans and the red kidneys. He saved his seed each year and he never failed to harvest a good crop. In the fall the vines were pulled and left stacked on poles in the field until the beans were dry enough to rattle in the pod. Then Father brought the stacks of dried bean vines into the barn to be "thrashed" and winnowed. The threshing was done by hand with Grandfather Smith's old flail; then the beans were put through a "winnower" which did a pretty fair job of separating them from the chaff and bits of dry stalk. Still, it took quite a while to pick over the beans every Friday night in preparation for the overnight soaking and the all-day baking on Saturday. One week we would have the red kidneys, next Saturday the white pea beans. Of course we had with them several kinds of relish: piccalilli, ketchup, mustard, or dill pickles. Mother always steamed two loaves of brown bread, baked a big pan of baking powder biscuits and sometimes made hot rolls, too. The leftovers were warmed up for Sunday breakfast. We thought everything tasted fully as good that way, especially when we poured on enough maple syrup so the beans were swimming in delicious sweetness.

❧

Pick over and wash
  4 cups dry beans

Cover with about 2 quarts cold water and leave to soak overnight.

Prepare for baking: Drain beans and cover with fresh water. Heat quickly to the boiling point. Then simmer until the thin outer skins are ready to burst. Test by taking a few beans on a spoon and blowing sharply. When the skins wrinkle and crack the beans are sufficiently parboiled. (Too much parboiling will make the beans mushy.)

Wash and score
  A 2-inch cube of fat salt pork

Put the beans into a 3-quart crockery bean pot. Push the pork down into the beans until all but the rind is covered.

Add
  ½ cup maple syrup
  Hot water to cover the beans

Bake in a preheated oven at 275° for 6-8 hours. Leave pot uncovered for the first hour or until pork rind is beginning to crisp. (Be careful not to burn beans on top.) Add hot water as needed to keep the beans moist. Serve with baked ham or frankfurters.
SERVES 12 OR MORE.

PARSNIPS

FATHER'S FAVORITE EARLY-SPRING VEGETABLE

The parsnip, a root vegetable which is woody and flat-tasting in fall, becomes crisp and fragrant, sweet to the taste after a winter's stay in the ground. When Father harvested the root vegetables he left the parsnip row untouched, a practice still followed in New Hampshire. As soon as the snow began to go Father became impatient for the ground in his garden to thaw enough so he could begin to dig parsnips. We like parsnips cooked the way Mother did them to please Father—scrubbed, peeled, sliced thin, and boiled until soft in salted water. Served with lots of butter and a dusting of pepper, the golden yellow slices are a very appetizing dish, we think. Esther's family likes the leftovers sautéed in butter. Cooked parsnips are also very good made into fritters and pan-fried.

DANDELION GREENS

Every spring our grandmothers dosed their children with sulphur and molasses and fed their families copious messes of boiled greens. The nauseating dose of sulphur mixed with black molasses was supposed to cleanse the children of winter's sluggishness. The wild greens were considered the best of spring tonics. Cowslip (gathered when in bud), mustard, milkweed, pigweed, and dandelion were the common weeds gathered and boiled. Dandelion greens were the most popular. We escaped the molasses and sulphur because Mother didn't hold with such old-fashioned notions. We ate dandelion greens—not as a tonic but because Father was so fond of them. New Hampshire families (count us with them) are still enthusiastic dandelion green eaters. Gathered while still small and tender, cooked to buttery softness in the old-fashioned way with a generous piece of salt pork in the kettle, served hot or cold with a dash of good sharp cider vinegar, dandelion greens are a dish fit for an epicure—or a Yankee.

SUCCOTASH

The Indians were said to have invented succotash—a mixture of dried corn and dried beans cooked in a pot over an open fire. The succotash we knew was made only in the season of fresh green corn and garden shell beans (bush beans). According to New Hampshire cooks (we share the opinion), there is no other proper combination for succotash.

⁂

Melt in a saucepan
  2 tablespoons butter

Add
  2 cups freshly boiled corn cut from the cob
  2 cups cooked shell beans
  About ½ cup light cream
  1 teaspoon salt
  ¼ teaspoon pepper

Heat just to the boiling point. SERVES 4.

Note: New England succotash is not made with lima beans. The bush beans Father raised were of the variety called "cranberry." As the beans matured the pods became speckled with bright red. The beans, shelled from the pods, were also speckled or tinged red. The shell beans (as we called them), put into a kettle with a piece of salt pork and boiled until soft, were served as the main vegetable at one meal. If succotash was to be made for another meal, an extra large quantity of shell beans would be cooked.

SWEET CORN CUSTARD

ADAPTED FROM THE BOSTON COOK BOOK, 1904

Use
> *12 ears tender sweet corn, freshly picked*

Cut through each row of kernels with the point of a sharp knife. Then with the back of the knife press out the pulp and leave the hull on the cob. There should be one cup of pulp or a little more.

Mix in a bowl
> *The corn pulp*
> *3 eggs beaten until light*
> *1½ cups milk, heated*
> *1 tablespoon sugar*
> *½ teaspoon salt*
> *1 tablespoon butter, melted*

Pour the mixture into a buttered 1½-quart oven-to-table casserole. Set the casserole into a dish of hot water. Bake in a preheated oven at 350° for 45 minutes.
MAKES 4 TO 6 SERVINGS.

SCALLOPED POTATOES WITH HAM

Prepare
> *4 cups potatoes, peeled and sliced thin*
> *1 small onion, sliced paper thin*
> *1 cup cooked ham, ground*

Mix
> *¼ cup flour*
> *1 teaspoon salt*
> *½ teaspoon pepper*

Butter a 2-quart, oven-to-table casserole. Put a layer of potato slices into the casserole. Add a thin layer of ground ham and several slices of onion. Sift on some of the flour mixture. Dot with butter. Repeat until all prepared vegetables and ham are used (casserole should be about three-fourths full). Dot top generously with butter. Bake in a preheated oven at 425° for 10 minutes.

Pour on
  2 cups hot milk

Bake at 425° for 60 minutes or until vegetables are tender. If potatoes become very brown on top, stir carefully or cover during last 15 minutes of cooking time.
SERVES 4 TO 6.

Note: Adding the hot milk after the potatoes have cooked for 10 minutes helps prevent curdling.

MAPLE-CANDIED SWEET POTATOES

Place in a saucepan
  4 medium or 6 small sweet potatoes, scrubbed
  1 teaspoon salt
  Water to cover

Bring to a boil and cook for 10 minutes. Cool.

Melt in a baking pan
  2 tablespoons butter
  3 tablespoons soft maple sugar

Peel the sweet potatoes and cut into slices ½-inch thick. Arrange slices in two layers in the baking pan. Soak each slice well with the melted butter-maple mixture. Cover pan with aluminum foil. Bake in a preheated oven at 450° for 30 minutes. Uncover and bake for 15 minutes.
SERVES 4.

SCALLOPED TOMATOES

ADAPTED FROM MOTHER'S RECIPE

Mix
> *2 cups soft bread crumbs*
> *1 teaspoon salt*
> *½ teaspoon white pepper*
> *¼ teaspoon celery salt*
> *⅛ teaspoon dried basil*

Purée
> *2 cups canned tomatoes*

Reserve ½ cup bread crumbs. Alternate remainder of bread crumbs and tomato purée in a 1-quart, buttered casserole, beginning with crumbs and completing with layer of tomatoes.

Toss the reserved crumbs with
> *1 tablespoon melted butter*

Spread buttered crumbs over the casserole. Bake in a preheated oven at 375° for 30 minutes.
SERVES 4.

ANNE'S SPINACH CASSEROLE

Cook and chop fine
> *Fresh spinach to measure 2 cups*

Mix together
> *The cooked spinach*
> *1 cup grated natural Cheddar cheese*
> *1 small onion, minced*
> *1 teaspoon salt*
> *½ teaspoon pepper*
> *2 eggs, well beaten*

Turn mixture into a greased casserole.

Sprinkle on top
  3 tablespoons fine bread crumbs
  2 strips crisp bacon, crumbled

Bake in a preheated oven at 350° for 45 minutes or until set.
SERVES 4.

DOROTHY'S PAN-FRIED SUMMER SQUASH

Use two young summer squash—yellow crook-neck or straight-neck.
Wash but do not peel. Cut off and discard ends. Cut into slices ¾-inch in thickness.

Put into a saucepan
  The squash
  Water to barely cover
  ½ teaspoon celery seed
  1 teaspoon salt

Boil for 8 minutes or until squash is just beginning to soften.

Drain.

Mix and spread on waxed paper
  1½ cups fine cracker crumbs
  1 teaspoon salt
  ¼ teaspoon pepper

Beat in a shallow bowl
  1 large egg with
  1 tablespoon milk

Dip squash slices in egg mixture. Coat well with cracker crumbs.

Heat in a large frying pan
  2 tablespoons butter

Fry squash slices until lightly browned on one side. Turn and brown.
Transfer to a heated platter and keep warm. Continue to fry, adding
butter as needed.
MAKES 4 TO 6 SERVINGS.

ANNE'S EGGPLANT SOUFFLÉ

Peel and cube
  2 medium-size eggplants

Place in a saucepan. Add
  Hot water to cover
  ½ teaspoon salt

Cook over low heat 10-15 minutes or until soft. Drain well and mash.

Prepare
  2 cups medium-thick white sauce

Mix
  The white sauce
  The mashed eggplant
  ¾ cup fine bread crumbs
  ½ cup grated mild cheese
  2 tablespoons finely snipped parsley
  1 teaspoon Worcestershire sauce
  1 teaspoon white pepper
  1 teaspoon salt
  A pinch of nutmeg

Stir in
  4 egg yolks, beaten until light

Fold in
  4 egg whites, beaten until stiff

Pour into a 2-quart soufflé dish or casserole. Bake in a preheated oven at 350° for 45 minutes.
SERVES 6 TO 8.

Note: Use only freshly picked eggplant. The skins should be smooth, firm, and glossy, rich purple in color.

Suggestion: If there is any Eggplant Soufflé left over, it will be just as good reheated.

STUFFED EGGPLANT

Cover with boiling salted water
  2 small eggplants, cut in half lengthwise

Parboil for 10 minutes. Drain, reserving a little of the cooking water. Remove the pulp taking care to leave skins intact. Chop the pulp.

Mix in a bowl
  The chopped pulp
  1 cup soft bread crumbs
  2 cups cooked ham, ground or chopped fine
  1 teaspoon scraped onion
  1 teaspoon salt
  ½ teaspoon pepper
  ¼ teaspoon celery salt
  2 tablespoons or more reserved water

Fill eggplant shells with the mixture.

Cover with
  ½ cup soft bread crumbs tossed with
  1 tablespoon butter, melted

Bake in a preheated oven at 375° for 35 minutes.
SERVES 4.

CORN CHOWDER

OLD NEW HAMPSHIRE STYLE

Put in a Dutch oven or heavy kettle
  A 1-inch cube fat salt pork, diced

Cook and stir over low heat until pork bits are crisp.

Add
  1 medium onion, diced

Cook over low heat, stirring until onion pieces are soft.

Add
 2 cups peeled, diced potatoes
 ½ teaspoon salt
 ¼ teaspoon pepper
 Cold water to cover

Bring to a boil and simmer for 10 minutes or until potato pieces are beginning to soften.

Add
 1 10-ounce package frozen whole-kernel corn

Add a little more water if needed. Bring again to a boil and simmer for 10 minutes.

Add
 2 cups milk

Heat. Serve over common crackers, split and toasted. SERVES 6.

SPLIT PEA SOUP WITH HAM

Our pea soup is made according to Mother's method, but we add extra seasoning and a little wine to enhance the flavor.

❧

Soak overnight
 A 16-ounce package of split green peas

Drain peas in a colander. Rinse well under the cold water tap. Combine in a deep, heavy kettle or Dutch oven
 The peas
 1 large or 2 medium onions
 2 bay leaves
 2 quarts cold water
 A large ham bone which has plenty of meat

Bring to a boil. Turn heat down and keep at a low boil, with kettle partly uncovered. Cook for 2 hours or until peas are very soft. Remove ham bone and reserve. Discard bay leaves and onion. Put peas and liquid through a medium-coarse wire strainer (or use a blender). Separate meat from bone. Discard all gristle and fat. Chop or shred meat (there should be about 2 cups).

Combine in the kettle
The strained peas (add water to make 2 quarts)
2 cups diced carrots
1 cup diced celery
1 medium onion, sliced
3 cups diced potatoes

Cook over low heat until vegetables are soft. Stir occasionally, to prevent sticking.

Add
The meat
¼ cup sherry
½ teaspoon pepper

Simmer until blended. Serve as a main course with johnnycake.
SERVES 8 TO 10.

❧ 24 ❧

Doughnuts and Cookies

*Doughnuts, spoon cakes, old-fashioned
and modern-day cookies, brownies,
and cookie bars*

FRANCES' DOUGHNUTS

Sift together three times
   6 cups all-purpose flour
   6 teaspoons double-acting baking powder
   1 teaspoon cinnamon
   1 teaspoon nutmeg
   ½ teaspoon ginger
   1 teaspoon salt

Beat slightly
   3 medium eggs (room temperature)

Add and mix
   1½ cups sugar
   1 cup milk (room temperature)
   ¼ cup melted butter (½ stick), cooled

Stir in to make a soft dough
   The flour mixture

Turn dough out onto a lightly floured board. Dust with flour and pat into a ½-inch thick rectangle. Leave to rest for 5 minutes. Form doughnut shapes with a cutter, arranging in rows in the order cut. Press the trimmings together and pat out into a rectangle. Cut and twist into cruller shapes. As soon as the dough is all cut, turn the doughnuts over with a spatula, beginning with the row first cut. Let rest for another 5 minutes. Fry in fat preheated to 380°. Beginning with the first cut, slide four at a time gently and quickly into the hot fat. Turn doughnuts as soon as they rise and keep turning until golden brown all over. Stand doughnuts on edge in rows to drain on absorbent paper.

Note: Frances has some tricks to insure good doughnuts. Handle dough gently and quickly. Preheat fat while dough is resting.

OLD-FASHIONED BUTTERMILK DOUGHNUTS
GRANDDAUGHTER JOANN BAILEY'S RECIPE

Sift together
>3½ cups all-purpose flour
>¼ teaspoon baking soda
>½ teaspoon cream of tartar
>1 teaspoon salt
>1 teaspoon nutmeg
>½ teaspoon ginger

Cream, using a large shallow-bowled spoon,
>2 tablespoons softened butter with
>1 cup sugar

Beat with a fork and add
>2 medium eggs

Mix in
>1 cup buttermilk

Stir in to make a soft dough
>*The flour mixture*

Have vegetable oil for frying preheated to 425°. (Joann uses an electric deep-fat fryer.)

Turn out the dough onto a lightly floured board. Flour your hands slightly and pat the dough into a rectangle ⅓-inch thick. Form doughnuts with a large, lightly floured cutter. Begin frying, 4 at a time, as you cut. Turn doughnuts quickly as they rise to the surface. Then turn again and keep turning until both sides are browned. (Frequent turning prevents cracking.) Drain doughnuts on paper towels. Make the trimmings into 2-inch sticks and fry. Let doughnuts cool to room temperature, then store in a tightly covered container.
MAKES 3 DOZEN.

Note: Eggs and buttermilk must be taken from the refrigerator 2 hours before you are ready to mix the dough.

Suggestion: While doughnuts are still warm, toss in a clean paper bag containing ½ cup sugar.

CHOCOLATE DOUGHNUTS

ADAPTED FROM A FOLEY FAMILY RECIPE

When the younger generation revived the art of making doughnuts at home, granddaughter-in-law Patty Foley Weeks got out her mother's long-unused recipe, adapted it for use in her own modern kitchen. Now, whenever Patty gets out the electric frying pan and the odor of hot chocolate doughnuts begins to waft from the kitchen, her children and their playmates come running. Soon the entire batch disappears.

꙳

Sift together
    1¾ cups plus 1 tablespoon all-purpose flour
    1½ teaspoons baking powder
    ¼ teaspoon cinnamon

Melt
    ¼ teaspoon butter with
    2 squares baking chocolate

Cream
    ½ cup sugar
    1 large egg, slightly beaten

Cream in the melted chocolate. Stir in alternately
    The flour mixture
    ½ cup milk

Refrigerate dough overnight. Place on a lightly floured board and roll to a thickness of ¼ inch. Form doughnuts using a 3-inch cutter. Allow the doughnut forms to rest on the cutting board for 10 minutes. Fry four at a time in vegetable shortening preheated to 425°. Cook for 2 minutes after all have risen to the surface. Turn and cook for 2 minutes. Drain doughnuts on absorbent paper. Roll in plain or powdered sugar.
MAKES 16 DOUGHNUTS AND 16 DOUGHNUT HOLES.

GRAMMIE PAGE'S SPOON CAKES

LITTLE "DOUGHNUT" CAKES AS MADE BY COUSIN MIN BACON

Mix
    2 cups buttermilk
    1 teaspoon baking soda

Stir in
    3½ cups sifted all-purpose flour
    ½ teaspoon salt

Add and beat until batter is fairly smooth
    1 large egg

Drop the batter from a mixing spoon into deep fat which has been heated to 370°. Fry until the spoon cakes are browned on one side. Turn and brown. Serve at once with bowls of warmed maple syrup for dunking.
SERVES 4 TO 6.

GRANDMOTHER SMITH'S SHIN-PLASTERS

AS ADAPTED BY COUSIN PEARL SMITH YORK

In the days before people could depend on the value of currency issued by the government, contracts and deeds often specified payment to be made in silver dollars. Paper bills were sometimes scornfully referred to as "shin-plasters." Perhaps because they were rolled as thin as paper, these molasses cookies acquired the same uncomplimentary name. It is undeserved because the cookies are gingery sweet—so fragile and crisp they break at a touch.

❧

Sift together
    3 cups all-purpose flour
    1 teaspoon ginger

½ teaspoon salt
1 teaspoon baking soda

Combine in a saucepan and heat to the boiling point
½ cup dark molasses
½ cup sugar
½ cup butter

Cool to room temperature. Add and beat well
1 large egg

Stir in to make a soft dough
The flour mixture

Chill at least 3 hours. Roll dough very thin. Cut cookies with a large cutter. Bake in a preheated oven at 350° for 3-5 minutes. (Caution: these cookies burn easily). Store in a covered container.
MAKES ABOUT 5 DOZEN.

GREAT-AUNT EMMA SANBORN'S SOFT MOLASSES COOKIES

Tastes in food may change with the times, but these rolled molasses cookies are still just as popular with children of all ages as those baked by Great-aunt Emma more than a hundred years ago.

Sift together
4 cups all-purpose flour
1 teaspoon baking soda
1 teaspoon ginger
¼ teaspoon salt

Cream
½ cup softened butter
1 cup sugar

Beat in
  1 large egg
  ½ cup heavy cream, well-soured
  ½ cup dark molasses

Mix in to make a soft dough
  The flour mixture

Chill dough for several hours or overnight. Flour board lightly. Roll one half of dough at a time to a thickness of about ¼ inch. Cut cookies with a large scalloped-edge cutter. Bake in a preheated oven at 350° for 15 minutes or until cookies are firm. Store in a covered jar. MAKES ABOUT 3 DOZEN.

Suggestion: These cookies are excellent eaten warm from the oven and equally good served with cold applesauce for a light dessert.

CRY-BABY COOKIES

Many years ago when New England housewives kept their molasses in stone jugs, mothers and aunties and grandmothers used the "light" New Orleans kind to make spicy little cookies so good that children ate every batch warm from the oven—and begged for more. When she was first married, Esther found the recipe for "Cry-Baby Cookies" printed on the woman's page of a farm magazine. The name was appealing so she clipped the recipe and pasted it into her notebook. After that, the cookies were tried by every beginner cook who copied from Esther's book and always with the same result! The cookies were a failure—tough and tasteless as sawdust. Perhaps there was a typographical error or maybe the recipe didn't work because of differences in the flour and molasses. That bad old recipe with the intriguing name remained a challenge, so we subtracted and added, measured and mixed. Now the mothers and aunties and grandmothers in our family all make Cry-Baby Cookies, perhaps not exactly the same as the original old-fashioned kind, but so good that the younger children can hardly wait for the delicious-smelling, spicy little "babies" to come out of the oven.

Sift together twice
> 2½ *cups all-purpose flour*
> 2 *teaspoons baking soda*
> ½ *teaspoon ground cloves*
> ½ *teaspoon allspice*
> ½ *teaspoon cinnamon*
> ¼ *teaspoon ginger*

Cream together until light
> ¾ *cup softened butter*
> 1 *cup sugar*

Add and beat in
> 1 *egg*

Mix in alternately
> *The flour mixture*
> 4 *tablespoons light molasses*

Chill dough. Roll into ½-inch balls. Dip in sugar. Place balls, sugared side up, on a greased cookie sheet. Bake in a preheated oven at 375° for 10 minutes.
MAKES 5 TO 6 DOZEN.

GRAMMIE PAGE'S SUGAR COOKIES

Grandmother Page didn't use a cook book and she never wrote down ingredients. She must have cooked by "pinches" and "handfuls" yet every new batch of her sugar cookies tasted just exactly as good as the last ones. Her cookies were generously large and prettier than ordinary round ones because she used a scalloped-edge cutter that imprinted a faint leaf design in the center of each cookie. Working from memory, using today's ingredients, we have duplicated Grammie Page's Sugar Cookies as nearly as possible. We use a large scalloped-edge cutter found in a New Hampshire antique shop. Although our cookies have no pretty leaf design, they are so highly prized by the children of our family that every baking must be counted and evenly divided, share and share alike.

Sift together
  4 cups all-purpose flour
  ½ teaspoon salt
  1 teaspoon cream of tartar

Cream
  1½ cups sugar with
  ¾ cup softened butter

Beat in
  2 eggs
  1 teaspoon vanilla
  ½ teaspoon lemon extract

Dissolve
  ½ teaspoon baking soda in
  ½ cup sour cream

Stir into creamed mixture
  The flour mixture
  Sour cream and soda

Chill dough for several hours or overnight. Roll out about a third of the dough at a time to a thickness of ¼-inch. Cut and place cookies on a greased cookie sheet. Brush with heavy cream or unbeaten egg white. Sprinkle lavishly with sugar. Bake in a preheated oven at 375° for 12-15 minutes or until cookies are flecked with delicate brown. Do not overbake. Sugar cookies should be crisp outside, a little soft inside. A 3-INCH SCALLOPED-EDGE CUTTER MAKES 40 COOKIES.

Note: We think sugar cookies should be stored in a crockery jar within easy reach of children.

FILLED COOKIES

A NEW ENGLAND BRIDE'S "RECEIPT," 1860

Sift together
> 2¾ *cups all-purpose flour*
> ½ *teaspoon baking soda*
> 1 *teaspoon cream of tartar*
> ½ *teaspoon salt*

Cream until light
> ½ *cup softened butter*
> 1 *cup sugar*
> 1 *teaspoon vanilla*

Add
> 1 *large egg, slightly beaten*

Stir in
> *The flour mixture*
> 2 *tablespoons heavy cream*

Chill dough.

FILLING

Mix in a saucepan
> 1 *cup chopped seeded raisins*
> ½ *cup sugar*
> ½ *cup orange juice*
> 1 *tablespoon finely grated orange peel*

Cook over low heat, stirring constantly until thick. Cool.

Roll out cookie dough into a thin sheet. Cut into rounds, using a 2½-inch cutter. Place a heaping teaspoon of filling on one round and cover with another. Crimp edges to seal. Brush tops with heavy cream. Bake in a preheated oven at 350° for 15 minutes or until cookies are speckled with brown.
MAKES 2½ DOZEN COOKIES.

MOTHER'S MAPLE ICEBOX COOKIES

Sift together
>   3½ *cups all-purpose flour*
>   ¼ *teaspoon salt*
>   1 *teaspoon cream of tartar*
>   ½ *teaspoon baking soda*

Cream together
>   1 *cup soft maple sugar*
>   ¾ *cup softened butter*

Add and cream in
>   1 *beaten egg*
>   ½ *teaspoon vanilla*

Stir in
>   *The flour mixture*
>   1 *cup broken walnuts*

Form dough into rolls about 1 inch in diameter. Chill in refrigerator. Slice into thin cookies. Bake in a preheated oven at 350° for 10 minutes or until delicately browned.
MAKES ABOUT 6 DOZEN.

DUNDEE OATMEAL COOKIES

ADAPTED FROM AUNT MARY'S RECIPE

Sift together twice
>   2 *cups all-purpose flour*
>   ½ *teaspoon baking soda*
>   ½ *teaspoon salt*
>   ½ *teaspoon cinnamon*
>   ¼ *teaspoon allspice*
>   ¼ *teaspoon nutmeg*

Cream
>   1 *cup softened butter*

½ cup sugar
½ cup light brown sugar (packed)

Beat in
2 medium eggs

Stir in
The flour mixture
½ cup dates, chopped
½ cup chopped walnuts or pecans
1 teaspoon grated orange peel
¼ cup orange juice
2 cups uncooked, quick-cooking rolled oats

Chill dough. Drop by teaspoon onto a greased cookie sheet (leave room for spreading). Flatten cookies with spoon. Bake in a preheated oven at 350° for 12 minutes or until lightly browned.
MAKES ABOUT 7 DOZEN COOKIES.

ANNE'S THUMB COOKIES

Sift together
2 cups all-purpose flour
¼ teaspoon salt

Cream together
1 cup softened butter
½ cup sugar

Beat in
2 egg yolks
1 teaspoon vanilla

Stir in
The flour mixture

Chill. Roll into small balls. Place on a greased cookie sheet. Press the middle of each cookie with your thumb to make a hollow.

Place in each hollow
  ¼ teaspoon jam or jelly

Bake in a preheated oven at 375° for 12 minutes.
MAKES ABOUT 4 DOZEN COOKIES.

McDOUGALL'S SHORTBREAD

FAVORITE OF THE WOOLDRIDGE FAMILY

Sift together
  2 cups all-purpose flour
  ¼ teaspoon salt
  ¼ teaspoon baking powder

Cream together
  1 cup softened butter
  ½ cup confectioners' sugar
  1 teaspoon vanilla

Work in
  The flour mixture

Roll into an 8 × 12-inch rectangle (dough will be about ½-inch thick). Cut into 2-inch squares. Place on a buttered cookie sheet, allowing space around each square. Bake in a preheated oven at 375° for 10-12 minutes or until cookies are a delicate brown.
MAKES 24 SQUARES.

PEANUT BUTTER COOKIES

EASY ENOUGH FOR CHILDREN TO MAKE

Sift together
  3 cups all-purpose flour
  1½ teaspoons baking soda
  ½ teaspoon salt

Cream together
  1 cup softened butter
  1 cup white sugar
  1 cup brown sugar (packed)
  1 cup creamy peanut butter

Beat in
  2 medium eggs
  1 teaspoon vanilla

Stir in
  The flour mixture

Chill. Form dough into small balls. Flatten with a fork. Bake in a preheated oven at 375° for 8 minutes.
MAKES ABOUT 5 DOZEN COOKIES.

DATE KISSES

Beat until quite stiff, using an electric mixer
  3 egg whites
  ½ teaspoon cream of tartar

Add and beat in a little at a time
  1½ cups sifted confectioners' sugar
  1 teaspoon vanilla

Continue to beat until mixture is smooth and very stiff.

Stir in
  1 cup chopped dates
  1 cup chopped pecan meats

Drop mixture by a teaspoon onto a greased cookie sheet. Bake in a preheated oven at 325° for 30 minutes. Turn off oven and leave cookies for 30 minutes more.
MAKES 2½ TO 3 DOZEN KISSES.

ALMOND MACAROONS

ADAPTED FROM A FRENCH RECIPE

Crush in an electric blender
About 2 cups blanched almonds

Put through a coarse sieve to make
1¼ cups coarse almond "meal"

Reserve large almond pieces for another use. Mix with the almond "meal"
1 small (or ½ large) unbeaten egg white

Add and mix in very thoroughly
½ cup sifted sugar
1 teaspoon almond extract

Work in, using your fingers
½ cup sifted sugar
1 small (or ½ large) unbeaten egg white

Chill the dough. Cover a greased cookie sheet with aluminum foil. Using a teaspoon, place dabs of dough on the cookie sheet. Flatten dough with a spoon. Bake in a preheated oven at 275° for 35 minutes. Cool for 5 minutes. Run an ice cube wrapped in a paper towel under the foil until each macaroon can be removed without breaking.
MAKES 4 DOZEN MACAROONS.

SPRITZ COOKIES

A BERQUIST FAMILY FAVORITE

Cream thoroughly, using your hands
2 cups softened butter with
1 cup sifted sugar

Add and beat in
3 teaspoons almond extract
1 large egg, slightly beaten

Stir in to make a dough
   3½ cups all-purpose flour (or a little more)

Chill dough slightly. Using a Swedish cookie press, form cookies on a buttered cookie sheet. Bake in a preheated oven at 375° for 10 minutes or until delicate gold.
MAKES ABOUT 6 DOZEN COOKIES.

Note: Any cookie press may be used. Genuine Spritz presses may be purchased from mail-order houses handling Swedish-made articles.

KATHY'S CHOCOLATE PECAN COOKIES

This easy to do recipe was developed especially for my granddaughter, Katherine Eddinger, and all other beginner cooks. Little sisters and brothers are always willing to eat up all the chocolate cookies that big sister bakes.

Sift together
   2½ cups all-purpose flour
   ½ teaspoon baking soda
   ¼ teaspoon salt

Beat together using an electric mixer
   1½ cups sugar
   ½ cup softened butter
   2 squares baking chocolate, melted
   ½ cup commercial sour cream
   1 teaspoon vanilla

Add and continue to beat for 2 minutes
   1 large egg

Beat in, a little at a time
   The flour mixture

Drop dough from a teaspoon onto a greased cookie sheet. Press a pecan half into top of each cookie. Bake in a preheated oven at 375° for 10 minutes. Using a spatula, loosen cookies at once from the cookie sheet.

Variation: Omit pecans and ice cookies with white frosting.

WENDY'S LEMON DROP COOKIES

The directions for making these delicious Lemon Drop Cookies are given here exactly as written by my twelve-year-old great-niece, Wendy Weeks, an accomplished cook.

✦

Use electric mixer for everything.

Cream
   2 cups white sugar
   ½ cup real butter (1 stick)

Beat in
   2 large eggs

Add and beat until smooth
   1 cup commercial sour cream
   ½ teaspoon baking soda
   ¼ cup lemon juice with grated peel of lemon

Add and mix in well
   3 cups sifted flour

Drop dough from a teaspoon onto a greased cookie sheet. Bake 15-18 minutes in a preheated 350° oven. Sprinkle with sugar while warm. MAKES ABOUT 48 COOKIES.

McGINTY'S COOKIES

FROM THE KITCHEN OF JEAN KENNETT

Sift together
  2 cups all-purpose flour
  ½ teaspoon baking powder
  1 teaspoon baking soda
  ½ teaspoon salt

Cream thoroughly
  1 cup softened butter with
  2 cups light brown sugar

Beat well and add
  2 large eggs

Add and mix well
  2 tablespoons milk
  The flour mixture

Chill dough. Drop by a measuring spoon (half-teaspoon) onto a greased cookie sheet. Bake in a preheated oven at 350° for 10 minutes or until cookies are set. Loosen cookies at once, using a spatula. Leave on the cookie sheet until cooled.
MAKES 5 DOZEN COOKIES.

Note: McGinty's Cookies should be thin and very crisp.

BANGOR BROWNIES

Brownies should be moist and chewy, with plenty of pecan meats and *very* chocolaty. We Smiths all agree that this recipe, dating from the nineteen twenties when we were learning to cook, is the best we have ever tried.

❧

Cream
>   ½ cup softened butter with
>   1 cup sugar

Stir in
>   3 squares melted chocolate
>   2 eggs, slightly beaten
>   1 teaspoon vanilla

Mix in
>   ½ cup all-purpose flour

Add
>   1 cup pecan meats, chopped

Spread batter in a greased 9-inch square pan. Bake in a preheated oven at 375° for 12-15 minutes or until done. Brownies should be soft inside. Cut into squares while warm.

DOROTHY'S BLOND BROWNIES

Sift together
>   1½ cups all-purpose flour
>   2 teaspoons baking powder
>   ½ teaspoon salt

Melt
>   ½ cup butter

Stir in
>   2 cups light brown sugar (packed)

Beat into cooled butter-sugar mixture
>   2 eggs
>   2 teaspoons vanilla

Stir in
>   The flour mixture
>   1 cup broken pecan meats

Spread batter in a greased 9-inch square baking pan. Bake in a preheated oven at 350° for 20 minutes or until done. Cut into bars.

ELLEN'S "TEACHER" BROWNIES

Blend thoroughly
> *½ pound butter, melted*
> *1 cup sifted flour*
> *¼ cup brown sugar, packed*

Spread evenly in a greased 9-inch square pan. Bake in a preheated oven at 350° for 10 minutes.

Sift together
> *¼ cup flour*
> *1 teaspoon baking powder*

Stir in
> *1 cup brown sugar, packed*
> *1 6-ounce package semi-sweet chocolate bits*
> *1 cup chopped walnut meats*
> *2 eggs, slightly beaten*
> *1 teaspoon vanilla*

Spread over the first cooked layer. Bake in a preheated oven at 350° for 30 minutes. Cut at once into bars.

"BRITTA'S" BROWNIES

FROM A SWEDISH KITCHEN

Sift together
> *1 cup all-purpose flour*
> *6 tablespoons cocoa*
> *1 teaspoon grated orange peel*
> *½ teaspoon baking powder*

Cream together
  1 cup sugar
  ½ cup softened butter

Stir in
  2 eggs, beaten

Mix in
  The flour-cocoa mixture

Spread batter in a greased 9 × 13-inch baking pan. Sprinkle on
  ½ cup thin-sliced blanched almonds

Bake in a preheated oven at 350° for 15 minutes. Be careful not to overbake. Cut at once into small squares or diamonds.

DATE BARS

OUR MOST POPULAR COOKIE BAR

Sift together
  1 cup all-purpose flour
  ½ teaspoon baking powder
  ¼ teaspoon salt

Cream
  1 cup sugar
  ⅓ cup softened butter

Beat in
  2 large eggs
  1 teaspoon vanilla

Stir in
  The flour mixture

Add
  1½ cups dates, quartered
  ½ cup broken walnuts

Spread batter in a greased 9-inch square baking pan. Bake in a pre-heated oven at 375° for 25 minutes or until done. Cut into bars at once. Sprinkle sugar on top. Leave bars in the pan until cool.

Suggestion: Substitute pecan meats for a different flavor. Omit sugar on top for a less sweet cookie bar.

PINEAPPLE SQUARES

GRANDDAUGHTER-IN-LAW SHEILA WEEKS' RECIPE

Sift together
  2 cups all-purpose flour
  1 teaspoon baking powder
  1 teaspoon baking soda

Cream together
  ½ cup brown sugar (packed)
  ½ cup white sugar
  ½ cup soft butter
  ½ teaspoon vanilla

Beat into creamed mixture
  1 egg

Stir into creamed mixture, in order,
  1 cup crushed undrained pineapple
  The flour mixture
  ½ cup chopped walnuts or pecans

Bake in a preheated oven in a greased 9 × 13-inch pan at 350° for 25 minutes. Cut into bars. Dust with confectioners' sugar or ice with thin frosting.

LEMON SQUARES

FROM THE KITCHEN OF IDA BERQUIST

BOTTOM LAYER

Mix together using a pastry blender or electric mixer
   ½ cup cold butter cut in pieces
   ¼ cup confectioners' sugar
   1 cup sifted all-purpose flour

Pat out this mixture in a greased 9-inch square baking pan. Bake in a preheated oven at 350° for 15 minutes. Do not overbake, mixture should be light golden. Let cool for 10 minutes.

TOP LAYER

Beat together
   2 eggs
   1 cup sugar
   ¼ teaspoon salt

Stir in
   2 tablespoons flour sifted with
   ½ teaspoon baking powder

Add
   2 tablespoons lemon juice
   2 tablespoons grated lemon rind

Spread this topping evenly over the baked portion in pan. Bake in a preheated oven at 350° for 20 minutes. Cut into squares. Dust top with confectioners' sugar.

ALMOND SQUARES

BOTTOM LAYER

Cream together
  1 cup flour
  2 tablespoons confectioners' sugar
  ½ cup butter

Pat into bottom of a greased 9-inch square pan. Bake in a preheated oven at 350° for 10 minutes.

TOP LAYER

Mix together
  2 eggs, beaten until light
  1¼ cups brown sugar
  2 tablespoons flour
  ¾ cup shredded coconut
  ¾ cup chopped almonds
  1 tablespoon almond extract

Spread over baked mixture. Bake in a preheated oven at 350° for 10 minutes or until slightly brown. Sprinkle with sugar. Cut into bars.

BUTTERSCOTCH MERINGUE BARS

BOTTOM LAYER

Sift together
  2 cups all-purpose flour
  1 teaspoon baking powder
  ¼ teaspoon salt

Cream
  ½ cup softened butter
  ½ cup sugar

Beat in
> 2 egg yolks
> 1 teaspoon vanilla

Stir in
> *The flour mixture*
> *4 tablespoons heavy cream*

Mix in
> *1 cup broken pecan meats*

Spread mixture evenly in a greased 7½ × 11-inch pan. Bake in a preheated oven at 350° for 15 minutes. Let cool for 10 minutes.

TOP LAYER

Beat until stiff and shiny
> *2 egg whites*

Beat in
> *1 teaspoon vanilla*

Fold in
> *1 cup sifted light brown sugar*

Spread this meringue over the baked mixture. Bake in preheated oven at 275° for 45 minutes. Cut into bars. Cool before removing from the pan.

MAPLE BUTTERNUT BARS

Sift together
> *1 cup all-purpose flour*
> *½ teaspoon baking powder*
> *¼ teaspoon salt*

Cream thoroughly
> *½ cup soft maple sugar*
> *½ cup softened butter*

Add and mix well
  2 large eggs, beaten until light

Stir in
  The flour mixture

Add
  ½ cup broken butternut meats (If butternuts are not available, substitute walnuts.)

Spread the butter in a greased 9-inch square baking pan. Bake in a preheated oven at 375° for 35 minutes. Cut into squares. Remove from pan.

Ice with Maple Butter (*see p. 411*).

BRANDIED CHRISTMAS FRUIT BARS

Prepare fruit several hours before making the fruit bars. Mix together in a shallow bowl and cover tightly
  1½ cups candied cherries, halved
  ½ cup citron, diced
  1 cup candied pineapple, diced
  5 tablespoons brandy

Sift together
  1¾ cups all-purpose flour
  1 teaspoon baking powder
  ¼ teaspoon salt

Cream together thoroughly
  ½ cup softened butter
  1 cup sugar

Beat in
  2 eggs
  2 tablespoons brandy

Stir in
  The flour mixture

Mix in
  The brandied fruits
  1 cup broken pecan meats

Spread the batter in a greased 9-inch baking pan. Bake in a preheated oven at 375° for 40 minutes. Fruit bars will be soft inside. Brush with more brandy, sprinkle with sugar and cut into bars. Cool before removing from the pan.

❧ 25 ❧

Cakes

Traditional and modern cakes, including gingerbread, cupcakes, sponge cakes, cheesecakes, fruitcakes, and upside-down cakes

ELLEN'S APPLESAUCE CAKE

OUR SIX-GENERATION "RECEIPT"

Sift together twice
>*2 cups all-purpose flour*
>*1 teaspoon baking powder*
>*½ teaspoon salt*
>*½ teaspoon each cinnamon, ground cloves, nutmeg*
>*Pinch of ginger*

Cream together
>*¾ cup sugar*
>*½ cup softened butter*

Mix together
>*¾ cup applesauce*
>*¼ cup molasses*
>*1 teaspoon baking soda*

Stir into creamed mixture. Mix in
>*The flour-spice mixture*

Add
>*½ cup broken walnut meats*
>*½ cup raisins*

Bake in a large greased loaf pan in a preheated oven at 350° for 60 minutes or until cake is done.

Variation: Substitute dates or citron for raisins. Omit nutmeats.

ESTHER'S DUTCH APPLE CAKE

Peel and slice thin
>*Cooking apples to measure 2 cups*

Sift together into a large bowl
>*1¾ cups all-purpose flour*

  1 cup sugar
  2 teaspoons baking powder
  ½ teaspoon salt

Place in a measuring cup
  1 large egg, unbeaten
  1 tablespoon melted butter

Add
  Milk to fill the cup

Add to the flour mixture
  Contents of the cup
  1 teaspoon vanilla

Beat well to make a smooth batter. Pour into a greased 9-inch square baking pan. Arrange the apple pieces over the top, pushing them down slightly into the batter.

Sprinkle with
  2 teaspoons sugar mixed with
  ¼ teaspoon cinnamon

Bake in a preheated oven at 375° for 35 minutes or until apple slices are soft and cake is done. Serve warm with whipped cream. MAKES 8 SERVINGS.

MAPLE GINGER CAKE

Granddaughter-in-law Sheila Weeks' recipe wins the praise of all who taste it.

Sift together
  2 cups all-purpose flour
  1 teaspoon baking soda
  ½ teaspoon ginger

½ *teaspoon allspice*
¼ *teaspoon salt*

Beat together
    1 egg
    1 cup maple syrup
    1 cup commercial sour cream

Sift in and beat well
    The flour mixture

Beat in
    2 tablespoons melted butter

Pour into a greased 9-inch square pan. Cook in a preheated oven at 350° for 30 minutes, or until cake is done. Serve with maple sugar or with Maple Sauce (*recipe follows*).

MAPLE SAUCE

Put into a double boiler
    2 egg yolks

Beat well. Cook over hot (not boiling) water.

Stir in slowly
    ⅔ *cup hot maple syrup*

Cook and stir until the mixture is the consistency of thin custard. Cool to room temperature. Fold in
    ½ *cup heavy cream, whipped stiff*
    1 teaspoon rum

GRANDMOTHER SMITH'S GINGERBREAD

ADAPTED FROM AUNT MARY'S COOKBOOK

Sift together
    2½ cups all-purpose flour
    ½ teaspoon cream of tartar
    ½ teaspoon nutmeg
    ¾ teaspoon ginger

Cream together
    ½ cup softened butter
    ½ cup sugar

Add and beat in thoroughly
    2 large eggs

Dissolve
    ¾ teaspoon baking soda in
    1 cup buttermilk

Stir into the creamed mixture
    The buttermilk-soda combination
    1 cup dark molasses

Add and mix until batter is quite smooth
    The flour mixture

Pour batter into a greased deep 9-inch square baking pan. Bake in a preheated oven at 350° for 35 minutes or until gingerbread is done.

MOTHER'S GINGERBREAD

Sift together
    2½ cups all-purpose flour
    1½ teaspoons baking soda
    ½ teaspoon salt
    ½ teaspoon ginger
    ½ teaspoon cinnamon
    ¼ teaspoon ground cloves

Cream thoroughly
  ½ cup softened butter
  ½ cup sugar

Add one at a time and beat well after each addition
  2 large eggs

Stir in alternately
  1 cup light molasses
  The flour mixture

Beat in
  1 cup boiling hot water

Pour the batter into a greased 9 × 13-inch baking pan. Bake in a pre-heated oven at 350° for 35 minutes. Serve warm with whipped cream.

ESTHER'S SOUR CREAM CAKE

In our grandmother's time, when butter was churned every week, sour cream was used lavishly in baking. The Weeks family enjoys the special flavor of this tender cake, made according to Grandmother Smith's century old "receipt"—except that Esther's directions are more explicit.

Sift together twice
  1¾ cups pastry flour
  1 teaspoon cream of tartar
  ½ teaspoon baking soda
  ¼ teaspoon salt

Beat until fairly smooth
  1 cup well-soured heavy cream with
  1 cup sugar
  1 teaspoon vanilla

Stir in
  2 eggs, beaten until light

Fold in
  The flour mixture

Pour batter into a greased 9-inch square baking tin. Bake in a pre-heated oven at 350° for 30 minutes or until cake is done. Serve plain or with vanilla ice cream.

Note: Esther often doubles the recipe and bakes the cake in a 9 × 13-inch pan.

ANNE'S ANGEL WING CUPCAKES

Mix batter for Sour Cream Cake (*see p. 289*). Bake in greased cupcake pans, filling them two thirds full. Make a lemon filling.

Mix
  1 cup sugar
  2½ tablespoons all-purpose flour

Add
  ¼ cup lemon juice
  Grated rind of two lemons

Melt in a double boiler
  1 teaspoon butter

Stir in
  The sugar-lemon mixture

Add a little at a time and cook, stirring until thick
  1 medium egg, slightly beaten

Cool the filling. Prepare and fill the cupcakes in the following manner: Cut a circular section from the top of each cake, making a hole about one-half inch deep. Leave the outside of the cake intact. Spoon filling into the cakes. Divide the circular cut sections in half. Replace on top of the cakes, reversing halves to form an angle making the angel wings. Sift confectioners' sugar generously all over the cakes.

Note: Bake cupcakes at 375° for 15-20 minutes.

MOLASSES SPICE CUPCAKES

Sift together three times
    2 cups all-purpose flour
    ½ teaspoon baking soda
    1 teaspoon cream of tartar
    1 teaspoon ginger
    ¼ teaspoon ground cloves
    ¼ teaspoon allspice

Cream
    ½ cup sugar with
    1 cup heavy cream, very well soured

Add and beat well
    2 large eggs

Stir in
    ⅓ cup light molasses

Add the flour mixture and beat only until smooth (do not overbeat). Spoon batter into greased deep muffin tin or cupcake pan (MAKES 12 CUPCAKES). Bake in a preheated oven at 350° for 30 minutes or until cakes are done. Remove from tin and let cool. Swirl Lemon Frosting thickly over tops of cakes (*recipe follows*).

LEMON FROSTING

Beat together, using an electric mixer,
    ⅓ cup soft butter
    2½ cups confectioners' sugar
    ¼-⅓ cup fresh lemon juice
    4 drops yellow food coloring

OLD-FASHIONED MARBLE CAKE

FATHER'S FAVORITE "PLAIN" CAKE

Mother made her Marble Spice Cake so often she could mix it up "with one hand tied behind her," as the old saying goes. We had forgotten how good this cake was until Granddaughter-in-law Patty Weeks copied the recipe from Esther's cookbook and tried it out for her family. Patty sometimes ices the cake with a brown-sugar frosting (*recipe for Penuche Frosting follows*) and thus makes Mother's everyday cake into an elegant party dessert, delicious and rich.

かなる

Sift together twice
   3 cups cake flour
   1 teaspoon baking powder
   ½ teaspoon salt

Cream together
   1 cup softened butter
   2 cups sifted sugar

Cream in
   4 large eggs, beaten until light
   1 teaspoon vanilla

Add alternately, beating after each addition,
   The dry ingredients
   1 cup buttermilk mixed with
   1 teaspoon baking soda

Divide the batter in half. Set aside one part. Fold into the second part
   ¾ cup flour sifted with
   ½ teaspoon baking soda and
   1 teaspoon each ground cloves, cinnamon, allspice

Stir into this spiced part
   ½ cup light molasses

Bake in 2 greased loaf pans for plain cake. Use a greased 9 × 13-inch pan for frosted cake. Spoon the batters into pan alternately—spiced and unspiced. Swirl with the spoon to produce a marbled effect. Bake in preheated oven at 350° for 30 to 40 minutes or until cake tests done.

PATTY WEEKS' PENUCHE FROSTING

Melt in a heavy saucepan
½ cup butter

Stir in gradually
1 cup brown sugar, packed

Add
¼ cup light cream

Bring to a boil, stirring constantly. Remove from heat. Cool to luke-warm or 120°. Stir in
2 cups confectioners' sugar, sifted

Note: This frosting will remain soft indefinitely if kept in the refrigerator.

THE NEW ENGLAND HOMESTEAD CHOCOLATE CAKE

Father had a notion that chocolate should be used only in candy. He often brought home a bag of chocolate drops from the grocery store. He hid the bag of candy in his clothes closet and passed the chocolate drops out sparingly, usually to pacify someone with hurt or indignant feelings. But chocolate cooked in his food he couldn't stand, so we never used to have chocolate cake when we were little. Early in their marriage Mother got into the habit of cooking only what suited Father, just as Grandmother Smith had always cooked exactly according to Grandfather's "dictates." We have no doubt that all the generations of Smith wives had done the same, clear back to Susanna, wife of Robert Smith, our ancestor who came to the Massachusetts Bay Colony in

1630. No wonder the Smith men had become the autocrats of their dinner table. Poor Father was doomed to be the last! The times were changing too fast and he had too many daughters. His unquestioned authority began to slip. True, when Esther had her hair bobbed without asking him (she knew what he would say) and I put on my first pair of white linen knickers, there were loud, stormy tirades and everyone crept around quietly for a day or two, but the hair stayed stylishly short and the knickers were worn out, giving way finally to shorts and slacks. Mother clipped a recipe from the Woman's Page of *The New England Homestead* and we began to have chocolate cake on the table. Mother compromised when it came to food and always made a white cake too, so Father had his frosted white cake and we enjoyed both chocolate and white. I always think of this particular chocolate cake with a bit of nostalgia for those skylarking years when boyfriends in their rattly old cars were constantly driving up to the farm to spend the evening. There were times when some boy was suspected of being fully as intrigued by the thought of Mother's chocolate cake as by the desire to spend the evening with one of us girls.

Sift together twice
   ¾ cup cake flour
   1 teaspoon baking soda
   4 tablespoons cocoa
   ¼ teaspoon salt
   1 large pinch ground cloves

Beat together
   1 large egg
   1 cup sifted sugar
   ¾ cup well-soured heavy cream
   1 teaspoon vanilla

Add and beat well
   The sifted flour mixture

Beat in just before putting cake into the oven
   ¼ cup boiling water

Bake in a greased 9-inch square pan in a preheated oven at 350° for 30 minutes or until done. Ice as desired.

FRANCES' DEVIL'S FUN CAKE

When our youngest brother Joe (Gardner) was away in service during World War II he often wrote telling us how homesick he was and how much he missed the good farm food. He once said he longed especially for a big piece of the dark chocolate layer cake Frances often made. The very first time Joe came home on leave, Frances made this Devil's Fun Cake just for him and he ate the whole cake, all by himself.

Sift together three times
 1¾ cups cake flour
 ¾ teaspoon baking soda
 ½ teaspoon salt

Put into a large bowl
 4 squares baking chocolate, cut into small pieces

Add and stir until chocolate is melted
 ¾ cup boiling water

Cool to lukewarm. Beat in
 ½ cup softened butter
 1 teaspoon vanilla
 1¾ cups sifted sugar

Add one at a time, beating after each addition
 3 large eggs

Add alternately, mixing only enough to make a smooth batter
 The dry ingredients
 ¾ cup buttermilk

Bake in 2 greased deep 9-inch layer-cake pans in a preheated oven at 350° for 35 minutes or until cake is done. Cool cakes. Meanwhile prepare a filling-topping.

Melt in a double boiler
 2 squares unsweetened baking chocolate with
 1 tablespoon hot water

Stir in
  2 lightly beaten eggs

Cook for 2 minutes stirring constantly. Remove from heat. Beat in a little at a time
  ¼ cup softened butter
  2 teaspoons vanilla
  Enough confectioners' sugar for spreading consistency

Put cake layers together, spreading filling between layers and over the top of the cake.

ALLYN'S COCOA CAKE

AN EASY-TO-MIX CAKE

Sift together
  1½ cups flour
  1 teaspoon baking powder
  ¾ teaspoon baking soda

Heat in a heavy saucepan
  ½ cup unsweetened cocoa
  1 cup water

Bring to a boil. Stir until mixture thickens slightly. Remove from heat and cool.

Cream together in a large bowl
  1 cup sugar
  ½ cup Crisco (or other vegetable shortening)
  ½ teaspoon salt
  1 teaspoon vanilla

Add one at a time, beating well,
  2 large eggs

Add and beat in the cooled cocoa mixture. Stir in the dry ingredients. Bake in a greased 9-inch cake pan in a preheated oven at 375° for 30 minutes or until cake is done.
Serve warm plain, or cool and ice with a butter frosting.

MOCHA POUND CAKE

ADAPTED BY GRANDDAUGHTER JOANN BAILEY

Sift together
  2 cups cake flour
  1¼ cups sugar
  1 tablespoon instant coffee
  ½ teaspoon salt
  ½ teaspoon cream of tartar
  ¼ teaspoon baking soda

Cream by hand or with an electric mixer
  ¾ cup softened butter

Stir in
  ½ cup cold water
  1 teaspoon vanilla

Mix in, stirring until dampened, then beating with electric mixer,
  The flour mixture

Add one at a time, beating after each addition,
  3 medium eggs

Add and beat until smooth
  2 squares unsweetened chocolate, melted

Pour the batter into a greased 9¼ × 5¼-inch loaf pan. Bake in a preheated oven at 325° for 50 minutes or until cake is done. Dust with confectioners' sugar. Serve with ice cream.

Note: This cake is best when freshly baked.

ESTHER'S ONE-EGG CAKE

AN OLD-TIME, INEXPENSIVE FAVORITE

Sift together
  1¾ cups cake flour
  1 cup sugar
  2 teaspoons baking powder

Put into a measuring cup
  1 large egg
  Enough milk to fill the cup

Beat the egg-milk mixture in a large mixing bowl. Add and beat
  1 tablespoon melted butter
  1 teaspoon vanilla

Add and blend thoroughly
  The flour mixture

Bake in a greased 9-inch square pan in a preheated oven at 350°
for 30 minutes or until cake is done.

Variations:
BOSTON CREAM PIE: Bake the cake in two greased 8-inch layer-cake
pans. Put the layers together with a vanilla-flavored cream-filling and
spread a thin chocolate icing over the top.

LEMON CREAM CAKE: Put the layers together with a lemon filling and
dust the top with confectioners' sugar.

MARY'S DUTCH CHERRY CAKE

Pit and let stand at least an hour
  Sour cherries to measure 2 cups plus 12 cherries

Drain and reserve juice.

Sift together
    1½ cups all-purpose flour
    2 teaspoons baking powder
    ¼ teaspoon salt

Place in a bowl and beat
    2 egg yolks
    ¼ cup melted butter
    ½ cup sugar

Add and mix to make a batter
    The flour mixture
    ½ cup milk

Add and mix in gently
    1 teaspoon almond extract
    2 cups cherries, drained

Beat until stiff and glossy and fold into the batter
    2 egg whites with
    ¼ cup sugar

Spread the batter in a greased 9 × 13-inch pan. Bake in a preheated oven at 350° for about 25 minutes. (Cake will be thin. Do not overbake.) Cut in squares and spoon on Cherry Sauce (*recipe follows*). MAKES 12 TO 16 SERVINGS.

CHERRY SAUCE

Mix in a saucepan
    1 tablespoon cornstarch
    ¼ cup sugar
    ¼ cup cold water
    1 cup reserved cherry juice (add water if needed)

Bring mixture to a boil. Add and stir until sauce is smooth
    1 tablespoon butter
    1 teaspoon almond extract
    12 cherries, pitted

MARY'S CINNAMON CAKE

AN EASY-TO-MIX CAKE

Sift together
  1½ cups cake flour
  ½ teaspoon salt
  2 teaspoons baking powder
  ½ teaspoon cinnamon

Cream together
  ⅓ cup softened butter
  1 cup sugar
  1 teaspoon vanilla

Add and beat well
  2 large eggs

Add alternately, beating after each addition,
  ½ cup milk
  The flour mixture

Spread batter in a greased 9-inch square baking tin. Sprinkle a mixture of ⅓ cup sugar mixed with 2 teaspoons cinnamon thickly all over the top of the batter. Bake in a preheated oven at 350° for 30 minutes, or until done. Cut in squares and serve warm.

Note: This cake is a favorite with children. Mother used to double the recipe, yet we ate the whole cake at one meal.

ANNE'S PRUNE SPICE CAKE

Sift together
  2 cups all-purpose flour
  1 teaspoon salt
  1 teaspoon baking soda
  1 teaspoon baking powder
  1½ teaspoons cinnamon

1 teaspoon nutmeg
1 teaspoon allspice

Cream with electric mixer
½ cup softened butter
1½ cups sifted sugar

Add one at a time, beating after each addition,
3 eggs

Mix in
1 cup cooked, drained prunes, chopped

Add alternately, beating after each addition,
1 cup buttermilk
The flour-spice mixture

Bake in 2 greased loaf tins in a preheated oven at 350° for 35 minutes or until cake is done.

Note: This cake keeps very well. It is good plain or with a brown sugar frosting. (*See recipe for Penuche Frosting p. 293.*)

ESTHER'S BLUEBERRY CAKE

Sift together
3½ cups all-purpose flour
3 teaspoons baking powder
½ teaspoon baking soda
½ teaspoon salt

Place in a large bowl and beat well
2 cups well-soured heavy cream

Beat in a little at a time
2 cups sifted sugar
2 teaspoons vanilla

Add one at a time, beating after each addition,
   4 large eggs

Stir in and mix to make a smooth batter
   The flour mixture

Add
   1½ cups fresh blueberries, lightly floured

Pour batter into a greased 9 × 13-inch pan. Bake in a preheated oven at 350° for 45 minutes or until cake is done.
MAKES 16 SERVINGS.

Suggestion: Serve as a dessert with Grandmother Smith's Hot Pudding Sauce flavored with 1 teaspoon lemon extract or 2 tablespoons fresh lemon juice. (*See recipe for Hot Pudding Sauce p. 362.*)

MOTHER'S WHITE MOON CAKE

The ladies of the Gilford Community Church and the Mt. Belknap Grange always used to pride themselves on the baked goods they brought to "sociables" in the village. Mother and her friends exchanged their most treasured recipes. Although we do not remember which of Mother's friends gave her this recipe, we believe there may be some good cook in Gilford, New Hampshire, who still makes this white party cake, using the original directions from a yellowed, hand-written cookbook.

Sift together three times
   3 cups cake flour
   3 teaspoons baking powder
   ½ teaspoon salt

Cream together in a large bowl
   2 cups sifted sugar
   ⅔ cup Crisco (or other white vegetable shortening)

Add alternately, beating after each addition,
1 cup milk
2 teaspoons vanilla
The flour mixture

Fold in lightly
5 egg whites, beaten until very stiff and glossy

Bake in 2 greased 9-inch layer-cake tins in a preheated oven at 350°
for 30 minutes or until cake is done. Cool slightly. Turn out cakes and
frost while they are still warm. Use a thin white icing between the
layers and on top. Let the top frosting run down over the sides of the
cake in driplets, thus adding a silvery appearance.

HICKORY NUT CAKE

FROM THE KITCHEN OF LOIS NELSON

Sift together
3 cups cake flour (reserving 1 tablespoon)
2 teaspoons baking powder

Cream thoroughly, using your clean hands
2 cups sifted sugar
⅔ cup softened butter

Add alternately, mixing well after each addition,
1 cup water (room temperature)
The flour mixture

Mix in
1 cup chopped hickory nuts or pecans (floured)

Fold in
5 egg whites, beaten until stiff and glossy

Bake in a greased 9 × 13-inch pan in a preheated oven at 350° for 45
minutes or until cake is done. Frost in the pan with this white icing
and decorate top of cake with nutmeat halves.

ICING

Beat until smooth, using the electric mixer,
3 tablespoons melted butter
3 tablespoons melted Crisco (or other white vegetable shortening)
5 tablespoons light cream
2½ cups sifted confectioners' sugar

SILVER CAKE

GRANDDAUGHTER SUSAN WOOLDRIDGE'S BIRTHDAY CAKE

Sift together three times
3 cups cake flour
4 teaspoons baking powder

Cream until very smooth
¾ cup Crisco (or other white vegetable shortening)
2 cups sugar
1 teaspoon salt
1 teaspoon vanilla
½ teaspoon almond extract

Beat in alternately, using an electric mixer,
The flour mixture
1 cup water (room temperature)

Add all at once and beat with a mixer for 2 minutes
6 egg whites

Spread batter in a greased 9 × 13-inch cake pan. Bake in a preheated oven at 350° for 45 minutes or until cake is done. Ice with a fluffy boiled frosting made with egg whites, or any favorite white frosting.

ESTHER'S NEVER-FAIL SPONGE CAKE

AN EASY-TO-MIX CAKE THAT LIVES UP TO ITS NAME

Sift together
2½ cups cake flour
4 teaspoons baking powder
¼ teaspoon salt

Beat in a large bowl
1 egg white

Add and beat until foamy
4 egg yolks

Add gradually, beating until light,
1¾ cups sifted sugar
1 teaspoon vanilla

Mix in alternately, beating until smooth,
1 cup boiling water
The flour mixture

Fold in smoothly and lightly
3 egg whites, beaten until very stiff

Bake in a 9-inch angel cake pan in a preheated oven at 325° for 45 minutes or until cake is done. Invert pan and cool. Serve plain or with a white icing.

THREE-EGG SPONGE CAKE

FROM THE KITCHEN OF A SWEDISH-AMERICAN COOK

Sift together three times
1 cup cake flour
1 teaspoon baking powder

Beat until foamy and very light
3 large eggs

Continue to beat while adding a little at a time
1 cup sugar

Fold in
The flour mixture

Stir in
⅓ cup hot water
1 teaspoon vanilla

Add, stirring in carefully and gently,
3 tablespoons melted butter

Butter an 8-inch tube pan. Dust bottom and sides with
2 tablespoons fine dry breadcrumbs

Turn batter into pan. Bake in a preheated oven at 350° for 50 minutes or until cake is done. Invert on a wire rack.

BOSTON SPONGE CAKE

FROM THE KITCHEN OF FRANCES RICHARDSON HIGGINS

Our recipe for 5-egg sponge cake came from the hand-written cookbook of a true Boston "blueblood." Among her ancestors were governors of the Massachusetts Bay Colony and captains who sailed their clipper ships around the Horn. The family fortune had dwindled away by the time she was middle-aged. Then this aristocratic Bostonian, who had never set foot in a kitchen except to supervise, soon became an expert cook and managed a successful tearoom and catering service for many years. To be served at a fancy tea party, Boston Sponge Cake should be frosted with a delicate pink icing and sliced thin. We like it even better cut while still warm into big wedges and served with cold milk. That is the way we first sampled the cake in the New Hampshire farm kitchen of our Bostonian friend's daughter.

✦

Sift together three times
1 cup cake flour
1 teaspoon baking powder

Beat until very light and foamy
  5 egg yolks (large eggs)

Add gradually, still beating hard,
  1 cup sugar
  1 teaspoon lemon extract
  1 tablespoon cold water

Mix in thoroughly but gently
  The flour mixture

Fold in to make a smooth batter
  5 egg whites, beaten until stiff and shiny

Bake in a 9-inch tube pan in a preheated oven at 350° for 50 minutes or until cake tests done. Invert pan on a wire rack until cake is cool.

JELLY ROLL

Sift together three times
  1½ cups cake flour
  2 teaspoons baking powder

Beat until stiff and glossy
  3 egg whites

Fold in
  1 cup sifted sugar
  3 egg yolks, beaten until foamy and thick

Mix in thoroughly but lightly
  The flour mixture

Spread batter evenly in a buttered 15½ × 10½-inch jelly roll pan. Bake in a preheated oven at 350° for 15 minutes. Turn cake quickly out onto a clean dish towel sprinkled with confectioners' sugar. If cake edges are crisp, cut off thin strips. Roll the cake in the towel and let stand a few minutes. Unroll and spread with jam or jelly. Roll up firmly. Dust the outside of the cake roll with confectioners' sugar and wrap in waxed paper and refrigerate. Cover cake with whipped cream just before it is to be served.

VERNA'S ANGEL CAKE

Sift together four times
　　1 cup cake flour
　　1 cup fine granulated sugar

Beat until foamy
　　11 egg whites (room temperature)

Continue to beat until egg whites are stiff and glossy, adding gradually
　　1 teaspoon cream of tartar
　　¼ teaspoon salt
　　1 teaspoon vanilla
　　¼ cup sifted sugar

Fold into egg white mixture smoothly, using a large shallow-bowled spoon or wire whisk,
　　The sifted flour-sugar mixture

Bake in a 10-inch tube pan in a preheated oven set at 325° for 60 minutes or until cake is done. Invert the pan and let stand until the cake is cool.

MOCK ANGEL CAKE

At times of the year when eggs were scarce Mother sometimes made this white cake which we considered almost as good as real angel cake. She used the yolks in a custard pudding.

Sift together four times
　　2 cups cake flour
　　2 teaspoons baking powder
　　1¾ cups sugar
　　1 teaspoon cream of tartar

Add and beat well
  1 cup boiling water
  1 teaspoon vanilla

Set batter aside and leave until it cools to room temperature.

Fold in
  5 large egg whites, beaten until stiff and glossy

Bake in 9-inch tube pan in preheated oven set at 275° for 60 minutes or until cake is done. Invert the pan and let stand until the cake is cool.

GOLD CAKE

FROM THE KITCHEN OF OLIVE FOWLER

Sift together three times
  3 cups cake flour
  2 teaspoons baking powder

Beat until foamy and light
  10 egg yolks

Continue to beat while adding a little at a time
  2 cups sifted sugar
  ¼ teaspoon salt
  ½ teaspoon nutmeg
  1 teaspoon lemon extract

Fold in alternately, thoroughly but lightly,
  The flour mixture
  1 cup cold water

Bake in a 10-inch tube pan in a preheated oven set at 350° for 60 minutes or until cake is done. Invert the pan on a wire rack. Let stand until cool. Serve plain or with a thin icing.

FRESH COCONUT POUND CAKE

ADAPTED FROM AN OLD "RECEIPT"

Use a fresh coconut with a bright brown shell. Pierce the "eyes" and drain off the milk. Crack and remove shell. Cut coconut into pieces and peel. Crush in an electric blender, doing a small amount at a time, or use a hand grater. Place any left-over coconut in plastic bags and freeze for future use.

Sift together twice
3 cups cake flour
2 teaspoons cream of tartar
1 teaspoon baking soda

Cream together thoroughly
½ cup softened butter
½ cup Crisco (or other white vegetable shortening)
1¾ cups sifted sugar

Add and beat well
4 egg yolks, beaten until light
1 tablespoon vanilla

Add alternately, mixing well,
The flour mixture
1 cup milk

Mix in
1 cup fresh, finely crushed coconut

Fold in
4 egg whites, beaten until stiff and glossy

Bake in 2 greased loaf tins in preheated oven set at 350° for 60 minutes or until cake is done. Frost with white icing and sprinkle fresh coconut on the cake or serve without icing.

Note: A 10-inch tube pan may be used. Pan should be inverted on a wire rack for cooling.

MADEIRA CAKE

ADAPTED FROM AN OLD ENGLISH RECIPE

Sift together three times
  2⅓ cups cake flour
  ½ teaspoon baking powder

Cream together thoroughly
  ½ pound softened butter
  2 cups sifted sugar
  1 teaspoon vanilla
  1 teaspoon almond extract

Beat into creamed mixture, one at a time,
  6 egg yolks

Continue beating until mixture is light and foamy. Add, two at a time, beating well after each addition,
  6 egg whites

Fold in lightly
  The sifted flour mixture

Bake in a 10-inch tube pan in a preheated oven at 325° for 75 minutes or until cake is done. Invert pan on a wire rack for cooling.

Note: Use three small bowls or teacups as you break eggs so you will have two whites in each bowl.

Suggestion: Try Madeira Cake sliced, toasted and buttered as the English do.

JESSIE'S HARVEST LAYER CAKE

Sift together three times
  2½ cups cake flour
  ½ teaspoon salt
  1 teaspoon baking soda

Cream by hand or with an electric mixer
   1 cup softened butter

Add gradually and continue beating until light and fluffy
   2 cups sifted sugar
   2 teaspoons vanilla

Add one at a time and beat well after each addition
   5 large eggs
   3 squares melted chocolate

Add alternately, beating after each addition,
   1 cup buttermilk
   The flour mixture

Bake in a greased 9 $\times$ 13-inch pan or in 2 9-inch layer cake pans in a preheated oven at 350° for 40 minutes or until done. Ice with any chocolate frosting preferred.

HOLIDAY LAYER CAKE

This favorite old cake "receipt" was rarely written down because the name "1-2-3-4 Cake" made the ingredients easy to remember. Jessie's Holiday Layer Cake is an up-to-date adaptation, easy to mix with an electric beater. Here is her never-fail recipe.

Sift together three times
   3 cups cake flour
   3 teaspoons baking powder
   ½ teaspoon salt

Cream in the large bowl of an electric mixer
   1 cup softened butter

Add, 2 tablespoons at a time, creaming after each addition,
   2 cups sugar

Beat in
   1 teaspoon vanilla

Add, one at a time, beating well after each addition,
   4 large eggs

Add alternately, beating until smooth after each addition,
   The flour mixture
   1 cup milk

Spread the batter evenly in 3 greased 8-inch layer pans. Bake in a pre-heated oven at 350° for 30 minutes or until cake is done.

FILLING FOR HOLIDAY LAYER CAKE

Grind
   6 dried figs
   ½ cup seedless raisins

Cover with boiling water. Let cool. Drain. Mix
   The ground fruits
   ½ cup chopped pecans
   1 cup butter frosting (made with ⅓ cup soft butter and 2½ cups confectioners' sugar).

Spread filling between cooled cake layers. Frost top and sides with butter frosting flavored with vanilla.

SURPRISE RIBBON CAKE

Jessie's three-layer Ribbon Cake is the prettiest of our collection. Her electric mixer method simplifies the making of this elaborate cake so that it is dependable, even when made by a beginner. The combination of flavors is an added delight.

❧

Sift together three times
   3 cups cake flour
   4 teaspoons baking powder
   1 teaspoon salt

Mix together and set aside
   2 tablespoons cold water
   2 tablespoons cocoa
   ⅛ teaspoon ground cloves
   ½ teaspoon cinnamon
   ⅛ teaspoon baking soda

Cream together until soft
   ¾ cup Crisco (or other white vegetable shortening)
   2 cups sifted sugar

Add alternately to the creamed mixture, beating constantly,
   1¼ cups water
   The flour mixture

Add all at once and continue beating for 2 full minutes
   4 unbeaten egg whites

Divide batter into three equal parts. As each is completed pour into a greased 8-inch layer pan.

Add to the first part
   1 teaspoon vanilla

Add to the second part
   1 teaspoon almond extract
   Few drops red food coloring

Add to the third part
   The cocoa mixture
   Few drops red food coloring

Bake in a preheated oven at 350° for 30 minutes or until done. Cool cakes. Prepare Seven-Minute Frosting or any white frosting according to directions in a basic cookbook. Put the cake together with the dark layer on the botton and the pink layer in the middle. Spread the fluffy white frosting between the layers and frost the cake thickly all over. The surprise comes when the white frosting is cut through revealing the pretty tricolored "ribboned" slices.

ALMOND-MACE LAYER CAKE

This cake is our most elegant, yet it is really just another version of the old basic "1-2-3-4 Cake."

∾�֎∾

Mix the batter for Holiday Layer Cake (*See p. 312*), sifting with flour
 ⅛ teaspoon mace

In place of vanilla, beat into the creamed ingredients
 2 teaspoons almond extract

Bake in 3 greased 8-inch layer-cake pans in a preheated oven at 350° for 40 minutes. Cool. Prepare Almond Cream Filling (*directions follow*).

ALMOND CREAM FILLING

Beat well together
 1 cup sugar
 2 large eggs

Beat in
 2 tablespoons flour
 1 tablespoon cornstarch moistened with ¼ cup cold milk

Add and blend
 2 cups scalded milk

Cook and stir in double boiler until mixture is thick. Remove from heat.

Stir in
 1 teaspoon almond extract
 1 cup blanched almonds, ground very fine

Cool and then chill the filling.

Stir in
 1 cup whipped cream

Put the cake together, spreading Almond Cream Filling between the layers. Frost the cake with the remaining filling. Refrigerate until ready to serve.

Note: Almond-Mace Layer Cake should be eaten within a day or two. Do not freeze.

ANNE'S SOUR CREAM CHEESECAKE

Mix
> 1¼ *cups graham cracker crumbs*
> ⅓ *cup melted butter*
> ¼ *cup sugar*

Line a 9-inch round, deep cake pan with this mixture, reserving ½ cup. Bake in preheated oven at 375° for 10 minutes. Cool.

Beat with an electric mixer
> 3 *large eggs*

Add, beating in a little at a time,
> 1 *pound softened cream cheese*
> ½ *cup sugar*
> ½ *teaspoon almond extract*

Turn this mixture into the cooled graham cracker crust. Bake in preheated oven at 375° for 20 minutes. Cool to room temperature.

Mix and pour onto the cake
> 1 *pint commercial sour cream*
> 1¼ *cups sugar*
> ½ *teaspoon almond extract*

Sprinkle top with
> *The reserved crumb mixture*
> ½ *cup thinly sliced, toasted almonds*
> ¼ *teaspoon nutmeg*

Bake in preheated oven for 20 minutes at 350° or until the cake is soft-set. Chill overnight before serving.

STRAWBERRY GLAZED CHEESECAKE

Mix together to make a crust
  12 graham crackers, crushed
  ½ cup ground walnut meats
  1 tablespoon sugar
  ¼ cup melted butter (½ stick)

Press the crust into a 9-inch spring form pan. Refrigerate.

Beat until light and thick, using an electric mixer,
  5 large eggs

Add gradually and continue to beat
  1½ cups sugar
  1 teaspoon vanilla
  ½ teaspoon lemon juice

Beat in a little at a time
  1½ pounds softened cream cheese
  2 cups commercial sour cream

Beat until the batter is very smooth without lumps. Pour onto the prepared crust. Bake in a preheated oven at 350° for 90 minutes. Turn off heat and leave the cake in the oven for 90 minutes. Let cake cool in the pan to room temperature.

Mix in a saucepan
  ¾ cup crushed strawberries
  1 cup sugar

Heat to the boiling point. Stir in
  1 package unflavored gelatin dissolved in
  ¼ cup cold water

Stir and cook for 2 minutes. Chill until very thick. Spread over top and sides of the cheesecake

Decorate top with ¼-½ cup whole, perfect strawberries. Refrigerate cake until ready to serve.
THIS RICH DESSERT SERVES 12.

Note: Substitute frozen strawberries when fresh fruit is not available.

LEMON CHEESECAKE

Use a round-bottomed, deep cheesecake pan, or attach a foil "collar" around the top of a deep 9-inch cake tin. Butter bottom and sides of pan and spread with fine bread crumbs.

Sift together
    3 tablespoons all-purpose flour
    ½ teaspoon cream of tartar
    ½ teaspoon salt

Blend very thoroughly until perfectly smooth
    1 pound softened cream cheese
    1 cup sugar

Beat in one at a time
    4 large eggs

Fold in gently, blending well,
    ¼ cup fresh lemon juice and grated peel of 1 lemon
    The flour mixture
    1 cup heavy cream, whipped very stiff

Spoon the batter into the prepared pan. Bake in a preheated oven at 275° for 2 hours. Turn off the heat and leave the cake in the oven for 1 hour.

Suggestion: Use a spring form pan 9 inches × 2½-inches deep if you wish to remove cake from pan before cutting.

AUNTIE'S BOILED CAKE

AS ADAPTED FOR ROYAL'S BIRTHDAY OR CHRISTMAS CAKE

Mix together in a saucepan
    1¼ cups cold water
    1 cup sugar
    ¼ cup butter (or vegetable shortening)
    ⅓ cup seedless raisins

⅓ *cup mixed candied fruits and peels*
1 *teaspoon cinnamon*
½ *teaspoon allspice*
½ *teaspoon nutmeg*

Bring mixture to a boil quickly. Stir a little when it starts to bubble. Remove from heat. Cool to lukewarm.

Sift together
  2¼ *cups all-purpose flour*
  1 *teaspoon baking soda*
  1 *teaspoon baking powder*

Add to the cooled spice-fruit mixture
  1 *large egg, beaten until light*

Stir in
  The flour mixture

Add
  ⅓ *cup broken walnut meats*

Bake in greased 9¼ × 5¼-inch loaf pan in a preheated oven at 350° for 40 minutes or until cake is done. The top should be glazed and slightly "crackled."

Note: For Royal's December 22nd birthday, Verna bakes double the recipe in a 10-inch tube pan. She uses either pale green icing with silver trimming or white icing and red trimming. Her daughter, Barbara Turner, decorates these Christmas cakes with bits of candied cherries, citron, and slivered almonds.

CANADIAN EMBASSY LIGHT FRUITCAKE

This cake is adapted from a recipe used for many years by the wife of a Canadian Embassy official. It is our best Christmas cake, one certain to please all fruitcake lovers because it is rich and moist without being heavy. We bake the cakes in November, planning enough for family use and for gifts. Then we wrap them in aluminum foil and store in a cool place to "ripen." After you have once used the recipe, you will find the cakes easy to make and the recipe one that never fails. Prepare these fruits the day before making cakes.

❧

Mix in a large shallow bowl or pan
   1 cup dates, coarsely cut
   1 cup citron, diced
   1 cup candied cherries, coarsely cut
   2 cups mixed candied fruit peels, diced
   1 cup candied pineapple, coarsely cut

Pour over the fruits and mix well
   ½ cup light rum

Cover the bowl tightly and set aside.

Grease and line with paper
   *5 1-pound cake pans**

Sift together
   2¼ cups all-purpose flour
   1 teaspoon baking powder
   ¼ teaspoon allspice
   ¼ teaspoon mace
   ¼ teaspoon cinnamon
   ¼ teaspoon nutmeg

Cream together in a 4-quart bowl
   1 cup softened butter
   1½ cups sugar

* Use small aluminum loaf pans approximately 7½" × 4" × 2" (usually marked 1-pound) for this and other fruitcake recipes in this book. Cakes of this size make good "kitchen" gifts. Greased pans may be lined with brown paper or heavy waxed paper. Aluminum foil may also be used, but do not grease pans when using aluminum foil.

Add one at a time and beat very thoroughly after each addition
   5 large eggs

Fill a measuring cup with
   ½ cup fresh orange juice
   ¼ cup molasses
   ¼ cup light rum

Add alternately to the creamed mixture, beating after each addition,
   The cupful of liquids
   The flour mixture

Mix in
   The prepared fruits

Mix in
   1½ cups broken pecan meats

Pack the batter into the prepared cake pans. Fill corners carefully. Bake in a preheated oven at 275° for 2 hours. Cool cakes in the pans for 10 minutes. Turn out onto a wire rack. Dip a pastry brush in rum and brush warm cakes all over, allowing rum to soak into the cakes. Wrap in aluminum foil and store in a cool place.

"JAPANESE" FRUITCAKE

ADAPTED FROM AN OLD "RECEIPT"

Mix the batter for Holiday Layer Cake (*see p. 312*). Divide into 3 parts. Bake 2 parts in greased layer cake pans in a preheated oven at 350° for 30 minutes or until cake is done.

Add to the third part
   ½ cup diced, candied pineapple
   ½ cup finely cut dates
   ½ cup chopped pecan meats
   ½ teaspoon cinnamon
   ½ teaspoon allspice
   ¼ teaspoon clove
   ¼ teaspoon nutmeg
   Pinch of ground ginger

Bake the dark batter in a layer-cake pan of the same size used for the lighter batter. Cool cakes.

FILLING-TOPPING

Mix in a heavy saucepan
  1 cup crushed, drained pineapple
  1 cup fresh, finely grated coconut
  2 tablespoons diced candied ginger
  ⅓ cup lemon juice and grated peel of one lemon
  1½ cups sugar
  1 tablespoon cornstarch

Cook over medium heat stirring constantly until the mixture is very thick. Cool to room temperature. Put the cake layers together, using the dark layer in the center. Spread the filling-topping between the layers and over the top of the cake.

Suggestion: Serve this rich cake after a light meal.

WHITE FRUITCAKE

Granddaughter Jeanne Berquist Eddinger always serves this white fruit-cake to her family and guests on Christmas Day. Jeanne thinks the cake is best when baked two weeks beforehand.

❧

Prepare these fruits the day before making cake. Mix in a large shallow bowl or pan
  2 cups diced citron
  2 cups halved candied cherries

2 cups candied pineapple, sliced in thin strips
½ cup brandy

Cover the bowl tightly and set aside overnight.

Grease and line with paper
5 1-pound cake tins

Sift together three times
3¾ cups all-purpose flour
½ teaspoon salt
½ teaspoon baking powder

Cream thoroughly, using your hands,
1½ cups softened butter
2 cups sifted sugar

Add and mix thoroughly, still using your hands,
6 egg yolks, beaten until light and foamy

Combine
¾ cup milk
¼ cup brandy
2 teaspoons almond extract

Add alternately to the creamed mixture, beating well after each addition,
The cup of liquid
The sifted dry ingredients

Mix in gently but thoroughly, using your hands,
The brandied fruits
1½ cups thinly-sliced blanched almonds

Beat
6 egg whites until foamy

Add to the egg whites
1 teaspoon cream of tartar

Continue beating until the egg whites are stiff and glossy. Fold into the cake batter gently. Mix until no streaks of egg white can be seen. Pack

the cake batter into the prepared 1-pound cake pans (7½″ × 4″ × 2″).
Bake in a preheated oven at 325° for 90 minutes or until cakes are done.
Cool cakes in the pan for 10 minutes. Turn out onto a wire rack. Dip a
pastry brush in brandy and brush cakes all over, allowing the brandy
to soak into the cakes. Wrap and store overnight. Brush the cakes again
with brandy. Repeat once or twice. Wrap in aluminum foil and store
in a cool place. A few hours before serving, ice with almond-flavored
frosting. Decorate with a poinsettia design made of blanched almonds
and red and green candied cherries.

CANDIED FRUITCAKE

Prepare fruits the day before making cake.

Mix in a large bowl
> *1 pound candied pineapple, cut in strips*
> *1½ pounds dates, cut crosswise in thirds*
> *1 pound whole candied cherries*

Pour over the fruit and mix well
> *½ cup brandy*

Cover tightly and set aside overnight.

Sift together
> *2 cups all-purpose flour*
> *2 teaspoons baking powder*

Beat together
> *4 large eggs*
> *½ teaspoon salt*
> *1 cup sugar*

Stir in
> *The flour mixture*

Mix into the dough, using your hands,
  8 cups whole pecan halves
  The brandied fruits

Pack the dough carefully into 5 greased 1-pound (7½″ × 4″ × 2″) loaf tins lined with paper. Bake in a preheated oven at 275° for 90 minutes. Let cakes cool 10 minutes in pan. Turn out and peel off paper. Using a pastry brush, soak cakes with brandy. Wrap and store in a cool place for several weeks before serving.

Note: Cut the cakes into slices ½-inch thick, then divide each slice into thirds, about the size of fudge pieces.

PINEAPPLE UPSIDE-DOWN CAKE

Melt and mix in a frying pan
  3 tablespoons butter
  ½ cup light brown sugar

Drain (reserving liquid) and sauté in the hot mixture
  8 canned pineapple slices

Spread hot butter-sugar mixture in a greased 11″ × 7″ baking pan.

Arrange pineapple slices on top in a single layer.

Sift together
  1½ cups all-purpose flour
  2 teaspoons baking powder
  ½ teaspoon salt

Cream together
  ½ cup butter
  ½ cup sugar

Beat in
  1 large egg
  1 teaspoon vanilla

Mix alternately into creamed ingredients
   ½ cup reserved pineapple juice
   The flour mixture

Spread batter over the pineapple slices. Bake in a preheated oven at 350° for 35 minutes or until cake is done. Turn out on plate upside down. Serve with whipped cream.
SERVES 6 TO 8.

MARY'S APPLE-FLOPPED CAKE

Peel and slice thin
   6 firm apples

Combine in a saucepan
   Apple slices
   Hot water to cover
   A bit of red food coloring

Bring to a boil and drain. Arrange apple slices in a buttered 9-inch square baking pan.

Sift together
   1 cup all-purpose flour
   1½ teaspoons baking powder
   ¼ teaspoon salt

Cream together
   ¼ cup softened butter
   ½ cup sugar

Beat into creamed mixture
   1 large egg
   ½ teaspoon vanilla

Add alternately, beating after each addition,
   The flour mixture
   1 cup milk

Spread the batter over the apple slices. Bake in a preheated oven at 350° for 35 minutes or until done. Turn cake out onto a board or platter, apple side up.

Serve hot with vanilla ice cream.
SERVES 6 TO 8.

❦ 26 ❦

Pies and Other Desserts

Pastry and pies, homemade mincemeat,

cobbler, puddings and sauces,

strawberry shortcake

FAMILY PASTRY OR PIE CRUST MIX

When it comes to making pies, the cooks in our family are all true experts, but only husbands and sons do the boasting. Each excellent pastry maker praises the skill of the others, but remains firmly set on using her own method. Amounts of flour and shortening used in making these wonderful pies all vary greatly, but none of our cooks can (or will) record ingredients accurately. I sent out a questionnaire, compared the answers, added and divided, but did not come up with a workable recipe. Then I scrambled the hints and suggestions and added a notion of my own to produce this composite. My greatniece, Pamela Weeks, collaborated to prove the recipe easy enough for a fifteen-year-old beginner. The final result is this mix—easy to handle, convenient to keep on hand, sure to make tender pie crust, and much less expensive than a packaged mix.

෴

Sift together into a large bowl
   7½ cups all-purpose flour
   3 teaspoons baking powder
   1 teaspoon salt

Cut in a little at a time, using a pastry blender,
   1 pound (2 cups packed) cold Crisco or other vegetable shortening

Makes about 9 cups.

Store in the refrigerator. Use 2-2½ cups mix to make a 9-inch pie. To mix the dough, stir in about ¼ cup ice water a little at a time. If you find you have too much water don't hesitate to add more flour. If you have too little water so the dough cannot be rolled out, add a little more water and try again. Crust made from this mix will stand quite a bit of handling and still be tender.

To make a baked pie shell: Line a pan with pastry, making a high crust by turning under ½ inch of pastry. Make this edge stand upright and then press into a fluted edge with fingers. Prick pastry with fork all over. Dot with tiny pieces of cold butter. Bake at 450° for about

12 minutes. Check after 5 minutes and if bubbles are forming in crust, prick carefully with silver fork (do not make large holes in crust).

GREEN APPLE PIE

SMITH-FAMILY STYLE

Peel, core, and slice
Hard green pie apples to make 4 cups

Stir together
2¼ cups Family Pastry Mix (see p. 331)
About ¼ cup cold water

Line a 9-inch pie plate using half of the pastry.

Fill with
The sliced apples, mounded in the center

Sift on
1 scant cup sugar
¼ teaspoon nutmeg
¼ teaspoon cinnamon

Dot with
1 tablespoon cold butter, cut into small pieces

Cover with a top crust, pressing edge with fingers or fork tines to seal. Prick crust and brush generously with heavy cream. Bake in a preheated oven at 450° for 10 minutes, then at 350° for 35-45 minutes or until apples are soft. Cut into 6 pieces and serve hot, smothered with maple syrup.

SALT PORK APPLE PIE

Line a deep 9-inch pie plate with pastry (*see p. 331*). Fill with
4 cups tart cooking apples, sliced

Spread with
1 cup sugar

Sprinkle on
¼ teaspoon cinnamon
1 large pinch nutmeg

Chop into very small bits
A ½-inch cube of fat salt pork

Dot the apples with the salt pork bits. Put on the top crust, pressing edge to seal. Brush with cream. Prick with a fork in several places. Bake in a preheated oven at 375° for 50 minutes or until apples are soft.

Note: The tiny pieces of salt pork melt and blend with the hot juices adding a delightful tang to the flavor of the apples. We used to eat this old-fashioned apple pie hot, covered with warm maple syrup.

MINCE PIE

Line a 10-inch pie plate with pastry (*see p. 331*). Prepare a lattice top.

Fill pie with
1 quart Jessie's mincemeat (recipe follows)

Sprinkle on
2 tablespoons brandy

Put on the lattice top. Brush with
1 tablespoon heavy cream

Bake in a preheated oven at 450° for 10 minutes. Reduce heat to 350° and bake for 30 minutes.
SERVES 8.

Note: Use 1 pint mincemeat to make an 8-inch pie.

Suggestion: Serve mince pie with medium-sharp Cheddar cheese.

JESSIE'S MINCEMEAT

MADE LIKE MOTHER'S

Use
> *A 5-6 pound piece of beef with bone in*
> *(Shank or heel of the round)*

Put into a large kettle
> *The meat*
> *2 teaspoons salt*
> *1 quart cold water*

Bring to a boil. Simmer until meat falls from the bone (about 3 hours). Cool in broth. Skim off and discard fat. Put meat (including some suet) through a food chopper, using finest knife.

Peel, core, and grind
> *Baldwin apples to make 12 cups*

Mix in a large heavy kettle (canning size)
> *4 cups ground cooked beef*
> *12 cups ground apples*
> *3 1-pound boxes seeded raisins, ground*
> *1 pound ground citron*
> *2 cups sugar*
> *2 cups meat broth (more if needed to make moist)*
> *2 cups boiled cider (see pp. 125–127)*
> *1 teaspoon cinnamon*
> *1 teaspoon allspice*
> *1 teaspoon ground cloves*

Cook very slowly 2-3 hours until ingredients are well blended. Stir occasionally so mixture will not stick to the pan. Apple pieces should be soft but not mushy.

Stir in
> *1 cup brandy*

Ladle into hot sterilized jars if mincemeat is to be kept indefinitely. Store mincemeat in covered containers in refrigerator for immediate use. MAKES 6 TO 8 PINTS.

Note: If Baldwins are not available, use any firm cooking apples. Sweet cider may be substituted for boiled cider. Brandy may be omitted (Mother never used "spirits" in cooking). For amount to use in making pie, *see preceding Mince Pie recipe.*

ANNE'S EASY MINCEMEAT

Heat in a large frying pan
   2 tablespoons butter

Add and stir until brown
   2 pounds ground beef
   ½ cup hot water

Mix in a large kettle
   The partially cooked meat
   1 cup beef suet, ground
   10 cups hard green tomatoes, ground and drained
   12 cups ground cooking apples, cored but not peeled
   2 oranges, seeded and ground
   1 lemon, seeded and ground
   2 pounds seeded raisins, ground
   ½ cup light molasses
   1 teaspoon salt
   1 tablespoon ground cloves
   1 tablespoon cinnamon
   1 cup cider vinegar
   2½ pounds light brown sugar
   1 10-ounce jar jelly, grape or apple

Cook over low heat for 2 hours. Stir frequently to prevent burning. Ladle into hot sterilized jars. Seal.
MAKES ABOUT 9 QUARTS.

Variation: For a richer mincemeat, add ½ pound ground citron. Add 1 cup brandy just before canning.

GREEN TOMATO MINCEMEAT

COUSIN MIN BACON'S RECIPE

Grind, using coarse knife or food chopper
Hard green tomatoes to measure 5 cups (3 pounds)

Drain and place in a kettle with enough cold water to cover. Bring to a boil and cook 5 minutes. Drain thoroughly.

Peel, core, and grind
Cooking apples to measure 4 cups (3½ pounds)

Combine in a large kettle
The tomatoes
The apples
1 pound seeded raisins
1 cup ground beef suet
1¼ cups cider vinegar
1 tablespoon salt
2 tablespoons cinnamon
1 tablespoon nutmeg
2 teaspoons ground cloves
4 tablespoons fresh lemon juice

Bring mixture to a boil over medium heat, then simmer for 2 hours. Stir occasionally to prevent burning. Pack into hot sterilized jars. Seal. MAKES 5 PINTS.

MARY'S SOUR CHERRY PIE

Line a deep 9-inch pie plate with pastry (*see p. 331*).

Fill with
4 cups sour cherries, pitted

Mix and spread over cherries
1 cup sugar
2 tablespoons flour
¼ teaspoon cinnamon

Cover with top crust. Make three slashes in crust. Bake in a preheated oven at 400° for 10 minutes. Turn oven to 325° and bake for 45 minutes. Serve warm.

Note: If our Family Pastry Mix is used, the top crust should be brushed with cream or spread with more shortening.

ANNE'S CHERRY SUNDAE PIE

Line a deep 9-inch pie plate with pastry (*see p. 331*).

Drain, and reserve juice from
   2 1-pound cans water-packed, sour red cherries

Mix in a saucepan
   1½ cups sugar
   2 tablespoons cornstarch
   1 teaspoon fresh lemon juice
   1½ cups cherry juice

Cook over low heat for 10 minutes or until mixture is clear and a little thickened. Stir constantly to prevent burning. Allow sauce to cool slightly.

Add
   ⅛ teaspoon almond extract

Mix
   The cherries
   2 tablespoons flour

Fill the pastry with cherries. Reserve 1 cup cherry sauce. Pour remainder over the cherries. Cover pie with top crust. Spread with cream. Slash crust. Bake in a preheated oven at 450° for 10 minutes, then at 350° for 30 minutes. Just before ready to serve, heat the reserved cup of sauce. Top each piece of pie with vanilla ice cream and hot cherry sauce.

ANNE'S CHERRY COBBLER

Drain and reserve juice from
1 can (No. 2½) sour red cherries or
1 package frozen sour red cherries

Sift together
1 cup all-purpose flour
2 teaspoons baking powder
¼ teaspoon salt

Cream together
¼ cup softened butter
⅓ cup sugar

Beat in alternately until mixture is smooth
The flour mixture
½ cup milk

Pour batter into a 2-quart casserole. Spoon fruit over the batter.

Pour on
1 cup reserved fruit juice

Bake in a preheated oven at 350° for 50 minutes. Serve warm with plain cream or vanilla ice cream.

BLUEBERRY PIE I

LIKE MOTHER MADE

Line a deep 9-inch pie plate with pastry (*see p. 331*).

Fill with
4 cups fresh or frozen wild blueberries

Mix and spread over berries
1 cup sugar
4 teaspoons flour

Dot with
    1 tablespoon cold butter, cut into bits

Put on the top crust, pressing edge to seal. Brush generously with cream. Slash or prick with a fork in several places. Bake in a preheated oven at 375° for 50 minutes.

Note: Pick over but do not wash wild blueberries unless they are dusty.

BLUEBERRY PIE II

USING CULTIVATED BLUEBERRIES

Pick over and wash
    4 cups blueberries

Line a 9-inch pie plate with pastry (*see p. 331*). Fill with the blueberries.

Mix and spread over the blueberries
    ¾ cup sugar
    1 tablespoon flour

Sprinkle on
    1 tablespoon lemon juice

Put on the top crust. Brush with cream. Bake in a preheated oven at 475° for 10 minutes. Reduce heat to 350° and bake for 35 minutes or until blueberries are soft and tender.

FRESH PEACH PIE

Line a 9-inch pie plate with pastry (*see p. 331*).

Fill with
    4 cups peaches, peeled and sliced

Mix and spread over peaches
   ¾ cup sugar
   1 tablespoon flour

Dot with
   1 tablespoon cold butter, cut into bits

Sprinkle with
   2 tablespoons brandy

Put on a top crust. Brush generously with cream. Slash or prick the crust in several places. Bake in a preheated oven at 450° for 10 minutes, then at 350° for 40 minutes or until peaches are tender. Serve plain or topped with vanilla ice cream.

Note: If peaches are very ripe and juicy, add 1 tablespoon flour.

FRESH PEACH CUSTARD PIE

Line a 9-inch pie plate with pastry (*see p. 331*).

Peel, slice, and purée in an electric blender
   3 cups ripe peaches

Blend to make a smooth paste
   1 cup sugar
   1 tablespoon flour
   4 tablespoons heavy cream

Stir in
   The mashed peach mixture
   3 large eggs, beaten until light
   1 tablespoon brandy

Pour peach custard into prepared pastry. Bake in a preheated oven at 450° for 10 minutes, then at 350° for 35 minutes or until custard is set. Serve cold with whipped-cream topping.

FRESH APRICOT PIE

Line a 9-inch pie plate with pastry (*see p. 331*).

Fill with
 4 cups unpeeled ripe apricots, washed and stoned

Mix and spread over apricots
 ¾ cup sugar
 ¼ teaspoon nutmeg
 1 tablespoon flour

Dot with
 1 tablespoon cold butter, cut into bits

Put on a top crust. Brush generously with cream. Slash or prick crust in several places. Bake in a preheated oven at 450° for 10 minutes, then at 350° for 30-40 minutes or until apricots are tender.

ESTHER'S OLD-FASHIONED RHUBARB PIE

Line a 9-inch pie plate with pastry (*see p. 331*). Prepare a top crust.

Wash and cut into pieces
 6-8 stalks fresh strawberry rhubarb

Place in a saucepan and cover with cold water. Bring to the boiling point. Drain and cool.

Measure and fill pastry with
 4 cups rhubarb pieces

Mix and spread on
 2 tablespoons flour
 1¼ cups sugar

Dot with
 2 tablespoons cold butter, cut into pieces

Put on the top crust. Bake in a preheated oven at 375° for 45 minutes.

RHUBARB CUSTARD PIE

FROM THE KITCHEN OF KATHERINA LUND

Line a 9-inch pie plate with pastry (*see p. 331*). Prepare a top crust.

Wash and cut into small pieces
  4 cups strawberry rhubarb

Add and mix
  1½ cups sugar
  ¼ cup flour
  3 large eggs, beaten

Pour the filling into the prepared pastry.

Dot with
  1 tablespoon cold butter, cut into small pieces

Put the top crust on. Bake in a preheated oven at 400° for 10 minutes, then at 350° for 50 minutes.

VERNA'S PINEAPPLE PIE

Line a 9-inch pie plate with pastry (*see p. 331*). Prepare pastry strips for a lattice top.

Mix in a saucepan
  1 No. 2 can crushed pineapple
  2 tablespoons cornstarch
  ⅓ cup sugar

Cook over low heat for 8 minutes, stirring constantly. Remove from heat. Stir in
  2 beaten egg yolks
  Juice of ½ lemon

Return to heat. Cook and stir for 2 minutes.

Blend in
   1 tablespoon butter
   1 tablespoon light rum (optional)

Cool filling. Turn into prepared crust. Put on the lattice top. Bake in a preheated oven at 450° for 10 minutes, then at 350° for 20 minutes.

MAPLE PUMPKIN PIE

Line a deep 10-inch pie plate with pastry (*see p. 331*).

Mix and beat well
   2 cups cooked or canned pumpkin
   ⅔ cup soft maple sugar (see p. 410)
   1 cup light cream or milk
   3 large eggs
   1 teaspoon cinnamon
   ½ teaspoon ground ginger
   ½ teaspoon nutmeg
   ½ teaspoon allspice
   ½ teaspoon salt

Bake in a preheated oven at 375° for 10 minutes, then at 325° for 45 minutes or until filling is set.

Suggestion: Serve pumpkin pie with a topping of sweetened, spiced whipped cream or in the old-fashioned way—with large wedges of "store" cheese.

ELLEN'S HONEY PUMPKIN PIE

Line a deep 9-inch pie plate with pastry (*see p. 331*).

Mix and beat until smooth
  2 cups home-cooked or canned pumpkin
  ½ cup white sugar
  ½ cup light brown sugar
  ½ teaspoon salt
  1 teaspoon cinnamon
  ½ teaspoon ground ginger
  ½ teaspoon nutmeg
  ⅓ cup strained honey
  1 cup light cream
  2 large eggs, slightly beaten

Pour the filling into the prepared pastry. Bake in a preheated oven at 425° for 10 minutes, then at 325° for 45 minutes or until filling is set.

Note: 1 cup undiluted evaporated milk may be used instead of the cream. Baking time will be shorter.

FRANCES' PUMPKIN CHIFFON PIE

Prepare a
  9-inch baked pie shell (see p. 331)

Beat together
  3 egg yolks
  ¾ cup sugar

Add and beat well
  ½ cup light cream
  1¼ cups cooked, strained pumpkin
  ½ teaspoon nutmeg
  ½ teaspoon cinnamon
  ½ teaspoon salt
  ¼ teaspoon ground ginger

Cook over boiling water until mixture is thick.

Stir in
    1 envelope gelatin softened in
    ½ cup cold water

Chill until mixture begins to firm.

Fold in
    3 egg whites beaten until stiff with
    ¼ cup sugar

Spoon mixture into prepared pie shell. Refrigerate until set. Decorate top with whipped cream.

Note: Substitute canned pumpkin if desired.

SQUASH PIE

AN OLD NEW HAMPSHIRE "RECEIPT"

Line a deep 9-inch pie plate with pastry (*see p. 331*).

Mix in a double boiler
    ¾ cup light brown sugar
    2 tablespoons butter
    2 cups cooked, mashed winter squash
    1 cup light cream
    1 cup milk
    ½ teaspoon cinnamon
    ¼ teaspoon allspice
    ½ teaspoon salt

Heat and stir until blended.

Stir in
    4 large eggs, beaten

Pour squash mixture into prepared pastry. Bake in a preheated oven at 425° for 10 minutes, then at 325° for 50 minutes or until pie is set.

Note: Substitute canned or frozen winter squash if fresh squash is not available.

GRANDMOTHER SMITH'S FROSTED LEMON PIE

FROM AUNT MARY'S COOKBOOK

Line a 9-inch pie plate with pastry (*see p. 331*). Do not refrigerate.

Mix together
    1 cup sugar
    3 tablespoons flour
    1 tablespoon cornstarch
    ¼ teaspoon salt

Cream in
    1 tablespoon softened butter

Mix in
    ¼ cup lemon juice and pulp
    2 tablespoons grated lemon peel

Add and beat well
    1 egg
    3 egg yolks
    1 cup cold water

Chill mixture. Pour into prepared crust. Bake in a preheated oven at 450° for 10 minutes, then at 325° for 30 minutes or until custard is soft-set.

Beat until foamy
    3 egg whites

Add and beat until glossy but not dry
    3 tablespoons sugar

Frost pie with meringue, making sure meringue extends to crust, and return to oven. Bake at 350° until frosting is delicately browned.

ELLEN'S LEMON SPONGE PIE

Line an 8-inch pie plate with pastry (*see p. 331*).

Cream together
   3 tablespoons softened butter
   1¼ cups sugar
   6 tablespoons flour
   ½ teaspoon salt

Beat in
   4 egg yolks
   ½ cup milk
   ½ cup lemon juice and grated peel of 1 lemon

Fold in
   4 egg whites, beaten until stiff

Pour into prepared pastry. Bake in a preheated oven at 375° for 10 minutes, then at 325° for 30 minutes or until filling is set.

AUNT MARY'S LEMON PIE

Prepare a
   9-inch baked pie shell (see p. 331)

Mix in a double boiler
   1 cup sugar
   3 tablespoons cornstarch
   4 tablespoons flour
   ¼ teaspoon salt

Moisten with
   ¼ cup lemon juice

Cook mixture over boiling water, adding a little at a time,
   1½ cups boiling water

Continue to cook, stirring constantly until mixture is very thick and will stand in firm peaks. Remove from heat.

Stir in
　4 egg yolks, slightly beaten

Return to heat. Cook, stirring constantly for 2 minutes. Remove from heat.

Add
　1 teaspoon butter
　1 teaspoon grated lemon peel

Cool mixture. Spoon into prepared pie shell.

Beat until stiff
　4 egg whites with
　3 tablespoons sugar

Spread mixture over pie. Bake in a preheated oven at 375° for 10 minutes or until meringue is a light golden brown.

LIME MERINGUE PIE

For this pie we use either Key limes or Persian limes.

Prepare an
　8-inch baked pie shell (see p. 331)

Mix in a double boiler
　1¼ cups sugar
　3 tablespoons cornstarch
　3 tablespoons flour
　¼ teaspoon salt

Moisten with
　¼ cup lime juice

Cook mixture over boiling water, adding a little at a time,
  1¼ cups boiling water

Continue to cook, stirring constantly, until mixture is very thick and will stand in firm peaks. Remove from heat.

Stir in
  4 egg yolks, slightly beaten

Return to heat. Cook, stirring constantly for 2 minutes. Remove from heat.

Add
  1 teaspoon butter
  1 teaspoon grated lime peel
  Few drops green food coloring (optional)

Let mixture cool to room temperature. Spoon into prepared shell.

Beat until stiff
  4 egg whites with
  3 tablespoons sugar

Spread mixture over pie. Bake in preheated oven at 375° for 10 minutes or until meringue is a light golden brown.

LIME CHIFFON PIE

Prepare a
  9-inch baked pie shell (see p. 331)

Mix together in a double boiler
  ½ cup sugar
  1 envelope plain gelatin
  ¼ teaspoon salt

Add
  ½ cup lime juice
  ¼ cup cold water

Heat over boiling water.

Add, a little at a time, stirring constantly,
   4 beaten egg yolks
   A few drops green food coloring
   1 teaspoon grated lime peel

Remove from heat. Chill until mixture begins to firm.

Stir in
   4 egg whites beaten until stiff with
   ½ cup sugar

Fold in
   1 cup whipped cream

Spoon mixture into prepared pie shell. Serve chilled.

ORANGE CHIFFON PIE

Prepare a
   9-inch baked pie shell (see p. 331)

Mix in a double boiler
   ½ cup sugar
   2 envelopes unflavored gelatin
   ⅛ teaspoon salt

Add and mix
   ¾ cup fresh orange juice
   ¼ cup fresh lemon juice

Cook over boiling water, stirring until hot. Remove from heat. Stir in
   4 egg yolks beaten with
   1 whole egg
   1 teaspoon finely grated orange peel

Return to heat. Cook, stirring continuously for just 2 minutes. Cool until mixture is lukewarm.

Fold in
   4 egg whites beaten until stiff with
   ½ cup sugar

Spoon mixture into prepared pie shell. Bake in a preheated oven at 450° for 10 minutes. Refrigerate until ready to serve. Cover with sweetened whipped cream.

Suggestion: For a more pronounced orange flavor, use orange juice instead of water when making the pie shell.

OLD HOME DAY CUSTARD PIE

GILFORD VILLAGE, NEW HAMPSHIRE

Line a deep 9-inch pie plate with pastry (*see p. 331*). Do not refrigerate.

Beat well together
   4 large eggs
   1 cup sugar
   1 cup hot milk
   1 cup light cream, heated
   ½ teaspoon vanilla

Strain. Chill thoroughly. Turn the chilled filling into the prepared pastry.

Sprinkle with
   ⅛ teaspoon nutmeg

Bake in a preheated oven at 450° for 10 minutes, then at 325° for 35 minutes or until custard is set.

Note: Custard pie is best when served the day it is made; otherwise refrigerate it.

ESTHER'S MAPLE CUSTARD PIE

Line a deep 9-inch pie plate with pastry (*see p. 331*). Do not refrigerate.

Scald and let cool to lukewarm
  1½ cups milk

Cream together
  ¾ cup soft maple sugar (see p. 410)
  2 tablespoons flour
  ½ teaspoon salt
  4 egg yolks, slightly beaten

Add the milk. Strain.

Beat to form soft peaks
  4 egg whites

Combine the strained custard mixture with the egg whites. Blend thoroughly but gently. Pour this filling into the prepared pastry. Bake in a preheated oven at 325° for 60 minutes or until custard is set. Cool pie; refrigerate it if you will not serve it immediately.

VERNA'S BUTTERSCOTCH PIE

Prepare a
  9-inch baked pie shell (see p. 331)

Mix in a double boiler
  3 tablespoons flour
  2 tablespoons cornstarch
  1 cup light brown sugar (packed)
  ½ teaspoon salt

Add and cook, stirring until mixture is thick and smooth,
  2 cups scalded milk

Stir in gradually and cook for 2 minutes
  3 large eggs beaten with
  ¼ cup sugar

Add
   2 tablespoons butter
   2 teaspoons vanilla

Cool filling to room temperature and spoon it into prepared pie shell. Refrigerate pie. To serve, cover top with a thin layer of sweetened whipped cream.

Variation: Place a layer of sliced bananas on the bottom of pie shell. Pour filling over bananas.

DATE CREAM PIE

Line a 9-inch pie plate with pastry (*see p. 331*). Bake in a preheated oven at 450° for 8 minutes. Cool to room temperature.

Combine in a saucepan and heat to the boiling point
   2 cups milk
   1 cup dates, pitted and chopped

Mix in a double boiler
   2 tablespoons flour
   2 tablespoons cornstarch
   ½ teaspoon salt
   ⅔ cup sugar
   ½ cup cold milk

Stir in
   The hot milk-date mixture

Cook over hot water for 10 minutes or until mixture has thickened enough to stand in peaks. Stir to prevent lumps. Remove from heat.

Add
   3 large eggs slightly beaten
   2 teaspoons vanilla

Cool to lukewarm. Pour this filling into the partially baked pie shell. Bake in a preheated oven at 325° for 35-40 minutes or until filling is set. Cool and refrigerate.

JESSIE'S COCONUT CREAM PIE

Prepare a
  9-inch baked pie shell (see p. 331)

Mix in a double boiler
  ⅔ cup sugar
  ⅓ cup flour
  ¼ teaspoon salt

Stir in a little at a time
  2 cups scalded milk

Cook over boiling water for 12-15 minutes until mixture is thickened.

Add and cook for 2 minutes
  3 beaten egg yolks

Stir in
  ¾ cup shredded coconut
  1 teaspoon vanilla

Cool to room temperature. Turn mixture into prepared pie shell.

Beat until stiff
  3 egg whites
  4 tablespoons sugar

Spread over the pie. Sprinkle on
  ¼ cup shredded coconut

Bake in a preheated oven at 350° for 10 minutes or until meringue is
lightly browned.

FRESH COCONUT CREAM PIE

OUR MOST ELEGANT CREAM PIE

Prepare a
  9-inch baked pie shell (see p. 331)

Puncture "eyes," drain and reserve "milk" from
  A ripe coconut

Combine
  Coconut "milk"
  Enough light cream to make 2 cups

Crack coconut and peel. Shred fine, using an electric blender or hand grater,
  The peeled coconut meat

Blend in a double boiler
  ½ cup coconut milk–cream mixture
  ⅔ cup sugar
  ¼ teaspoon salt
  3 tablespoons flour

Add and cook, stirring until mixture is thick,
  1½ cups coconut milk–cream mixture

Remove from heat. Add
  3 beaten egg yolks

Return to heat. Cook, stirring constantly for 2 minutes.

Mix in
  1 cup shredded fresh coconut
  1 tablespoon butter
  ½ teaspoon vanilla
  1 teaspoon light rum

Cool to room temperature. Fill prepared shell.

Beat until stiff
  3 egg whites with
  4 tablespoons sugar

Spread over the pie.

Sprinkle over the top
  ¼ cup shredded fresh coconut

Bake in a preheated oven at 375° for 12 minutes or until meringue is golden.

MAPLE PECAN PIE

None of us baked pecan pies until Ellen returned from a visit to North Carolina, bringing the recipe for this traditional Southern dessert. We have substituted maple syrup for molasses, thus adding a touch of New England.

❧

Line a 9-inch pie plate with pastry (*see p. 331*).

Cream together
  ¼ cup sugar
  2 tablespoons softened butter

Add and blend
  ⅔ cup white corn syrup
  ⅓ cup maple syrup

Stir in
  4 large eggs, beaten
  1 cup broken pecan meats
  1 teaspoon vanilla
  ⅛ teaspoon salt

Pour mixture into the pastry.

Arrange over the top
  Whole pecan halves

Bake in a preheated oven at 325° for 45 minutes or until filling is set.

Suggestion: Forget calorie charts and serve Maple Pecan Pie topped with sweetened whipped cream.

MOTHER'S FRIED PIES

The Fried Pies that Mother made were a marvelous combination of hot doughnuts, hot applesauce flavored with boiled cider, and maple syrup. Mother used to make this dessert for our Saturday noon dinner usually at the time of year when she was making Boiled Cider Applesauce (*see p. 360*). She mixed a dough not quite as sweet as for her regular doughnuts. She made the doughnut forms without holes, using a large cutter so that the finished doughnuts were about as big as a saucer. The "pie" was made by putting two of these large doughnuts together like a layer cake. A generous amount of Boiled Cider Applesauce was spread between the doughnuts and over the top. Everyone poured on maple syrup to suit himself. This description of Fried Pies is given as a historic "receipt." Mother's Fried Pies are remembered fondly by all of my generation and by the older grandchildren who used to visit at High Maples Farm.

MOTHER'S APPLE DUMPLINGS

Use
  4 cups Family Pastry Mix (see p. 331)

Peel and slice thin
  Tart apples to measure 4 cups

Mix
  8 tablespoons sugar
  1 teaspoon cinnamon
  ¼ teaspoon nutmeg

Mix pastry with cold water as for pie crust. Divide into 8 parts. Roll out circles 9 inches in diameter. Mound ½ cup sliced apples in center of each circle. Fill apples with a heaping tablespoon of the sugar-spice mixture. Dot each mound with
  1 teaspoon cold butter

Fold and pinch edges of pastry circles up around apples, making open cups. Brush pastry with cream. Place dumplings in greased baking

pans so edges do not touch. Bake in a preheated oven at 375° for 35 minutes or until apples are soft. Serve warm with Grandmother Smith's Hot Pudding Sauce (see p. 362).
MAKES 8 SERVINGS.

Note: Double the sauce recipe. Flavor with 2 teaspoons vanilla and 2 of nutmeg.

VERNA'S APPLE ROLL

Sift into a bowl
   2 cups all-purpose flour
   1 teaspoon salt
   3 teaspoons baking powder

Cut in, using a pastry blender,
   6 tablespoons cold butter

Stir in to make a soft dough
   ⅔ cup milk

Roll on a floured board into a rectangle ¼-inch thick. Spread with
   2 tablespoons soft butter

Fill with
   2 cups chopped apples
   ⅓ cup chopped dates

Mix and sprinkle over the fruit
   ½ cup sugar
   ½ teaspoon cinnamon

Roll as for jelly roll. Cut into slices 1-inch thick. Bake in a preheated oven 10 minutes at 400°. Reduce heat to 350°. Bake for 20 minutes or until apples are soft.
MAKES 8 SERVINGS.

Suggestion: Serve hot with vanilla ice cream or Grandmother Smith's Hot Pudding Sauce (*see p. 362*) flavored with nutmeg.

Variation: Omit dates and use ½ cup seedless raisins, or include ¼ cup chopped pecans.

GREAT-GRANDMOTHER SMITH'S APPLE PANDOWDY
AN 1840 "RECEIPT"

Grandfather Smith lived with the illusion that nobody, even Grandmother, could equal his mother's cooking. He recollected with fondness the particular dishes that had been his boyhood favorites, among them Apple Pandowdy. Of course, Great-grandmother Harriett used no recipe books, but her old-fashioned apple dessert was doubtless made like the following, adapted from a very old cookbook.

❦

Butter a deep 10-inch pie plate or 8-inch round cake pan.

Fill with
4½ cups sliced cooking apples

Dot with
2 tablespoons cold butter, cut into bits

Mix together and spread on
⅓ cup sugar
¼ teaspoon nutmeg
½ teaspoon cinnamon
½ teaspoon salt

Drizzle on
⅓ cup light molasses

Cover with a thick pastry crust, ½ inch thick (make with 2 cups Family Pastry Mix, *p. 331*). Spread with cream. Prick crust with fork all over. Bake in preheated oven at 375° for 60 minutes. Cut the crust into the apples. Serve warm with thick cream.
MAKES 8 SERVINGS.

BOILED CIDER APPLESAUCE

In the fall when the Pound Sweets were ready to use, Mother made quantities of Boiled Cider Applesauce, some to eat up right away and more to be canned for winter use. She peeled and quartered as many of the big yellow-green apples as would fill her largest kettle. She drizzled boiled cider over the apples, added an equal amount of hot water and a cupful or more of sugar. She let the kettle simmer on the back of the stove where the apple pieces would stay whole as they softened and cooked to a tangy, brown sweetness. Although Pound Sweets and back-of-the-stove cooking are part of the long-ago past, Boiled Cider Applesauce is still very much enjoyed by our family. When Esther makes this kind of applesauce, she uses Red Delicious apples and oven-cooks the sauce in her large bean pot. Verna likes to use Cortland apples as well as Red Delicious.

❧

Place in a 3-quart casserole or large bean pot
　8 cups firm, sweet apples, peeled, cored, and quartered

Pour over the apples
　½ cup boiled cider

Add, measuring into cup used for the boiled cider
　½ cup sugar
　½ cup boiling water

Cover and cook in a preheated oven at 300° for 2 hours or until apple pieces are soft and rich brown in color. Stir gently several times during the cooking. Slow cooking and careful stirring insures uniform absorbing of the boiled cider flavor.
MAKES ABOUT 3 PINTS.

Note: This recipe is given chiefly for its historic value. It is not practical to reduce sweet cider by boiling in the kitchen and the commercial product is now difficult (but not impossible) to obtain even in New England.

PINK APPLESAUCE

Wash, discard stems and blossom ends and cut into quarters
5 pounds very red cooking apples

Combine in a large kettle
The apples
About 3 cups cold water

Bring to a boil and cook over low heat until apples are very soft. Put through a food mill.

Add and stir to dissolve
2 (or more) cups sugar

Note: A few drops of red food coloring may be added if desired.

Suggestion: Serve Pink Applesauce warm with cookies as dessert. Serve cold with roast pork as a relish.

FULLER PUDDING
A SMITH FAMILY "RECEIPT" OF THE 1880's

Sift together
1 cup all-purpose flour
½ teaspoon baking soda
¼ teaspoon cinnamon
¼ teaspoon nutmeg
¼ teaspoon ground cloves

Beat together
1 large egg
½ cup milk
½ cup light molasses
¼ cup melted butter

Beat in to make a smooth batter
The dry ingredients

Pour batter into a buttered 1-quart mold. Place mold on a rack in a large kettle or food blancher. Add boiling water until it comes halfway up around the mold. Steam for 2 hours. Serve hot with Grandmother Smith's Hot Pudding Sauce (*see below*).
SERVES 8.

Note: Mother flavored sauce for Fuller Pudding with 1 teaspoon vanilla and a pinch of nutmeg.

GRANDMOTHER SMITH'S HOT PUDDING SAUCE

Melt in a double boiler
   1 tablespoon butter

Stir in gradually to make a smooth mixture
   1 cup sugar
   4 tablespoons flour

Add a little at a time stirring constantly until the sauce is thick and clear
   2½ cups boiling water

Add flavoring as desired according to the pudding to be served.
SERVES 6 TO 8.

FLAMING CHRISTMAS PUDDING

We have adapted the recipe for old-fashioned Fuller Pudding to make a rich yet light and delicate steamed pudding. It is more quickly made and better suited to modern tastes than the traditional suet steamed pudding.

Sift together
    1¼ cups all-purpose flour
    ¼ teaspoon salt
    ½ teaspoon baking soda
    ⅓ teaspoon allspice
    ¼ teaspoon ground cloves
    ¼ teaspoon cinnamon
    ¼ teaspoon ground ginger

Beat together
    1 large egg
    ½ cup milk
    ½ cup dark molasses
    ¼ cup melted butter

Beat in to make a smooth batter
    The sifted dry ingredients

Stir in
    1 cup Brandied Fruits (recipe follows), chopped fine and lightly floured

Pour batter into a buttered 1-quart mold. Cover. Place mold on a rack in a large kettle or food blancher. Add boiling water until it comes halfway up around the mold. Steam for 2 hours. Invert the mold for 20 minutes or until pudding is somewhat cooled. Uncover and turn out. Brush warm pudding with brandy. Wrap in aluminum foil and store to "ripen."

To serve: Reheat pudding in aluminum foil. Put on a serving dish and top with a sprig of holly. Pour ½ cup warmed brandy over the pudding. Light and carry to the table flaming. Serve with Fluffy Brandy Sauce or Grandmother Smith's Hot Pudding Sauce (*see pp. 362 and 364*) flavored with brandy to taste.
SERVES 8.

BRANDIED FRUITS

We prepare Brandied Fruits early in November for use in Flaming Christmas Pudding (*see p. 362*) and for cake filling.

❧

Place in layers in equal quantities in a small crock
    Whole dates, stoned
    Whole candied cherries
    Slices, or half slices of candied pineapple

Fill the crock to within an inch of the top. Pour in brandy to cover the fruits. Cover the crock tightly and set away until needed.

Note: We use 1 pound cherries, 1 pound pineapple and 1½ pounds dates.

FLUFFY BRANDY SAUCE

Beat together thoroughly, using electric mixer,
    ½ cup softened butter
    2 cups sifted confectioners' sugar
    3 tablespoons brandy

Beat in
    1 egg yolk

Fold in
    1 stiffly beaten egg white

Pile into a bowl. Serve chilled.
MAKES ABOUT 2 CUPS.

CHERRY BRANDY SAUCE

Try making this delicious sauce when fresh sweet cherries are in season. You will find it quick and easy to do. Spooned over ice cream the sauce makes a dessert elegant enough to impress all your guests— even the recipe-collecting connoisseurs.

❧

Measure into a saucepan
1 cup (packed) dark, sweet cherries, stoned
½ cup sugar
¾ cup water

Bring to a boil. Turn heat down to simmer. Cook for 5 minutes or until cherries are soft. Strain, and reserve cherries.

Measure into the saucepan
1 cup of the juice (add water if necessary)
2 teaspoons cornstarch mixed with
2 tablespoons cold water

Cook over low heat, stirring constantly for 5 minutes or until mixture looks clear.

Add
1 tablespoon brandy

Pour the sauce over the reserved cherries. Refrigerate. Spoon over vanilla ice cream.
MAKES 6 SERVINGS.

Note: Use only a fine brandy and excellent quality ice cream.

Suggestion: Warm the sauce over hot water before serving.

CHOCOLATE STEAMED PUDDING

AN OLD-TIME BOSTON RECIPE

Sift together
  2 cups all-purpose flour
  2 teaspoons baking powder

Beat together
  2 eggs
  1 cup sugar

Stir in alternately
  The flour mixture
  1 cup milk

Add
  4 squares chocolate melted with
  2 tablespoons butter

Pour batter into greased 1-quart pudding mold. Cover and steam for 2 hours. Invert the mold for 20 minutes. Uncover and turn out. Serve warm with Fluffy Pudding Sauce (*recipe follows*).

FLUFFY PUDDING SAUCE

Beat with electric mixer until thoroughly blended
  2 tablespoons softened butter
  1 cup confectioners' sugar
  2 teaspoons vanilla

Stir in
  1 cup cream, whipped stiff

SERVES 6.

BRICK OVEN INDIAN PUDDING

AN ANCIENT NEW HAMPSHIRE "RECEIPT"

Mix to make a smooth paste
  ½ cup stone-ground, yellow corn meal
  ¼ cup cold milk

Heat in a double boiler
  3¾ cups milk

Add the corn meal paste to the hot milk gradually. Cook and stir for 10 minutes or until mixture is slightly thickened.

Mix in well
  ⅔ cup dark molasses, preferably West Indian
  1 large egg, beaten
  ¼ teaspoon nutmeg
  ¼ teaspoon cinnamon
  ½ teaspoon salt
  ½ cup raisins

Pour mixture into a greased 2-quart baking dish. Bake in a preheated oven at 325° for 30 minutes.

Stir in
  ¼ cup cold water

Bake for 30 minutes.

Again stir in
  ¼ cup cold water

Bake for 60 minutes longer. Let pudding stand for 30 minutes. Serve with thick cream.
SERVES 6 TO 8.

QUICK INDIAN PUDDING

Mix in a double boiler
1 cup milk
1 cup light cream
2 tablespoons quick-cooking tapioca
2 tablespoons sugar
½ cup molasses
2 tablespoons butter
3 tablespoons yellow corn meal

Heat, stirring constantly, until mixture is near boiling point and is well blended. Remove from heat.

Stir in
2 eggs beaten until light
1 teaspoon vanilla

Pour mixture into a buttered baking dish. Set dish in hot water. Bake in a preheated oven at 325° for 15 minutes. Stir, cover the dish and continue baking for 45 minutes or until pudding is set.
SERVES 6.

Variation: Omit vanilla and flavor with 1 tablespoon dark rum.

Suggestion: Serve hot with vanilla ice cream, or cold with plain cream —the way Mother used to do.

FRANCES' INDIAN PUDDING

A REFINEMENT OF AN OLD-TIME FAVORITE

Heat in a double boiler
1 quart milk

Stir constantly for 20 minutes while adding gradually
6 tablespoons white corn meal

Remove from heat. Mixture should be creamy smooth.

Stir in
  3 beaten eggs
  ½ teaspoon salt
  ½ teaspoon cinnamon
  ½ teaspoon nutmeg
  ¼ teaspoon ground ginger
  1 cup applesauce
  1 cup light molasses
  2 tablespoons butter
  1 tablespoon golden rum

Turn mixture into a buttered casserole.

Pour over the pudding
  1 cup cold light cream

Set baking dish in a pan of hot water. Bake in a preheated oven at 350° for 60 minutes or until set. Serve hot with vanilla ice cream. SERVES 6.

ANNE'S DOUBLE-BOILER BREAD PUDDING

Butter and cut into small cubes
  3 slices white bread

Place in a large double boiler
  ½ cup light brown sugar, packed

Add
  ½ of the bread cubes

Spread on top
  ½ cup light brown sugar

Add
  The remaining bread cubes

Blend and pour on
  2 cups milk
  3 medium eggs beaten until light
  ¼ teaspoon salt
  1 teaspoon vanilla

Cover and cook over boiling water for 70 minutes. Do not remove cover while cooking. Turn pudding out onto a serving dish. The brown sugar will have made a delicious caramel sauce. Spoon sauce over each serving.
SERVES 6.

CHOCOLATE BREAD PUDDING

Heat in a double boiler
  2 cups milk
  2 squares unsweetened chocolate

Mix in
  2 tablespoons butter
  1 cup sugar
  ¼ teaspoon salt
  1 teaspoon vanilla
  1½ cups soft bread crumbs

Stir in
  4 large eggs, beaten until light

Pour into a greased 2-quart casserole set in warm water. Bake in a preheated oven at 325° for 60 minutes or until set. Serve hot or cold with whipped cream.
SERVES 6.

Variation: Add 1 tablespoon brandy. Serve pudding with Fluffy Brandy Sauce (*see p. 364*).

SMITH FAMILY CUSTARD PUDDING

AS MOTHER MADE IT

Combine in a saucepan and heat to the boiling point
  4 cups rich milk
  1 cup seedless raisins, rinsed in cold water
  1 cup sugar
  ½ teaspoon salt

Beat until light
  6 large eggs

Allow milk to cool a little. Strain beaten eggs into the milk and mix.

Add
  2 teaspoons vanilla

Pour mixture into a buttered 2-quart baking dish. Set the dish in a pan of warm water. Bake in a preheated oven 325° until a silver knife comes out clean (about 90 minutes). Serve cold with whipped cream or plain.
MAKES 12 OR MORE SERVINGS.

CUSTARD BREAD PUDDING

FROM THE KITCHEN OF GRACE MUNGER

Heat to boiling point, using a heavy saucepan
  2 cups milk
  1 tablespoon butter

Stir in, as the milk heats,
  ¼ cup sugar
  ¼ cup seedless raisins

Remove from heat. Crumble into the milk and let cool
  2 slices fresh white bread with crusts removed

Stir in
> *1 egg slightly beaten*
> *¼ teaspoon salt*
> *¼ teaspoon nutmeg*

Pour into a buttered casserole set into a pan of hot water. Bake in a preheated oven at 375° for 15 minutes, then at 350° for 30 minutes or until custard is set.
SERVES 6.

Variation: Omit raisins. Place 2 tablespoons strawberry jam in the casserole before pouring in the custard. After the pudding is cooked, cool, turn upside down on a serving dish, and decorate with whipped cream.

Suggestion: Serve warm or cold with maple syrup, hard sauce, or sweetened whipped cream flavored with nutmeg.

VERNA'S APPLE CUSTARD PUDDING

Prepare
> *1 cup tart applesauce*

Heat
> *1 cup light cream*

Crumb in the electric blender
> *1 slice soft white bread*

Toss crumbs with
> *2 tablespoons melted butter*

Beat
> *2 medium eggs until light*

Mix
> *Beaten eggs*
> *Heated cream*
> *1 teaspoon vanilla*
> *⅓ cup sugar*

Turn applesauce into a buttered 2-quart casserole. Spread on buttered crumbs. Pour on liquid mixture. Bake in a preheated oven at 350° for 30 minutes or until custard is set. Serve with cream or vanilla ice cream.
SERVES 6.

ELLEN'S CARAMEL CUSTARD

Scald
  2 cups milk
  2 cups light cream

Remove from heat. Add
  ½ cup sugar
  1 teaspoon vanilla
  ¼ teaspoon salt

Stir in
  5 medium eggs, well beaten

Caramelize in a heavy frying pan
  ¾ cup sugar

Stir constantly over medium heat until sugar is entirely melted, making a smooth golden syrup. Turn syrup into a rounded 2-quart baking dish. Tip the dish to spread the syrup onto the sides. Strain liquid over the caramelized sugar.

Bake in a preheated oven at 325° for 90 minutes or until custard is set. Chill. Serve with the caramel syrup spooned over the custard.
SERVES 6 TO 8.

Note: For a less rich custard, omit cream and use 4 cups of milk.

RICE CUSTARD PUDDING

ADAPTED FROM A SWEDISH RECIPE

Melt in a double boiler
  2 tablespoons butter

Add
  ⅓ cup long-grain rice, rinsed
  1 cup cold water

Cook over boiling water, stirring now and then until water has been almost absorbed.

Add
  2½ cups cold milk
  ½-inch stick cinnamon

Continue cooking for 30 minutes, stirring gently 2 or 3 times. Remove from heat. Discard cinnamon stick.

Stir in
  1 tablespoon butter
  ½ cup sugar
  ½ teaspoon salt
  1 teaspoon vanilla

Beat together and mix in
  4 large eggs
  1 cup light cream

Add
  ⅓ cup seedless raisins

Pour mixture into a buttered 2-quart casserole or baking dish. Set dish in a pan of warm water. Bake in a preheated oven at 325° for 15 minutes. Stir. Bake for 30 minutes or until pudding is soft-set. Serve cold with plain or whipped cream.
SERVES 8 GENEROUSLY.

Variation: Omit raisins and serve the Swedish way with lingonberries, or with stewed cherries or raspberries used as a sauce.

MAPLE RUM CUSTARD PUDDING

Heat in a double boiler
 1 cup milk
 1 cup light cream
 ⅓ cup soft maple sugar (see p. 410)

Stir in
 5 eggs, beaten until light
 2 tablespoons golden rum
 1 tablespoon butter
 ½ teaspoon salt

Strain hot mixture into a buttered, 1½-quart baking dish.

Sprinkle on
 ¼ teaspoon nutmeg

Set baking dish into a pan of warm water. Bake in a preheated oven at 325° for 60 minutes or until custard is set. Serve cold with whipped cream or shavings of maple sugar.
SERVES 6 TO 8.

MOLASSES SPONGE PUDDING

ADAPTED FROM AN OLD-TIME "RECEIPT"

Butter a 9-inch square baking pan. Spread over bottom of the pan
 1 cup applesauce

Sift together
 1½ cups all-purpose flour
 1 teaspoon baking soda
 ¼ teaspoon cinnamon
 ½ teaspoon allspice
 ¼ teaspoon salt

Beat with an electric mixer
 2 large eggs

Add and continue beating
1 cup light molasses
4 tablespoons melted butter

Add alternately, beating after each addition,
The flour mixture
½ cup boiling water

Pour the batter over the applesauce. Bake in a preheated oven at 350°
for 45 minutes. Serve warm with whipped cream.
SERVES 6.

MAPLE SPONGE

Heat in a double boiler
1 cup heavy cream

Dissolve
1 tablespoon gelatin in
⅓ cup cold water

Beat
Yolks of 2 large eggs with
½ cup maple syrup
Pinch of nutmeg

Add slowly to the hot cream. Cook and stir over boiling water for
5-8 minutes or until a thin custard is formed. Remove from heat and
stir in the gelatin.

Beat until very stiff
Whites of 2 large eggs

Pour the hot custard slowly into the egg whites, beating as you pour.
Chill mixture until it is beginning to set. Beat again. Pour into a 1-
quart mold and refrigerate for several hours. To serve, unmold and
crumble bits of soft maple sugar over the pudding, or decorate with
whipped cream and chopped walnuts.
MAKES 4 TO 6 SERVINGS.

LEMON SOUFFLÉ

Beat together in a double boiler
 5 egg yolks
 1 cup sugar

Stir in
 1 cup light cream, scalded

Cook and stir for 2 minutes or until spoon is barely coated. Strain.

Add and stir in
 ½ cup lemon juice and grated peel of 1 lemon
 A pinch of nutmeg

Fold in
 5 egg whites beaten very stiff

Turn into 2-quart soufflé dish. Set dish in a pan of hot water. Bake in a preheated oven at 325° for 90 minutes. Turn off heat and leave in oven for 60 minutes. Chill.
SERVES 8.

STEAMED BLUEBERRY PUDDING

LIKE MOTHER USED TO MAKE

Sift together
 1½ cups all-purpose flour
 1½ teaspoons baking powder
 ¼ teaspoon salt

Cream
 1 cup sugar
 6 tablespoons (¾ stick) softened butter
 1 teaspoon vanilla or lemon extract

Add one at a time, beating well with an electric mixer after each addition,
 3 egg whites

Stir in alternately
The flour mixture
⅓ cup milk

Fold in
1 cup floured blueberries

Pour mixture into a greased 1-quart pudding mold. (Mold will be about three-fourths full.) Cover mold and set it on a rack in a deep kettle. Add boiling water to come half way up the mold. Cover the kettle and steam for 2 hours. Add more water if needed. Uncover mold and turn out pudding. Serve warm with Grandmother Smith's Hot Pudding Sauce (*see p. 362*) flavored with lemon.
Serves 6.

Suggestion: Double the sauce recipe and set a bowl on the table for extra helpings.

YANKEE TRIFLE

The idea for our New England style "trifle" was borrowed from the English. Although we have used old-time Yankee ingredients—including the liquor—we must disclaim any family history for this dessert. The very idea of using the "demon rum" in cooking or any way at all would have horrified our prohibitionist Grandmother Smith, who never permitted *any* kind of "spirits" to be brought into her home. Mother was a little more tolerant. She always kept one bottle of brandy on hand, high out of reach on the top shelf of a dark closet in the back hall. That brandy (strictly for medicinal use) lasted all through the Prohibition Era. As for us, we refuse to allow any pangs of New England conscience to spoil the pleasure of making and serving this delicious dessert.
Yankee Trifle is really three desserts in one, made separately and combined before serving.

STEP I

Bake a Boston Sponge Cake (*see p. 306*) and hide most of it away for a day or two so it will not be eaten up.

STEP II

Make Rich Custard Sauce:

Beat together in a double boiler
  4 eggs
  ⅔ cup sugar
  ½ teaspoon salt

Heat over simmering water, stirring until hot.

Add a little at a time
  2 cups light cream, heated

Cook, stirring (or beating with a wire whisk) for 10 minutes or until custard is smooth and thick.

Add
  1 teaspoon golden rum

Cool and refrigerate.
MAKES 3 CUPS.

STEP III

Make Raspberry Sauce:

Drain
  1 10-ounce package frozen raspberries, thawed

Reserve raspberries.

Mix in a double boiler and heat
  ¼ cup of the raspberry juice
  2 tablespoons cornstarch
  2 tablespoons sugar

Add
　　½ cup raspberry juice, heated

Cool slightly and pour over reserved raspberries. Refrigerate.

Note: Add lemon juice if there is less than ½ cup of raspberry juice remaining.

Put the trifle together several hours before serving time to allow ingredients to blend. Use a large glass bowl. Make a layer of finger-sized cake pieces on bottom and sides of bowl. Using a pastry brush, moisten the cake pieces with golden rum. Spoon Raspberry Sauce over the cake. Cover with chilled Rich Custard Sauce. Serve with sweetened rum-flavored cream.
MAKES 8 TO 10 SERVINGS.

Note: Fresh raspberries are not often available so we have suggested using frozen fruit. We use Old Mr. Boston Rum just for sentiment's sake. Substitute another brand of rum or use brandy if you wish.

BAKED PEARS IN ELDERBERRY WINE

Peel, cut in half and core
　　4 hard winter pears

Put in a saucepan and bring to a boil
　　½ cup sugar
　　½ cup hot water

Place pears cut side down in a shallow baking pan.

Combine and pour over the pears
　　The sugar syrup
　　3 tablespoons Esther's Elderberry Wine (see p. 388)
　　1 tablespoon brandy

Cover and bake in a preheated oven at 350° for 20 minutes. Remove cover. Prick pears in several places and turn cut side up. Bake uncovered for 20 minutes or until pears can be pierced easily with a fork. Using a slotted spoon, lift pears from the baking pan and place in a glass serving dish. Boil syrup until it is reduced to approximately ¼ cup. Cool slightly and pour over pears.

Refrigerate.
SERVES 4.

Note: Cherry Heering makes a good substitute for the Elderberry Wine.

STRAWBERRY SHORTCAKE

Wash and drain
    1 quart fully ripe strawberries

Hull and crush, reserving 6 or more perfect berries. Sweeten to taste.

Sift together
    2 cups all-purpose flour
    1 teaspoon baking soda
    2 teaspoons cream of tartar
    ¼ teaspoon salt

Work in with a pastry blender or knife
    1 cup commercial sour cream

Mix to make soft dough.

Cut into small pieces
    ½ stick cold butter

Turn dough out onto a floured board. Roll or pat into a rectangle. Beat flat with a rolling pin to a thin sheet. Dot with one-third of the butter pieces. Roll up the dough and repeat, beating twice more into a thin sheet, dotting each time with butter. Roll out into a large flat sheet about ⅜-inch thick. Cut into 12 rounds (use a 4-inch cutter). Place 6 rounds on a greased baking sheet. Dot with butter. Top with remaining rounds. Bake in a preheated oven at 450° for 12 minutes.

Separate halves. Spoon crushed strawberries over bottom half. Replace top and cover with more strawberries. Serve with plain cream or sweetened whipped cream. Decorate with the reserved berries. SERVES 6.

❦ 27 ❦

Preserves, Pickles and Relishes

Grape ketchup, jams, jellies, wine, pickles, piccalilli, and other relishes including chili sauce, chowchow, and chutney

GRANDMOTHER SMITH'S GRAPE KETCHUP
COPIED FROM AUNT MARY'S COOKBOOK

Farm families relished this spicy sauce long before commercial tomato ketchup appeared on the grocers' shelves. Even if we wished to make ketchup by this laborious process we could not get the ingredients, for wild grape vines have disappeared (from much of New Hampshire anyway), so it's just for sentimental reasons that we include grandmother's "receipt" here.

9 pounds of wild grapes
4½ cups sugar
2 tablespoons ground cinnamon
1 tablespoon ground allspice
1 tablespoon ground cloves
1 quart good cider vinegar

Scald grapes. Sieve. Add sugar and spices. Boil 15 minutes. Cool. Add vinegar.

This is all there was to the "receipt." We assume that grandmother bottled the ketchup, unless there was no need because her family ate it up so fast!

ESTHER'S SPICED GRAPE SAUCE

Wash and remove stems from
    3½ pounds fully ripe Concord grapes

Crush grapes thoroughly and place in a large kettle. Add
    1 cup water

Bring to a boil, then simmer for 15 minutes, stirring to prevent burning. Remove from heat and put through a food mill. Discard seeds and skins.

Place in a large kettle
  5 cups grape pulp
  5 cups sugar
  1 teaspoon cinnamon
  ½ teaspoon allspice
  ½ teaspoon ground cloves
  2 tablespoons cider vinegar

Bring to a boil over high heat. Boil hard for 1 minute stirring constantly. Remove from heat at once.

Add
  ½ bottle fruit pectin

Stir for 5 minutes, skimming to remove foam. Can in hot sterilized jars. Seal.
MAKES 7 HALF-PINT JARS.

Suggestion: Serve with hot or cold lamb or other roast meat.

WILD BLACKBERRY JAM

Nowadays, blackberries, once grown on nearly every New Hampshire farm, are rarely found under cultivation, yet there are many places where the wild berries grow, and old blackberry patches, flourishing untended, have mingled with the true wild species. These sweet little "gone wild" berries are well worth picking but it is best to get the landowner's permission (if he can be located). No matter how hot the day, we don't gather up pails and set out until we have donned stout jeans, old leather jackets, cotton gloves with the fingers cut out and leather shoes (the barbs will go right through sneakers). Blackberries and cream for supper assuage the pain of small wounds suffered despite precautions. In cold weather, Wild Blackberry Jam on the breakfast table brings back memories of the towhee that sang above our heads while we hunted the ripest berries through a tangled briar thicket.

Grind in a food chopper, using medium knife,
   2 quarts ripe, wild blackberries

Mix well in a large saucepan
   7 cups sugar
   4 cups ground blackberries and juice

Bring mixture to a boil over high heat. Keep at a full rolling boil for 1 minute, stirring constantly. Remove from heat.

Add
   ½ bottle fruit pectin

Continue to stir the jam for 5 minutes. Skim to remove foam.

Pour into hot sterilized jars. Seal.
MAKES ABOUT 7 HALF PINTS.

WILD ELDERBERRY JELLY

Watch for the time in late August when the elderberry bushes show color. Harvest before the berries are dead ripe or you will find the birds have been there before you and stolen away the prize. Snip off the large stems and drop the berry clusters into a basket. A full bushel will make two or three batches of jelly, depending on the ripeness of the berries.

∾✺∾

To prepare the juice remove the large stems from about 3 pounds of elderberries. A few very small stems may be left on. Place berries in a colander and run cold water over them. Drain. Put the berries through a food-chopper using the finest knife. Don't worry about the tiny stems, grind them along with the berries.

Place in a saucepan
   The elderberries
   1 cup cold water

Heat to the boiling point. Simmer for 15 minutes. Strain through a damp (double thickness) cheesecloth bag. Squeeze the bag gently while the berries are still warm.

Measure into a large saucepan
   3 cups elderberry juice (a little water may be added if needed)
   ½ cup strained lemon juice
   7 cups sugar

Mix well. Bring to a boil over high heat stirring constantly.

Add
   1 bottle fruit pectin

Bring again to a boil and boil hard for 1 minute, stirring constantly.

Remove from heat. Skim. Pour into hot sterilized jars. Seal.
MAKES ABOUT 7 HALF PINTS.

ESTHER'S ELDERBERRY WINE

Seasons when there is a full crop and somebody will volunteer to gather the wild berries, Esther starts some elderberry wine. Whenever we happen to be in New Hampshire at the right time, we hunt the roadsides and borders of wooded areas where the bushes seem to thrive. For a share in the wine, gathering and helping prepare the fruit is a small price to pay—and fun besides, we think. Elderberry wine has a delightful "wild" taste hard to describe.

෴

Snip elderberries from large stems with scissors and wash.

Put into a large canning kettle
   9 pounds sugar
   3 gallons pure spring water

Heat, stirring until sugar is dissolved. Bring to a boil and continue boiling for 5 minutes without stirring. Skim.

Add
>   *1 quart prepared elderberries, packed*

Cook and stir for 5 minutes until the berries are well mixed with the sugar solution. Cool to lukewarm.

Add
>   *½ cup fresh lemon juice*
>   *1 package dry yeast dissolved in*
>   *¼ cup lukewarm water*

Pour mixture into a 5-gallon stoneware crock. Cover with cheesecloth. Stir thoroughly 3 times each day for the next 6 days. On the 7th day strain through cheesecloth.

Add
>   *3 pounds seedless raisins*

Pour mixture back into crock. Cover tightly and leave undisturbed until New Year's Day. Bottle and cork.
MAKES ABOUT 10 QUARTS CLEAR WINE.

SPICED CRABAPPLE JELLY

Wash and cut into quarters (do not peel or remove seeds)
>   *5 pounds ripe crabapples*

Combine in a large kettle
>   *The crabapples*
>   *5 cups cold water*
>   *½ cup cider vinegar*

Tie in a small cheesecloth bag and push down into the apples
>   *2 tablespoons cloves*
>   *2 tablespoons mace blades*
>   *2-inch stick cinnamon, broken*

Cover kettle. Cook over low heat until apples are very soft. Mash the apples. Strain through a damp cheesecloth bag.

To make the jelly using bottled pectin:

Measure into a large saucepan
   5 cups juice (add water if necessary)
   7½ cups sugar
   ¼ - ½ teaspoon red food coloring (optional)

Bring to a boil over high heat, stirring constantly. Add
   ½ bottle pectin

Bring again to a full boil and boil for 1 minute, stirring constantly. Remove from heat. Skim. Pour into hot sterilized jars. Seal.
MAKES ABOUT 8 HALF-PINTS.

VERNA'S SPICED CIDER JELLY

Measure into a large saucepan
   2 cups sweet cider
   3½ cups sugar
   1 tablespoon cloves tied in a small cheesecloth bag
   1 tablespoon red cinnamon candies

Mix well. Bring to a boil over high heat, stirring constantly.

Add
   ½ bottle fruit pectin

Bring again to a boil and boil hard for 1 minute, stirring constantly. Remove from heat. Skim off foam and discard bag with cloves. Pour into hot sterilized jars. Seal.
MAKES A LITTLE MORE THAN 3 HALF-PINTS.

CRANBERRY-QUINCE JELLY

Jellies and jams made from the fruit of the quince tree were once highly valued in New England. Nowadays the tree is so rarely grown that the fruit which ripens in October cannot be found in the markets every year. When we are fortunate enough to have quinces given to us or can buy the fruit, we like to make jelly combining the quinces with apples or mixing the juice with that of another fruit as in this recipe.

Prepare the juices separately, then measure the correct amount of juice for each lot and store in the freezer until it is convenient to make the jelly.

~✼~

Wash cranberries, pick over and discard stems.

Combine in a large saucepan
4 cups cranberries
4 cups water

Bring to a boil. Cover saucepan and simmer for 10 minutes. Drain through a damp jelly bag. Squeeze the bag gently.
MAKES ABOUT 4 CUPS.

Prepare the quinces in quantities as convenient. Wash fruit and remove stem ends. Wipe with paper towel to remove fuzz. Quarter and put through a food chopper.

Place in a large saucepan
The quince pulp
Cold water to cover

Bring to a boil. Cook for 15 minutes. Drain through a damp jelly bag. Squeeze the bag gently.

To complete the jelly:

Measure into a large saucepan
2¼ cups quince juice
¼ cup fresh lemon juice
2 cups cranberry juice
7½ cups sugar

Bring to a boil over high heat stirring constantly. Add
½ bottle fruit pectin

Bring to a full boil and boil hard for 1 minute, stirring constantly. Remove from heat. Skim. Pour into hot sterilized jars. Seal.
MAKES ABOUT 7 PINTS.

SPICED CRANBERRY SAUCE

Pick over and wash
  1 pound fresh cranberries

Place in a deep 4-quart kettle
  The cranberries
  1½ cups sugar
  ½ teaspoon cinnamon
  ¼ teaspoon nutmeg
  ½ teaspoon allspice
  1½ cups boiling water

Heat in uncovered kettle until boiling point is reached. Turn heat to low and simmer for 20 minutes or until sauce is thick. Stir gently several times. Serve as a sweet relish with meat or fowl.
MAKES 4 CUPS.

PA'S PICKLES

Grandfather left the preparation of the family's food strictly up to Grandmother, while reserving the exclusive privilege of judging and criticising the finished product when it was set before him. The one exception to this rule was cucumber pickling, a job he would trust to no one but himself. The pickling process used by Grandfather more than a hundred years ago (and no doubt still earlier by the Smiths of Sanbornton) has been used ever since in our family and is basically the same as described in recent U. S. Department of Agriculture bulletins.

The old "receipt" as told to Aunt Mary:

For 1 peck small cucumbers, use 1 cup salt, alum size of a robin's egg. Make into brine. Scald 4 or 5 times. Can in 2 quart jars in hot vinegar. Add onions or whole spices if wanted. Put grape leaves on top of pickles before covering.

Note: Grape leaves were laid over the top of pickles—whether packed in glass or in large stone jars—a means of preventing pickles from turning soft in the brine.

SOUR CUCUMBER PICKLES

GRANDFATHER SMITH'S METHOD

Wash and place in a large stoneware crock
   4 pounds small fresh cucumbers

Heat to the boiling point
   2½ quarts water
   ⅓ cup pure salt
   Piece of lump alum, size of walnut

Pour the hot brine over the cucumbers. Let stand 24 hours. Pour off brine and reheat it to boiling point. Skim brine and pour over cucumbers. Let stand 24 hours and repeat brining process on 2 successive days (3 times in all). Drain the cucumbers and wash in cold water.

Heat in a large kettle
   2½ quarts cider vinegar

Pack the pickles in hot jars. Fill jars with the hot vinegar. Seal or cover tightly.
MAKES ABOUT 6 PINTS.

Variation: DILL PICKLES. Place a head of fresh dill in the bottom and on top of each jar of pickles.

MUSTARD PICKLES. Use the same process as for Sour Pickles. Add and heat with the vinegar

1 cup brown sugar mixed with ¼ cup dry mustard.

Note: Lump alum can be bought in markets or from drugstores.

SWEET CUCUMBER PICKLES

SMITH FAMILY METHOD

Wipe and place in a large stoneware crock
½ peck (4 quarts) small fresh cucumbers

Heat to the boiling point to make a brine
3 quarts water
½ cup pure salt
Piece of lump alum, size of walnut

Pour the hot brine over the cucumbers. Let stand 24 hours. Pour off brine and reheat it to the boiling point. Skim and pour over cucumbers. Let stand 24 hours and repeat brining process on 2 successive days (3 times in all). Drain cucumbers. Wash in cold water. Wash the crock and replace the cucumbers.

Heat in a large kettle.
2 quarts cider vinegar
1 cup sugar
1 cup water
½ cup mixed pickle spices tied in a cloth bag

Boil together for 5 minutes to blend. Pour the hot syrup over the cucumbers. Let stand for 24 hours. Drain off the syrup. Add to syrup
1 cup sugar

Heat syrup again to boiling point and pour over pickles. Repeat this process on 2 successive days adding 1 cup sugar each time. On the fourth day, drain the pickles and pack in hot jars. Heat the syrup to the boiling point and fill jars. Seal.
MAKES 6 PINTS.

GRAMMIE PAGE'S RIPE CUCUMBER PICKLE

Wash, peel, seed, and cut into quarters
Ripe yellow cucumbers to measure 3 quarts, packed

Combine in a kettle and bring to a boil
3 quarts cold water
½ cup pure salt
1 teaspoon powdered alum (or small piece lump alum)

Cool brine slightly. Place cucumbers in a 2-gallon crock and cover with brine. Let stand overnight. Drain in a colander.

Combine in a kettle and bring to a boil
3 cups cider vinegar
1 cup cold water
2 cups sugar
1 teaspoon cinnamon
1 teaspoon ground cloves
1 teaspoon allspice

Add half of the drained cucumbers to the hot vinegar-spice mixture. (Lift cucumber pieces with a slotted spoon to keep whole). Simmer for about 30 minutes or until cucumbers can be pierced by a straw. Pack into hot jars (again lifting with slotted spoon), cover with hot syrup and seal. Repeat the simmering process with remaining cucumbers and can as before.
MAKES ABOUT 4 PINTS.

SWEET RIPE CUCUMBER PICKLE

RECIPE OF THE YEATON FAMILY, EPSOM, NEW HAMPSHIRE

Wash and peel
8-10 large yellow cucumbers

Remove seeds and cut into 2-inch cubes (cubes should measure about 3½ quarts).

Place in a large kettle
> *The cucumber cubes*
> *Hot water to cover*

Bring to a boil. Simmer for 10 minutes or until cucumbers are just beginning to soften. Drain. Place in a gallon crock.

Combine in a large saucepan
> *6 cups sugar*
> *2 cups white vinegar*
> *½ teaspoon oil of clove*
> *½ teaspoon oil of cinnamon*

Bring to a boil and cook 1 minute or until liquid is clear. Pour the hot syrup over cucumbers and let stand overnight. Drain off the syrup and heat again to the boiling point. Pour over cucumbers and let stand a second time overnight. On the third morning, heat the cucumbers in the syrup to the boiling point. Pack into hot sterilized jars and seal.
MAKES ABOUT 7 HALF-PINTS.

GREAT-AUNT ELIZA'S MUSTARD PICKLE

ADAPTED BY COUSIN PEARL SMITH YORK

Place in a stone crock
> *2 quarts unpeeled, chopped cucumbers*
> *1 quart small pearl onions, peeled*
> *1 large head cauliflower broken into small pieces*
> *4 green peppers, seeded and chopped*

Mix in a large kettle
> *4 quarts cold water*
> *1 cup pure salt*

Bring to a boil. Pour over the vegetables and let stand overnight. Turn vegetables and brine into a kettle and bring to a boil. Remove from heat at once. Drain vegetables in a colander.

Mix in a 1-quart measuring bowl or pitcher
> *1 cup flour*
> *3 cups sugar*
> *1 tablespoon turmeric powder*
> *1 tablespoon dry mustard*

Add
> *Cider vinegar to fill the measure*

Mix vinegar with dry ingredients to make a thick paste.

Combine in a kettle
> *The paste*
> *1 quart cider vinegar*

Cook over very low heat, stirring constantly until mixture is thick and clear. Add drained vegetables and cook enough to heat through. Stir gently in order not to break up vegetables while keeping mixture from burning. Pack in hot sterilized jars. Seal.
MAKES 8 PINTS.

MAPLE BREAD AND BUTTER PICKLES

GRANDDAUGHTER-IN-LAW PATTY WEEKS' RECIPE

Wash and slice thin
> *Young, green cucumbers to measure 8 cups*

Mix in a crock or large enameled kettle
> *The sliced cucumbers*
> *1 sweet red pepper, seeded and diced*
> *3 large onions, sliced thin*

Sprinkle over vegetables
> *¼ cup pure salt*

Let stand 3 hours. Drain in a colander and rinse with cold water.

Combine in a 4-quart saucepan or kettle
   1 cup white sugar
   1 cup soft maple sugar, packed
   ½ teaspoon turmeric powder
   ¼ teaspoon celery seed
   1 tablespoon mustard seed
   2 cups cider vinegar

Bring slowly to the boiling point. Cook for 5 minutes to blend spices. Add drained vegetables to the hot syrup. Cook over medium heat until syrup is just beginning to bubble. Pack into hot sterilized jars. Seal. Makes about 4 pints.

MOTHER'S PICCALILLI

Wash, remove stem ends, and slice
   1 peck (approximately 12 pounds) hard green tomatoes

Peel and slice
   8 medium-sized onions

Layer the sliced vegetables in a stone crock or enameled kettle.

Sprinkle over vegetables
   1 cup pure salt

Let stand overnight.

Drain vegetables well and place in a large kettle. Mix and cover vegetables with
   2 parts water (approximately 4 cups)
   1 part cider vinegar (approximately 2 cups)
   ½ teaspoon powdered alum

Bring to a boil. Simmer for 12 minutes. Drain and discard liquid. Return vegetables to kettle.

Add
   1½ quarts cider vinegar
   3 cups sugar

Tie in a small cheesecloth or organdy bag and add
  2 teaspoons allspice
  2 teaspoons ground cloves
  2 teaspoons dry mustard
  2 teaspoons cinnamon
  2 teaspoons ground ginger

Bring to a boil and simmer 15 minutes. Discard bag of spices. Can in hot sterilized jars. Seal.
MAKES 9 PINTS.

Note: Powdered alum can be purchased at drugstore.

VERNA'S WHITE MOUNTAIN PICCALILLI

Wash, remove stem ends, and chop fine, using a knife,
  5 pounds hard green tomatoes (3 quarts)

Place chopped tomatoes in a stone crock or enameled kettle.

Add
  2 large onions, peeled and chopped
  1 large sweet red pepper, seeded and chopped

Add and mix
  ⅓ cup pure salt

Let stand overnight. Drain.

Mix in a large kettle
  3 cups cider vinegar
  2 cups white sugar
  1 cup light brown sugar

Tie in a small cheesecloth or organdy bag and add
  1 teaspoon cinnamon
  1 teaspoon allspice
  1 teaspoon ground ginger
  ½ teaspoon dry mustard
  Pinch of black pepper

Bring to a boil and cook for 5 minutes to blend spices. Add drained vegetables and simmer for 25 minutes. Discard bag of spices. Can in hot sterilized jars. Seal.
MAKES 5 PINTS.

SANBORNTON PICCALILLI

A WALLIS FAMILY RECIPE, 1865

Wash, remove stem ends, and slice thin
1 peck (8 quarts) hard green tomatoes

Remove seeds and stems and chop coarsely
4 sweet green peppers
3 hot red peppers

Peel and slice thin
8 large onions

Pack in layers in a stone crock. Salt each layer using
1 cup pure salt

Let stand overnight. Drain thoroughly in a colander.

Combine in a large kettle
The drained vegetables
2 quarts cold water
1 pint cider vinegar

Bring to a boil and cook 20 minutes. Drain well in a colander.

Return vegetables to kettle. Add
1 quart cider vinegar mixed with
1 pound light brown sugar

Place in a small cheesecloth or organdy bag and add
3 tablespoons dry mustard
2 tablespoons cinnamon
1 tablespoon ground cloves

1 tablespoon ground ginger
1 tablespoon allspice

Bring to a boil and cook over low heat for 15 minutes or until the tomatoes can be pierced with a straw. Discard bag of spices. Pack in hot sterilized jars and seal.
MAKES ABOUT 10 PINTS.

JESSIE'S GREEN RELISH

Wash, peel, and cut into convenient size for grinding
Onions to make 3 cups
1 medium head new green cabbage
10 or 12 green tomatoes, stem ends removed
12 sweet green peppers, seeded
6 sweet red peppers, seeded

Measure
½ cup table salt

Put vegetables through food chopper using finest blade. Layer the ground vegetables in a large preserving kettle. Sprinkle each layer with a portion of the salt. Cover. Let salted vegetables sit for several hours or overnight, as convenient. Rinse vegetables. Drain. Return to kettle.

Mix and add
4 cups sugar
4 cups cider vinegar
4 tablespoons mustard seed
1 tablespoon celery seed

Bring vegetables just to boiling point, stirring to prevent sticking. Simmer for just 5 minutes. Seal in hot sterilized jars.
MAKES 8 PINTS.

Note: Be sure to use fresh spices. Avoid overcooking in order to preserve crispness and color of the vegetables.

ANNE'S POTTSFIELD RELISH

Grind, using the coarse blade of food chopper,
   7 large, fully ripe tomatoes, stem ends removed
   12 large green tomatoes, stem ends removed
   Onions to measure 2 cups
   3 small sweet green peppers, seeded
   2 small hot red peppers, seeded
   1 small head green cabbage

Place in a large enameled kettle or stone crock and mix.

Chop fine and add
   1 bunch celery

Add and mix in
   ¾ cup pure salt

Let stand overnight. Place vegetables in a colander to drain. Press lightly to drain thoroughly.

Place drained vegetables in a large kettle. Mix and add
   6 cups sugar
   8 cups mild cider vinegar
   1 teaspoon ground cloves
   1 teaspoon cinnamon

Bring mixture to a boil. Simmer for 60 minutes. Stir occasionally to prevent sticking. Pack into hot, sterilized jars.
MAKES ABOUT 8 PINTS.

MARY'S HOT-DOG RELISH

FROM THE KITCHEN OF INA MORGAN, NEW HAMPSHIRE

Grind, using coarse knife of food chopper,
   Green tomatoes to measure 4 quarts
   1 medium-sized head of green cabbage, cored
   4 medium-sized green peppers, stem ends and seeds removed

2 sweet red peppers, stem ends and seeds removed
10 medium-sized onions, peeled

Place ground vegetables in a stoneware crock or enameled kettle.

Mix with
    ¾ cup pure salt

Let stand 60 minutes. Drain thoroughly.

Mix in a large kettle
    6 cups cider vinegar
    2 pounds light brown sugar
    ½ ounce celery seed
    2 tablespoons ground turmeric
    4 tablespoons mustard seed

Heat to the boiling point and cook 5 minutes to blend spices and vinegar. Add the drained vegetables and cook over low heat for 60 minutes. Stir occasionally to prevent sticking. Pack into hot, sterilized jars. Seal.
MAKES ABOUT 14 PINTS.

HOT SWEET RELISH

FROM A NEW HAMPSHIRE KITCHEN

Grind, using coarse knife of food chopper,
    12 hot green peppers, seeded
    12 hot red peppers, seeded
    15 medium-sized onions, peeled

Mix ground vegetables in a large crock or enameled kettle. Cover with boiling water and let stand 15 minutes. Drain. Cover with boiling water a second time and let stand 10 minutes. Drain.

Combine in a kettle
    1 cup cider vinegar
    3 tablespoons pure salt
    3 cups sugar

Bring this mixture to a boil and cook 5 minutes to blend spices. Add the drained vegetables. Cook for 15 minutes stirring enough to prevent burning. Pack in hot sterilized jars. Seal.
MAKES 4-5 PINTS.

Note: When handling hot peppers, use rubber gloves to avoid burning your hands.

CHILI SAUCE

A FAVORITE OF THE NAYLOR FAMILY

Grind, using coarse knife of food chopper (measurements after grinding),
   4 quarts meaty ripe tomatoes, peeled and stem ends removed
   2 cups onions, peeled
   1 cup sweet red peppers, stem ends and seeds removed
   1 cup green peppers, stem ends and seeds removed
   1 small hot red pepper, stem end and seeds removed

Add
   3 tablespoons table salt
   ½ cup sugar

Cook in a heavy kettle over low heat. Stir constantly until mixture begins to thicken.

Add
   2½ cups cider vinegar
   1 teaspoon cinnamon
   1 teaspoon allspice

Continue cooking, stirring often to prevent sticking, until mixture becomes a thick sauce (at least 3 hours). Pour into hot sterilized jars and seal.
MAKES 10 PINTS.

Note: Plum tomatoes will give the best results.

ELLEN'S QUICK MUSTARD CHOWCHOW

Wash and cut into small pieces
2 large heads of cauliflower (about 3 quarts)

Peel and chop
Onions to measure 1 quart

Heat to make a brine
4 quarts water
2 cups pure salt

Combine vegetables in a stone crock or enameled kettle. Add brine. Let stand overnight. Drain and rinse in cold water.

Mix in a kettle
2½ cups flour
12 tablespoons dry mustard
2 tablespoons turmeric powder
5 cups sugar

Add a little at a time to make a smooth paste
2 quarts cider vinegar
2 quarts cold water

Cook until thickened, stirring constantly to prevent burning.

Add
The drained vegetables
2 4-ounce cans pimento, drained and chopped
2 10-ounce jars tiny, sweet gherkins, drained and chopped

Cook over low heat until vegetables begin to soften. Stir constantly but gently in order not to break up vegetables more than necessary. Pack in hot, sterilized jars. Seal.
MAKES 6 QUARTS.

GREEN MANGO CHUTNEY

FROM THE KITCHEN OF MARTHA BOHGREN

This chutney, a mixture of exotic fruits and familiar vegetables, originated in the West Indies, but we think it is quite in keeping with the highly spiced relishes of our old-fashioned New England collection. The original recipe called for tamarind and fresh ginger root; this adapted version uses hard green apples and candied ginger which are easier to obtain. The chutney must be made in late July when the unripened mangoes and hard green apples can be found in city markets. The preparation is time-consuming but worthwhile, since the unusual blend produces such a delightful relish.

ᲢᲔᏴᲔᎦ

Measure fruits and vegetables after they are prepared.

Mix in a large kettle
  *4 cups green mangoes, peeled, sliced from the seed, and chopped
    into small cubes*
  3 cups hard green apples, peeled and grated
  2 cups seedless raisins, chopped
  ⅓ cup candied ginger, chopped fine
  1 cup onions, peeled and chopped fine
  ½ cup sweet peppers, seeded and chopped
  1½ teaspoons hot red pepper, seeded and diced
  3 cloves garlic, peeled and minced
  2 cups brown sugar
  1 tablespoon salt
  ½ teaspoon mace
  1 tablespoon mustard seed
  2 cups cider vinegar

Bring mixture to a boil and simmer for 30 minutes. Stir enough to prevent burning. Can in hot, sterilized jars. Seal.
MAKES 6 TO 8 HALF-PINTS.

❈ 28 ❈

Candies

Maple sugar specialties, fondants, pop-
corn treats, pulled candy, and fudges

MAKING MAPLE SUGAR AND MAPLE CANDY AT HOME

Maple butter, maple fondant for maple fudge and fondant balls, and the soft maple sugar used in recipes are more easily obtained and much less expensive if made at home. For best results, use Fancy or Grade A quality pure maple syrup—at least one month old, because newly made syrup has a tendency to make the maple sugar and maple butter or fondant very coarse in texture. In hot weather, or when syrup older than six months is used, cook it four to six degrees higher in temperature than our recipes call for.

⁓⋇⁓

To make maple products at home you will need several easily obtained pieces of equipment:

SAUCEPAN

Use a fairly heavy, deep metal saucepan of 2 to 3-quart capacity. A large pan allows for the bubbling of syrup and helps to prevent boiling over onto the range.

THERMOMETER

The use of a standard, easily-read candy thermometer is important. Always take the temperature reading when the thermometer is in an upright position.

SHALLOW DRIPPING PAN

A flat rectangular pan with rounded corners approximately 9 inches by 12 inches is suitable for cooling hot uncrystallized syrup when you make maple butter or maple fondant.

WOODEN PADDLE OR WOODEN SPOON

A smooth wooden paddle with an elongated handle and medium-broad flat base is best to use when you work maple butter or maple fondant.

Such a paddle can be easily made from hard wood. A wooden spoon with a broad shallow bowl is best for stirring soft sugar. The spoon may also be used for stirring maple butter, but this is more tiring to the hands than the wooden paddle.

FORK

For washing down crystals which accumulate on the sides of the pan, use a fork with dampened cheesecloth (or organdy) covering the tines. The cloth should be tied on so that no loose threads can fall into the syrup.

DOUBLE BOILER

An ordinary double boiler of 2-quart capacity is necessary for melting the finished fondant when you make maple fudge.

SOFT MAPLE SUGAR

Pour into kettle or saucepan
  1 quart pure maple syrup

Add
  ¼ teaspoon butter (size of a small shelled peanut)

Bring syrup to a boil and cook rapidly until candy thermometer registers 230°. Allow syrup to cool for a few minutes. Stir with a large spoon until a pronounced grain can be noted. Pour at once into tins or wide-mouth jars.
MAKES ABOUT 2 POUNDS.

Note: The pan of hot, uncrystallized syrup may be set into a second pan of cold water and left without being moved for 10 minutes before the stirring is begun. This method improves color and makes a finer grained sugar but requires a longer period of stirring.

MAPLE BUTTER

Maple butter is a smooth, creamy spread with just a slight grain, made entirely of pure maple syrup. The tiny piece of added butter "boils off" but keeps the syrup from foaming over to make a sticky mess on the stove. Use good quality maple syrup, the simple equipment we have suggested, and follow directions. Your homemade maple butter will be just as fine (and very much less expensive) than the products sold at country stands.

~❈~

Pour into a saucepan
  3 cups maple syrup

Add
  ¼ teaspoon butter (size of a small shelled peanut)

Bring the syrup to a boil as quickly as possible and continue to boil rapidly until the thermometer registers 232° (234° to 236° in warm weather). If impurities rise to the surface, skim while syrup is bubbling. Using the dampened cheesecloth-covered tines of a fork, wash down any crystals which accumulate on the sides of the pan. This procedure helps to keep the sugar crystals small and uniform. When the correct temperature is reached, pour the syrup quickly and without stopping into the dripping pan. Let the uncrystallized mass cool until you can feel no heat when you hold your hand close to the surface. Gradual cooling is better than rapid cooling because the sugar crystals will be smaller and more uniform. An efficient method of cooling is to set the pan on a rack in the bottom of the kitchen sink, pour the syrup into it. Have a continuous flow of water from the cold faucet around the pan. However, the pan should not be moved and water must not splash into the syrup. So if the continuous flow of water is not practical, simply set the pan into a larger pan containing ice water.
Begin working the syrup as soon as it is properly cooled. Using the wooden paddle, manipulate the mass, moving as much as possible into the center of the pan. Lift and stir with the paddle. Continue collecting from the corners; try to keep the entire mass moving. It is not at all necessary to work rapidly or strenuously, but once the procedure is started it should be continued at a steady, even rate. If the syrup is

allowed to cool so that working is very difficult, the pan may be set into hot water for a few seconds to loosen the syrup around the edges and make stirring easier.

The cold sticky mass will lose its transparency as it is manipulated, gradually becoming opaque, thinner, and lighter in color. In the final stage, the maple butter becomes quite stiff again, loses its glossy surface and may crumble if it is cooked to the higher temperature. It is easy to tell when the maple butter needs no more stirring and is done. Pack maple butter in glass jars or tin cans with tight covers. If it should be too firm to pack easily, store in the refrigerator in a covered bowl. After standing, the maple butter will soften.

Suggestion: Use maple butter to spread on toasted crackers, or dough-nuts. Warm slightly and use as a spread for waffles or pancakes, as an icing for cakes. Or eat from a spoon like candy (favorite of the children in our family).

MAPLE BUTTERNUT FUDGE

STEP I

Use
   3 cups maple syrup

Follow the procedure for making maple butter (*see p. 411*). Cook until the temperature of the syrup reaches 234° for new syrup, 236°-238° when weather is warm or when you use syrup more than 6 months old. Begin stirring when the cooked syrup is still slightly warm (cooking to the higher temperature makes stirring more difficult). The stirred candy will be quite firm and will crumble. The candy may now be stored in the refrigerator or you may proceed at once to Step 2.

STEP II

Remelt the candy in a double boiler. Care must be taken to keep the water boiling. The candy should be cut and lifted with a knife during the melting process. *It should not be stirred at all with a spoon while it is heating.* Cutting with a knife hastens the process, prevents coarse grain, and insures even texture. Heat only until the candy can be poured (consistency of pancake batter). Just before the melted candy is ready to be poured, stir quickly and gently with a large spoon, adding

*1 cup broken butternuts**

Pour into a buttered 9 × 9-inch square pan. If desired, candy may be smoothed with a knife or spatula dipped into hot water. Cut into squares. Leave in the pan until cooled.

* Walnuts or pecans may be used if butternuts are not available.

MOTHER'S MAPLE FONDANT BALLS

First on the list of our favorite holiday sweets we would put maple fondant balls topped with butternut halves. Mother never made this particular delicacy except at the Christmas season. Then she always planned to make up several batches well ahead of time. The fondant was best, she felt, when it had been allowed to ripen, so as it was finished she put it in bowls, covered it with a dampened cloth, and set the bowls out in the cold, ell kitchen. When the time came to finish up all the different varieties of candy just before Christmas Day, we helped do the candy balls. We cut off pieces of the cold fondant to roll between our lightly buttered palms until we could form the candies which came out more or less spherical, depending on experience and sticky little hands doing the rolling. We decorated the fondant balls with butternut halves pressed down firmly.

Several years ago a Christmas issue of Life Magazine featured all-time favorite holiday foods. One entire colored page showed a tempting spread of homemade candies. Nestled in pretty bonbon papers, displayed on a footed cut glass dish, were plain old-fashioned maple fondant balls, topped with pecan meats instead of butternuts. Coming across our candies there was like receiving a gift from the past. The recipe given was excellent, though not simplified enough for a novice candy maker (in our opinion). The following directions for making maple fondant just like Mother's, as nearly as we can remember, have been written down especially for Granddaughter Patty Smith, who has inherited a taste for real maple candy although she is too young to remember her Grandmother Smith and the candies that were made every Christmas at High Maples Farm.

༄

Put in a 2-quart heavy saucepan which has a smooth, rounded bottom
  2 cups best quality maple syrup
  ¼ teaspoon butter

Cook according to instructions for making Maple Butternut Fudge (*see p. 412*).

Take special care to remove crystals that form on sides of pan during cooking. When candy thermometer registers 236°-238°, remove saucepan from heat and set into a pan of cold water. Remove the thermometer and let fondant cool without moving the pan. When the fondant is lukewarm (test by holding your hand close to the surface), begin to stir, using a wooden paddle or large shallow-bowled spoon. Try to keep the entire mass moving as much as possible. Work away from the side of the pan toward the center, using an over and over movement to incorporate air into the candy. This will help to make the finished fondant smooth-grained and light in color. After you have stirred for approximately 10 minutes, the candy will become easier to manipulate, will change color and appear creamy. Scrape the candy quickly onto a lightly buttered platter, take the warm fondant into your hands and knead it into a ball. At this point you must work fast. A helper will be very useful. Continue the kneading until all lumps are removed and the fondant is very smooth. If the fondant becomes sticky from the heat of your hands so that kneading is difficult, rinse your hands quickly in very cold water, dry thoroughly and continue the kneading. Place the finished fondant in a lightly buttered bowl, cover with plastic film wrap and set in the refrigerator to ripen for a day or longer.

To finish the candies, cut off a piece of fondant about the size of a walnut. Butter your hands slightly. Roll the fondant into a ball. Place on a buttered platter. Press a butternut or pecan half onto the candy. MAKES 30 TO 36 FONDANT BALLS.

WHITE SUGAR FONDANT

Fondant-stuffed dates and white fondant balls topped with walnut halves were always part of our Christmas candy-making. The fondant used as a base was cooked and worked in the same manner as the maple fondant.

～✥〜

Put into a 2-quart heavy saucepan which has a smooth, rounded bottom
> *2 cups sugar*
> *1½ cups cold water*

Bring to a boil, stirring constantly.

Add
> *⅛ teaspoon cream of tartar*

Cover and let steam over low heat for 5 minutes. Remove cover. Using a candy thermometer, cook without stirring to 238°. Use a fork with a cloth swab dipped in cold water to wipe down crystals which form during cooking. Cool candy, stir and work into fondant, using the method described in recipe for Maple Fondant (*see p. 413*). Place finished fondant in a covered bowl and let stand in the refrigerator for a day or longer.
MAKES ABOUT 1 POUND.

STUFFED DATES

Use
> *8-9 dozen large soft dates, split and pitted*
> *1 pound White Sugar Fondant (see above)*
> *Nutmeats, bits of candied fruits*

Divide fondant into four parts and flavor as desired. The flavorings Mother used included extracts of vanilla, peppermint, lemon, and wintergreen. These old-time favorites are still very good but if you prefer a modern touch try the following or experiment with your own combination.

Combine, working with your fingers

I

¼ pound fondant
¼ teaspoon almond extract

II

¼ pound fondant
2 teaspoons Cointreau
3 or 4 drops orange food coloring

III

¼ pound fondant
2 teaspoons Crème de Menthe
3 or 4 drops green food coloring

IV

¼ pound fondant
2 or 3 drops oil of peppermint
3 drops red food coloring

Add bits of candied cherries, citron, pineapple, or nutmeats as you stuff the dates. Place stuffed dates on waxed paper and allow to "harden" for 24 hours before using.
EACH ¼ POUND OF FONDANT STUFFS AT LEAST 2 DOZEN DATES.

SUGARED POPCORN

Just before Christmas when all the candies had been made, Mother always "sugared" some popcorn because Father liked that better than any other holiday treat. Molasses corn balls were made at other times of the year. Grandson Bob Weeks and his family are enthusiastic popcorn eaters, so at Christmas they always have both molasses corn balls and some of the old-fashioned sugared popcorn known to the children as "Great-Grampa Smith's Christmas candy."

Pop enough popcorn to make
 4 quarts (about 1 cup kernels)

Discard all unpopped kernels and place corn in a large pan.

Combine in a heavy saucepan
 2 cups white sugar
 1 cup water
 ⅛ teaspoon cream of tartar

Cook without stirring until candy thermometer registers 270°

Remove from heat. Stir in
 2 tablespoons butter
 6-8 drops food coloring (optional)
 ½ teaspoon vanilla

Pour mixture over corn and stir until all kernels are coated.

Let cool until corn can be handled. Separate quickly into small clusters. Spread on waxed paper and leave until glaze is dry.

POPCORN BALLS
GRANDDAUGHTER-IN-LAW SHEILA WEEKS' RECIPE

Pop enough popcorn to make
 3 quarts (about ¾ cup kernels)

Discard all unpopped kernels. Place corn in a large pan.

Melt in a heavy saucepan
 1 tablespoon butter

Add and bring to a boil, stirring constantly,
 1 cup light molasses
 ½ cup white sugar

Cook over medium or low heat until candy thermometer registers 270°. Remove from heat and pour over the corn. Mix well to coat all kernels. Butter your hands lightly. As soon as corn has cooled enough to be

handled, shape balls about three inches in diameter. Use only enough pressure to make balls hold their shape.
MAKES 12.

WHITE PULLED CANDY

GRANDDAUGHTER-IN-LAW SHEILA WEEKS' RECIPE

Both molasses and white taffy (which we called "pulled" candy) used to be included in our holiday candy-making. When we were young, evening molasses-taffy pulls were often held after sliding or skating parties. As we remember, making the taffy was not considered difficult then, but we do not know anyone who now makes the molasses pulled candy at home. Perhaps today's molasses is too refined to make good taffy. We do know this recipe for white pulled candy is infallible.

✧

Melt in a heavy saucepan
   3 tablespoons butter

Add
   2 cups white sugar
   ½ cup white vinegar

Heat, stirring constantly, until sugar is dissolved. Boil until candy thermometer registers 260°. Pour into a buttered, shallow pan or pie plate. As mixture cools around sides, fold toward center. When cool enough to handle, butter your hands lightly and pull until candy loses its transparent shine and becomes a soft, opaque white.

Add while pulling
   ½ teaspoon vanilla or few drops peppermint oil

If candy becomes sticky, rebutter your hands. Cut in small pieces with shears and place on buttered platter to harden.
MAKES 36 PIECES ABOUT 1 INCH IN LENGTH.

Note: This quantity may be divided among 3 or 4 small "pullers."

AUNTIE'S BROWN SUGAR FUDGE

TRADITIONAL SMITH FAMILY CHRISTMAS CANDY

Mix
> *4 cups light brown sugar, packed*
> *1 cup light cream*

Cook over low heat, stirring until sugar particles are dissolved. Boil until candy thermometer registers 242°, or until soft ball stage is reached. Remove from heat.

Stir in at once
> *1 cup marshmallow crème*
> *2 teaspoons vanilla*

Beat until creamy.

Stir in
> *1 cup broken pecans*

Pour into a buttered 7½ × 11-inch pan. Cut candy into squares while still warm.

MAPLE DIVINITY FUDGE

Heat in a heavy saucepan
> *1½ cups maple syrup*
> *1½ cups sugar*
> *⅛ teaspoon butter*

Stir only until sugar is dissolved. Cook until candy thermometer registers 248°. Meanwhile, beat until stiff
> *¼ cup egg whites (1 large or 2 small eggs)*

Pour the syrup slowly over the egg white, beating to mix thoroughly.

Add
> *1 teaspoon light rum (optional)*

Continue to beat until the mixture is creamy or until you can notice a very slight grainy texture.

Mix in quickly
    1 cup broken pecans

Spread fudge in a slightly buttered 9 × 9-inch pan. Cut into 25 squares. Allow candy to cool completely before removing from pan.

CHERRY DIVINITY FUDGE

Put into a large saucepan
    4 cups sugar
    1 cup white corn syrup
    1 cup cold water

Heat slowly, stirring until sugar is dissolved. Cook without stirring until 250° is reached. Meanwhile, beat until very stiff
    2 egg whites

Pour the syrup in a thin stream into the egg whites, beating constantly until the mixture begins to stiffen and lose its glossy appearance. Add
    2 teaspoons vanilla
    1 cup broken pecans
    ⅓ cup red candied cherries, cut fine
    ⅓ cup green candied cherries, cut fine

Continue to stir until candy is too stiff to pour and is slightly grainy. Spoon and pack the candy into a buttered 9 × 13-inch pan. Mark the candy into squares and leave in the pan until cooled.

Variation: Omit cherries and substitute broken walnuts for the pecans.

CHOCOLATE MARSHMALLOW FUDGE

Put in a heavy saucepan
3 cups sugar
1 cup light cream
⅛ teaspoon salt
4 ounces unsweetened chocolate, broken into pieces

Heat slowly. Stir constantly until chocolate is melted, then stir only enough to keep the fudge from burning. Cook over medium heat until candy thermometer registers 234°-236°. Remove fudge from heat and let stand 5 minutes.

Add
1 cup marshmallow crème
2 teaspoons vanilla

Beat until candy loses its glossy appearance. Add
1 cup broken walnuts

Pour into a slightly buttered 9 × 9-inch pan. Cut into 25 pieces. Remove from pan when partially cooled.

Index

Index